IAA Reports, No. 15

THE AKHZIV CEMETERIES

THE BEN-DOR EXCAVATIONS, 1941–1944

MICHAL DAYAGI-MENDELS

Dedicated to the memory
of
Ruth Hestrin

ISRAEL ANTIQUITIES AUTHORITY

JERUSALEM 2002

Publications of the Israel Antiquities Authority

Editors-in-Chief:
Ayala Sussmann and Zvi Gal

Series Editor:
Ann Roshwalb Hurowitz

Preliminary editing: Inna Pommeranz

Front cover: Background, facsimile of a page from Ben-Dor's notebook; foreground, three musicians
(photo: P. Lanyi; courtesy of the Israel Museum)

Back cover: Background, facsimile of a page from Ben-Dor's notebook; foreground, group of pottery
(photo: P. Lanyi; courtesy of the Israel Museum)

Typesetting and layout: Phylis Naiman
Graphics: Natalia Zak, Irina Berin and Phylis Naiman
Cover design: Lori Lender, Ann Abuhav
Production: Lori Lender
Printed at Keterpress Enterprises, Jerusalem

ISBN 965-406-144-9
© THE ISRAEL ANTIQUITIES AUTHORITY 2002
POB 586, Jerusalem 91004

CONTENTS

ABBREVIATIONS

AASOR	*Annual of the American Schools of Oriental Research*
ABSA	*The Annual of the British School at Athens*
ADAJ	*Annual of the Department of Antiquites of Jordan*
AfO	*Archiv für Orientforschung*
AJA	*American Journal of Archaeology*
AJBA	*Australian Journal of Biblical Archaeology*
ANET	*Ancient Near Eastern Texts* J.B. Pritchard ed. Princeton 1969
'Atiqot (ES)	'Atiqot (English Series)
BA	*Biblical Archaeologist*
BAR	*Biblical Archaeology Review*
BASOR	*Bulletin of the American Schools of Oriental Research*
BBSAJ	*Bulletin of the British School of Archaeology in Jerusalem*
BMB	*Bulletin du Musée de Beyrouth*
EI	*Eretz Israel*
HTR	*Harvard Theological Review*
IAA Reports	Israel Antiquities Authority Reports
IEJ	*Israel Exploration Journal*
IMJ	*Israel Museum Journal*
JAOS	*Journal of the American Oriental Society*
JNES	*Journal of Near Eastern Studies*
NEAEHL	*The New Encyclopedia of Archaeological Excavations in the Holy Land.* E. Stern ed. Jerusalem 1993
PEQ	*Palestine Exploration Quarterly*
QDAP	*Quarterly of the Department of Antiquities in Palestine*
RSF	*Rivista di Studi Fenici*
RB	*Revue Biblique*
RDAC	*Report of the Department of Antiquities, Cyprus*
ZDPV	*Zeitschrift des Deutschen Palästina-Vereins*

PREFACE

Excavations of the Akhziv cemeteries, which comprised part of the Phoenician cultural sphere, have yielded a wide assemblage of Phoenician material, outstanding in terms of its quantity and variety. Due to the small number of excavations in Phoenicia itself, most of the information concerning the Phoenicians has been obtained from sites outside Phoenicia.

The two cemeteries of Akhziv described here, er-Ras and ez-Zib (Buqbaq), were excavated in 1941–1944 by Immanuel Ben-Dor on behalf of the Department of Antiquities of the Mandatory Government. Excavations in these cemeteries were resumed in 1958, 1960, 1963 and 1980 by Moshe Prausnitz on behalf of the Israel Department of Antiquities and the University of Rome. Additional excavations at the site were carried out by Elat Mazar on behalf of the Hebrew University, Jerusalem, in 1988–1994.

Ben-Dor passed on notes on his excavations to Ruth Hestrin, who was to be responsible for publishing the report. A facsimile of two of these notebook pages form the cover's background. Shortly after we began preparing the information for publication, Ruth fell ill and was unable to continue work on the project that had been so important to her. She managed to work on only a small part of the present publication before her death in 1993. Her input was sorely missed. This report is dedicated to her memory.

I wish to thank the directors of the Israel Antiquities Authority for enabling the closure of this project, initiated in Mandatory time, and the Israel Museum for facilitating my work.

The project was carried to fruition by all those who assisted in the preparation of this publication: Noga Ginsburg, for participating in the initial phase of this project, especially in the descriptions of the cemeteries; Shlomit Cohen and Na'ama Yahalom, as well as Miyoung Im, for their meticulous assistance; Nancy Benovitz for her tireless efforts in the initial stage of editing and for retyping the manuscript; Noga Ze'evi for preparing the drawings; Yoram Lehman and Marina Salzberger for photographing the objects and Peter Lanyi for the color photographs; Natalia Zak and Irina Berin for preparing the plans for publication; and Phylis Naiman for the layout; as well as the conservation and photography departments of the Israel Museum.

Benjamin Sass and Amir Golani reviewed the jewelry; Christian Hermann provided important information concerning the amulets; Yuval Goren carried out the petrographic analyses on some of the vessels; Ayelet Gilboa offered invaluable remarks; Ronny Reich advised on the tomb typology; and Prof. Ephraim Stern reviewed the manuscript in its final stages.

The manuscript was submitted in 1995 and selectively updated. Inna Pommerantz edited the text, Ann Roshwalb Hurowitz offered invaluable suggestions and brought the book to press, and Ayala Sussmann coordinated the project.

The Dorot Foundation for Education and Archaeology, Miriam and the late Arnold Frankel, New York, and Martin Blumenthal, New York, the Israel Museum and the Israel Antiquities Authority generously supported this project.

I wish to thank them all.

PHOENICIAN SITES ALONG THE EASTERN MEDITERRANEAN COAST

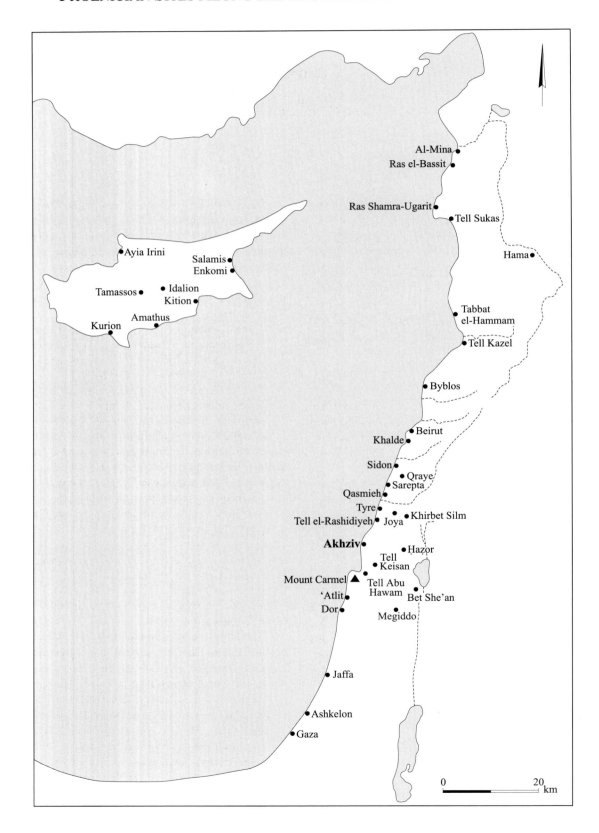

CHAPTER 1

INTRODUCTION

Akhziv (biblical Achzib) is located on the northern coast of Israel, about 14 km north of 'Akko. The site was settled from the Middle Bronze Age to the Crusader period.

Achzib is mentioned twice in the Bible as a Canaanite city which the tribe of Asher failed to defeat (Joshua 19:29; Judges 1:31). In Assyrian records, Akzibi is referred to as a fortified city, conquered by Sennacherib in 701 BCE during his third campaign, along with Sidon, Sarepta and 'Akko (Luckenbill 1924:110).

Josephus described the town as situated on the seashore, calling it by its Greek name, Ekdippa (*Ant.* V, 85; XIV, 343; *War* I, 257). The Talmud mentions it several times as a town located on the border of the country and on the road leading northward from 'Akko. At the time, the town had a Jewish community and a synagogue.

In the Crusader period, the town was known as Casal Lamberti, while in Moslem times, it became ez-Zib, retaining the biblical name Achzib.

Excavations carried out on the northern part of the mound by Moshe Prausnitz revealed Middle Bronze Age fortifications which were destroyed at the beginning of the Late Bronze Age. There is some evidence of renewed building activity in that period, but by the end of the Late Bronze Age the fortifications were again in ruins. In the Iron Age, Akhziv enjoyed its greatest expansion. The two major Phoenician cemeteries situated east (er-Ras) and south (ez-Zib/Buqbaq) of the city date from this period. These cemeteries were in use without interruption well into the beginning of the Persian period.

Ben-Dor's Excavations at Akhziv, 1941–1944

In his diaries, Immanuel Ben-Dor described his archaeological work at Akhziv as follows:

> The presence of ancient tombs has been known since the early twenties. In March 1921 the Department of Antiquities of the Mandatory Government of Palestine received a note from an otherwise unknown person, Edmondo Durighello, who reported that he excavated about one hundred tombs near the village of ez-Zib. He employed for this purpose some two hundred workers from the neighboring villages. His activities seem to have been concentrated in the southern, Buqbaq cemetery. He says that the tombs contained merely funerary objects without 'any artistic interest.' He notes, however, the presence of a number of clay figurines, to which he rightly ascribes an Egypto-Phoenician style.
>
> The Inspector of Antiquities, Y. Ory (Lederman) mentions in his report of May 1921 that an ancient cemetery probably exists south-east of the village.
>
> In the summer of 1941 I came on an unofficial visit to the seaside resort of Nahariya, 6 km south of Achziv. I was informed by the late Dr. Otto Stiehl of Nahariya, an enthusiastic friend of antiquities, that some of the villagers of ez-Zib are engaged in looting ancient tombs. They offered some unusual pieces of unbroken pottery and clay figurines for sale in Nahariya. Since Dr. Stiehl knew the location of the tombs he accompanied me to the site. Several open shafts were visible with heaps of freshly dug-out earth, a quantity of broken red burnished and plain pottery lay about.
>
> Two rectangular slabs of limestone lay face down near an opening of one of the tombs (later named Tomb I), and on being overturned they proved to bear inscriptions, each consisting of no more than two lines of incised letters in Phoenician script. The sun was setting and there was not much more to do but to secure the two inscriptions, to bring them to Jerusalem and to report to the Department. It was decided to begin excavating the tombs, first of all in order to prevent further looting and then to study the character of the cemetery. Later, Mr. Naim Effendi Makhouly, then Inspector of the northern district, was given the task of excavating some tombs. He was assisted by Najib Effendi Nasser, Junior Inspector of Antiquities, who was in charge of keeping the inventory of finds and keeping a diary.
>
> Subsequently I joined the dig at various times, particularly in the subsequent seasons, sometimes leading the team and sometimes giving merely advice.

Ben-Dor later amended the diary:

> The actual excavation was carried out at intervals, in the autumn of 1941, in the winter of 1942, in the summer of 1943 and in the spring of 1944. Each season lasted about one month. Then came 1947 with its troubled times, culminating in the division of Jerusalem. The objects from the Akhziv cemeteries were naturally housed in the Rockefeller Museum, apart from the small finds. Since a cold war persisted between the two states there was no possibility of seeing the material until the unification of Jerusalem in 1967.

The Southern Cemetery—Ez-Zib (Buqbaq)

The southern cemetery is situated on the Mediterranean shore, *c.* 1 km south of the tell. The name Buqbaq is onomatopoeic and derives from the peculiar sound produced by the seawater gushing through hollows in the rock.

Ben-Dor reports that the cemetery extends over an area of more than 5000 sq m of sand dunes. Depending on its location, the depth of the sand layers varies greatly; while it is merely 10 cm thick in the northern part of the site, it reaches a depth of over 2 m in the south. Below the sand is a layer of marl, with occasional pockets of rock chips or black soil. Further below is the bedrock, consisting of soft porous sandstone. The whole area is covered with sparse vegetation. There is nothing whatsoever on the surface that indicates the presence of tombs. How the tomb robbers discovered the tombs remains a puzzle; they may have accidentally come upon the first tomb and then probed for more. Fortunately, the robbers did a slipshod job, and large quantities of restorable and even complete pottery vessels, as well as small objects, could still be recovered from the looted tombs.

The search for new tombs proceeded with the digging of a series of trial trenches. Ben-Dor dug trenches 3–5 m wide, which branched off from one main trench across the area. Besides uncovering new tombs, these trenches yielded a great quantity of pottery, some dated later than the tombs, but for the most part contemporary, as well as a relatively large number of cult objects (chalices) and lamps, indicating that certain funerary rites may have been held outside and between the tombs.

The Eastern Cemetery—Er-Ras

This cemetery is located to the east of the tell, on a rock-spur which, in recent times, was planted mainly with olive groves. The limestone rock here is much harder and more solid than in the southern Buqbaq cemetery.

Analysis of the Material

Analyzing the material from the two cemeteries excavated by Ben-Dor was not an easy undertaking. Various factors played a role here: the long period that had elapsed since the excavation, the rather inadequate methods of recording information, the incomplete surveying of tombs which can no longer be located, and the damage caused by man (war) and nature (insects). A serious information gap, among others, is the lack of data concerning burials, in particular with regard to the type of burial—inhumation or cremation—as well as the presence of skeletal material and the position, number, gender and age of the deceased. Moreover, no information exists regarding the disposition of the objects in relation to the burials.

Not all the tomb plans are available. The missing plans may have been lost over the years, or perhaps were never drawn up in the first place. Some tombs were described in the excavation diary but have no plan, whereas others have plans but lack written descriptions. In addition, the information on the tombs provided in the excavator's diary is often self-contradictory. The plans do not indicate the scale (although we have attempted to calculate scales), nor in many cases, the orientation of the tombs. We do not have a general plan of the ez-Zib (Buqbaq) cemetery, and therefore the relation of one tomb to another also remains unknown.

The material listed as "finds from trenches" has not been analyzed in this publication, due to lack of information concerning stratigraphy and other features in the trenches.

The aim of this publication is the presentation of the extraordinarily rich repertoire of Phoenician pottery, small finds and terracottas recovered from the Akhziv tombs. In comparison to previous publications of Phoenician pottery uncovered at sites in the Phoenician homeland, the Akhziv repertoire surpasses most of them in its rich and varied assemblages.

An attempt was made to date the tombs according to the pottery typology; however, given the lack of sufficient information, we could not deal with stratigraphic matters.

CHAPTER 2

TOMB TYPOLOGY OF THE EZ-ZIB AND ER-RAS CEMETERIES

Most of the tombs are shaft tombs hewn into the *kurkar* rock, with a single burial chamber and a rock-cut roof; a more elaborate variant of this tomb has one to three rock-cut niches in the walls of the burial chamber. A few tombs have an open ceiling and were roofed with stone slabs. A single trough tomb was recorded, as well as one masonry tomb. There was no evident consistency in terms of size, depth or orientation of the tombs.

Both the ez-Zib (Buqbaq; designated 'Z') and er-Ras (designated 'ZR') cemeteries can be described as being fairly uniform in terms of the tomb types they contain. However, for many of the tombs excavated by Ben-Dor, no plan is available, merely a description in the excavation diary (see cover); in some cases, there is neither a plan nor a description.

The scanty recording of the excavations at Akhziv (see Chapter 1) limits our ability to analyze the Phoenician burial customs at the site. We shall nonetheless attempt to arrive at a number of conclusions regarding these cemeteries, and shed some light on their importance.

Three main tomb types can be distinguished:

Type 1: Shaft Tomb, Single Chamber with Rock-Cut Roof

These tombs have a vertical shaft, sometimes with a stairway along one of the walls, or a number of notches or footholds to facilitate the descent. The shaft is either square or rectangular in section.

The burial chamber is reached through an opening which, in some tombs, is still blocked by the original slab. Most of the tombs have a single burial chamber, either square or rectangular in shape. One tomb has a double chamber, reached by a single shaft. Benches hewn into the rock run along and parallel to the chamber's walls. The chamber walls are either vertical or slope slightly inward toward a flat or convex rock-cut ceiling.

Although this type of tomb appears in both cemeteries, it is more common in er-Ras.
Tombs of Type 1: Z I, Z V, Z IX, Z X, ZR III, ZR XVII, ZR XVIII, ZR XXI, ZR XXV, ZR XXVII, ZR XXVIII, ZR XXIX, ZR XXX, ZR XXXI, ZR XXXIV, ZR XXXVI, ZR XXXVII, ZR XXXVIII.
Plan Lacking: ZR I, ZR II, ZR IV, ZR V, ZR VII, ZR VIII, ZR IX, ZR XI, ZR XIII, ZR XLI, ZR XLII, ZR XLIII.

Type 1.1: Shaft Tomb, Single Chamber with Rock-Cut Niches and Roof

This tomb type is similar to Type 1 in all respects, with the exception of the one to three niches hewn into the walls of the burial chamber. They vary in shape and size. Some were cut to floor level, while others are shallow troughs. Usually, a rock-cut partition remained between it and the main chamber. A greater effort seems to have been made in preparing tombs of this type, perhaps indicating that they were used by a larger family or were in use for a long period of time.
Tombs of Type 1.1: ZR XV, ZR XVI, ZR XIX, ZR XX, ZR XXII, ZR XXIV, ZR XXVI, ZR XXXV.
Plan Lacking: ZR VI, ZR X, ZR XII, ZR XIV.

Type 2: Shaft Tomb, Single Chamber, Roof of Stone Slabs

These tombs have a vertical shaft, square or rectangular in section, usually without a stairway.

An opening, in some cases still blocked by the original stone slab, leads into the burial chamber. In most cases, this is a single, square or rectangular chamber. The walls are either vertical or slope toward the open ceiling, forming a truncated pyramid with an open top covered with flat stone slabs, placed transversally. In some tombs, the slabs were found *in situ*.

Tombs of Type 2: Z II, Z III, Z IV, Z VI, Z XIII, Z XVI, Z XVII, Z XVIII, Z XIX, Z XX, Z XXI.

Type 3: Trough Tomb

This tomb type, of which there is only one example, is an elongated, rectangular, shallow rock-cut pit. The tomb was found open, but originally had probably been covered with stone slabs.
Tomb of Type 3: Z XIV.

Type 4: Masonry Tomb

There is one masonry tomb, consisting of a rectangular structure, built entirely above surface level.
Tomb of Type 4: ZR XXXIX.

DISCUSSION

The er-Ras cemetery contains mainly tombs of Type 1 and its variant, Type 1.1. Most of the tombs in the ez-Zib cemetery, on the other hand, belong primarily to Type 2, though four tombs are of Type 1 (the sole double-chambered tomb in the cemetery), one of Type 3 (unique in the ez-Zib cemetery), and one is of Type 4.

Many examples of Iron Age shaft tombs have been recorded, particularly along the Phoenician coast. Rock-cut tombs consisting of a square shaft and a single burial chamber, dating from the 8th–7th centuries BCE, were also excavated by Benjamin Mazar in Jerusalem (E. Mazar and B. Mazar 1989:49–55). Similar tombs, consisting of a vertical shaft and a burial chamber of irregular shape, occasionally with a trench-like pit in the floor and rock-cut benches along the walls, continue into the Persian period. This suggests a link between Phoenician Iron Age and Persian-period burial practices, though the types of pottery found in the tombs differ (Stern 1982:80).

In general, the tombs in the er-Ras cemetery at Akhziv resemble those discovered at 'Atlit, which date to the Persian period (Johns 1933), although the former are more uniform. In Akhziv, the tombs consist of a vertical shaft with a burial chamber located at a right angle to the lower part of the shaft, with the entrance to the chamber being blocked by a vertical slab. In 'Atlit, however, the burial chamber was located directly below the vertical shaft, and the slab was laid horizontally over the entrance to the chamber, separating it from the shaft. Only one tomb at 'Atlit (Tomb L19) has a chamber which opens at right angles to the shaft, but it lacks a blocked doorway (Johns 1933:68–69).

Johns reports the presence of interments in the shafts. Because information is scarce, it is uncertain whether the same is true at Akhziv. The shafts are not as deep as those at 'Atlit, which are 4–5 m in depth. The 'Atlit shafts also have holes and knobs to facilitate access. As at Akhziv, burial niches were commonly found at 'Atlit.

Tomb Z I of the ez-Zib cemetery consists of a shaft ending in a vestibule leading to two chambers. At 'Atlit there are a few examples of this tomb type (L21b, L23, L23b, L35).

Further instances of Phoenician cemeteries are known from the city of Arvad at Amrit. These consist of tombs reached by a deep vertical shaft, sometimes with a stairway running along one of the walls. Some shafts have footholds to facilitate the descent. At the bottom of the shaft a doorway leads to a chamber. The number of chambers varies.

The cemetery at Sidon contains Phoenician tombs similar to those at Akhziv. These have a rectangular vertical shaft and a doorway cut through one of its sides (Perrot and Chipiez 1885:162, Fig. 102). The doors leading to the chambers were opened only for burial and the dead were placed directly on the floor. Some of the Sidon tombs are monumental, with a large *dromos*, and a complex arrangement of chambers. Some of the Akhziv tombs may also have had a *dromos*, but were not described as such due to inadequate recording.

Renan (1864:75, 410) maintained that the shaft tombs at Byblos represented the earliest examples of Phoenician tombs. He noted that the arrangement of the shafts and the way in which they opened into the chambers seemed Egyptian in style.

A few Phoenician cemeteries were excavated along the Phoenician coast. The excavations were carried out mainly at the monumental masonry tombs, which most likely indicated people of high rank. Information concerning the commoners' cemeteries is fairly scanty (Saidah 1966).

Rock-hewn tombs approached by a shaft or *dromos* were known in Cyprus from the Late Bronze Age to the Roman period (Karageorghis 1970:223). The chamber tomb, which was popular in Cyprus in the Cypro-Archaic period, had benches around the chamber, occasionally replaced by rock-cut niches.

It is noteworthy that the custom of burial in shaft tombs, already evident in Palestine in the Middle Bronze Age, was not popular in the Late Bronze Age; it was resumed in the Iron Age, and continued into the Persian period. As demonstrated above, this type of burial was common in the Phoenician sphere, and reached Phoenician settlements in the western Mediterranean (Harden 1962:105–114; Gras, Rouillard and Texidor 1991).

CHAPTER 3

THE EZ-ZIB (BUQBAQ) CEMETERY: TOMBS, POTTERY AND SMALL FINDS

Tomb Z I (Type 1; Plan 3.1; Figs. 3.1–3.3)

The plan of this tomb is unique in this cemetery. Although it was opened by looters, it is by far the richest in terms of the quantity and variety of the pottery types it contained.

The tomb consists of a rock-cut shaft ending in a vestibule, leading to two chambers (I East and I West). Several pointed-base jars were found in an upright position in the marl surrounding the shaft opening. The shaft is roughly rectangular in plan (1.25 × 1.37 m; depth 1.60 m). The shaft bottom forms a passage oriented north–south, with two benches along the opposite short sides. Large, rough stone slabs placed transversally south–north covered the shaft mouth. The northern slab was removed and later replaced by the looters.

At the bottom of the shaft, in the middle of each long side, a low threshold (width *c.* 0.75 m) leads into a chamber. The two slabs found on the passage floor probably closed the chamber openings. The floor of both chambers is 0.60 m lower than the floor level of the shaft; a rectangular slab (thickness 0.30 m), discovered on the floor of the western chamber near the entrance, may have served as a step. The western chamber is rectangular in shape (2.00 × 2.75 m; height 1.50 m), while the eastern chamber is nearly square (2.00 × 2.13 m; height 1.60 m). The chamber walls slope slightly toward the ceiling. In the center of the ceiling in the western chamber, there is a circular hole (diam. 0.20 m) blocked with stones.

Both burial chambers were found disturbed. The eastern chamber was particularly rich in finds, containing a large number of pottery vessels, including some types which occur only in this tomb, as well as some small finds. The western chamber held many broken vessels, as well as some charred wood and a horse figurine. Only a few finds were recovered in the passage. Two tomb stelae were located outside the shaft of the tomb (see Cross, Appendix 1: Nos. 2, 3).

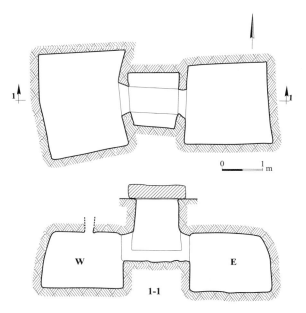

Plan 3.1. Tomb Z I, plan and section.

Chronology. This tomb is not only the richest of those excavated by Ben-Dor but is also among the earliest in the Akhziv cemeteries. The earliest vessels here include bowls (Types B10 I, B11 I)* and pilgrim flasks (Type PF1), as well as a Cypriot barrel-shaped juglet of Bichrome III ware (Type CP9), dating from the late 11th–10th century BCE. The fact that the tomb was in continuous use down to the 7th century BCE is attested by the presence of the red-slipped and burnished jugs which form about one-third of the pottery assemblage. It should be noted that both chambers contained contemporaneous pottery.

---

*The pottery typology is developed in Chapter 5.

Catalogue of Finds, Tomb Z I, Eastern Chamber
(For pottery types see Chapter 5. Fr = fragment; * = illustrated in Fig. 3.1.)

No.	Object	Type	IAA No.	Description	Dimensions (cm)	
Pottery						
1	Bowl	B1 I	70-7862	Reddish-brown coarse ware, white grits.	H 6.0	D 16.5
2	Bowl	B1 I	70-7863	Reddish-brown coarse ware, white grits.	H 3.7	D 15.0
3	Bowl	B1 I	70-7864	Grayish-brown coarse ware.	H 4.0	D 7.0
4	Bowl	B1 I	70-7874	Reddish-brown coarse ware.	H 5.0	D 17.0
5*	Bowl	B2 III	70-7861	Reddish-brown coarse ware.	H 5.0	D 20.0
6	Bowl	B2 III	70-7871	Reddish-brown coarse ware.	H 5.0	D 20.0
7*	Bowl	B2 IV	70-7879	Reddish-brown coarse ware.	H 4.5	D 18.0
8	Bowl	B2 IV	70-7870	Reddish-brown coarse ware, white grits.	Fr	
9*	Bowl	B3 I	70-7876	Brownish coarse ware.	H 4.0	D 20.0
10	Bowl	B3 I	70-7873	Brownish-buff coarse ware, white grits.	Fr	
11	Bowl	B3 I	70-7869	Brownish-gray coarse ware.	H 2.5	
12	Bowl	B3 I	70-7877	Brownish-buff coarse ware.	H 3.0	D 17.0
13*	Bowl	B8 IV	70-7866	Brownish-buff ware, well-levigated, burnished.	H 5.0	D 17.0
14*	Bowl	B10 I	70-7856	Reddish-brown ware, red-slipped on both sides. Black-painted decoration.	H 6.0	D 19.5
15*	Bowl	B11 I	70-7867	Reddish-brown ware, white grits. Black-painted decoration.	H 5.5	D 18.5
16*	Storage jar	SJ3	70-7882	Yellowish-buff brittle ware.	H 30+	W 20.0
17	Storage jar	SJ3	70-7881	Yellowish-buff ware.	Fr	
18	Storage jar	SJ4	70-8443	Reddish-buff ware. Rim folded over, flattened horizontally.	Fr	
19*	Storage jar	SJ4	70-7880	Reddish-brown ware.	H 52.5	W 24.0
20	Jug	JG2 I	44.247	Orange-buff ware, red-burnished.	H 19.5	W 11.0
21	Jug	JG2 I	70-7776	Orange-buff ware, red slip, burnished.	H 21.0	W 11.5
22	Jug	JG2 I	70-7778	Orange-buff ware, red slip, burnished.	H 21.5	W 12.5
23	Jug	JG2 I	70-7779	Orange-buff ware, red slip, burnished.	H 12+	W 11+
24	Jug	JG2 I	70-7777	Light buff ware, red slip, burnished.	H 20+	W 11.0
25	Jug	JG2 I	70-7783	Orange-buff ware, red slip, burnished.	H 17+	W 11+
26	Jug	JG2 I	70-7785	Orange-buff ware, dark red slip, highly burnished.	H 17.5+	W 12+
27	Jug	JG2 I	70-7796	Orange-buff ware, red slip, burnished.	H 15.5+	
28	Jug	JG2 I	70-7797	Orange-buff ware, red slip, burnished.	H 11+	W 8.5+
29	Jug	JG2 I	70-7803	Orange-buff ware, red slip, burnished.	H 8+	
30	Jug	JG2 I	70-7781	Orange-buff ware, red slip, burnished.	H 10+	
31	Jug	JG2 I	70-7794	Orange-buff ware, red slip, burnished.	H 13+	
32	Jug	JG2 I	70-7784	Orange-buff ware, red slip, burnished.	H 18.0	W 10.5
33*	Jug	JG2 II	70-7775	Light buff ware, red slip, burnished.	H 21.5	W 12.0
34	Jug	JG2 II	70-7780	Orange-buff ware, red slip, burnished.	H 14.5	
35	Jug	JG2 II	70-7782	Orange-buff ware, red slip, burnished.	H 11+	
36	Jug	JG2 II	70-7801	Orange-buff ware, red slip, burnished.	Fr	
37	Jug	JG4 II	70-7805	Reddish-brown ware, dark red slip, burnished.	H 8+	
38*	Jug	JG5 I	70-7786	Buff ware, thick dark red slip, burnished.	H 18.5	W 10.0
39	Jug	JG5 I	70-7788	Brownish-buff ware, red slip, burnished.	H 15.5	W 9.5
40	Jug	JG5 I	70-7792	Brownish-buff ware, red slip, burnished.	H 12+	W 11.0
41	Jug	JG5 I	70-7789	Brownish-buff ware, red slip, burnished.	H 11+	W 9.5
42	Jug	JG5 I	70-7790	Brownish-buff ware, red slip, burnished.	H 18+	W 10.5
43	Jug	JG5 I	70-7787	Brownish-buff ware, red slip, burnished.	Fr	
44	Jug	JG5 I	70-7800	Brownish-buff ware, red slip, burnished.		W 12.0

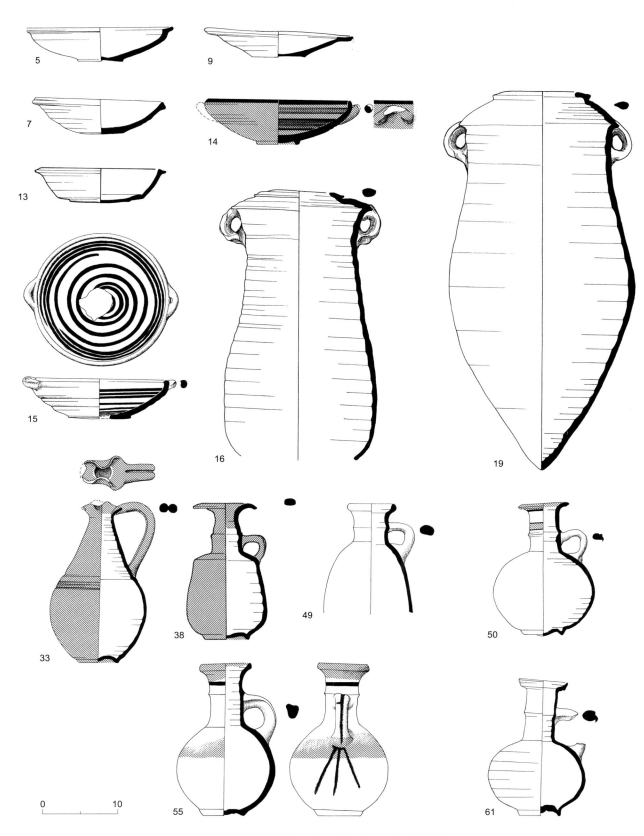

Fig. 3.1. Tomb Z I, eastern chamber, selected finds.

Catalogue of Finds, Tomb Z I, Eastern Chamber (contd., Fig. 3.1)

No.	Object	Type	IAA No.	Description	Dimensions (cm)	
45	Jug	JG5 I	70-7791	Grayish-brown coarse ware, red slip, burnished.	Fr	
46	Jug	JG5 I	70-7793	Orange-buff ware, red slip, burnished.	Fr	
47	Jug	JG5 III	70-7802	Orange-buff ware, red slip, burnished.	Fr	
48	Jug	JG5 IV	70-7813	Orange-buff ware, red slip, burnished.	Fr	
49*	Jug	Misc.	70-7827	Reddish-brown coarse ware, white grits.	H 16.5+	W 11.5
50*	Jug	JG6 I	70-7819	Grayish ware, well-levigated, whitish slip. Black- and red-painted decoration.	H 18.0	W 12.5
51	Jug	JG6 I	70-7809	Pinkish-yellow ware, white grits. Black- and red-painted decoration.	Fr	
52	Jug	JG6 I	70-7807	Pinkish-yellow ware. Black- and red-painted decoration.	Fr	
53	Jug	JG6 I	70-7816	Pinkish-buff ware. Black- and red-painted decoration.	H 15.5+	W 10.0
54	Jug	JG6 I	70-7810	Pinkish-buff ware. Black- and red-painted decoration.	Fr	
55*	Jug	Misc.	67-87	Pinkish-red coarse ware. Black- and red-painted decoration.	H 21.0	W 12.5
56	Jug	JG6 III	70-7907	Brownish-buff ware. Black- and red-painted decoration.	Fr	
57	Jug	JG6 III	70-7808	Brownish-buff ware. Black- and red-painted decoration.	Fr	
58	Jug	JG6 III	70-7812	Brownish-buff ware. Black- and red-painted decoration.	Fr	
59	Jug	JG6 III	70-7806	Brownish-buff ware. Black- and red-painted decoration.	Fr	
60	Jug	JG5 IV	70-7798	Brownish-buff ware, red slip, burnished.	Fr	
61*	Jug	JG6 V	67-88	Grayish-brown coarse ware, white grits.	H 19.5	W 12.5
62	Jug	JG6 V	70-7826	Coarse reddish-brown ware.	H 17.5+	W 12.0
63	Jug	JG7 III	70-7820	Brownish-buff ware.	Fr	
64	Jug	JG7 IV	70-7815	Brownish-buff ware.	Fr	
65*	Pilgrim flask	PF1	70-7851	Orange-buff ware. Red-painted decoration.	H 11.0	W 6.5
66	Pilgrim flask	PF1	70-7850	Orange-buff ware. Black-painted concentric circles.	H 10.5	W 6.0
67	Pilgrim flask	PF1	70-7849	Grayish coarse ware.	H 10.0	W 6.5
68	Pilgrim flask	PF1	70-7854	Reddish-brown ware.	H 7+	W 7.0
69	Pilgrim flask	PF1	70-7853	Brownish-buff ware.	H 6+	W 6.0
70	Pilgrim flask	PF1	70-7852	Orange-buff ware. Black-painted concentric circles.	H 7+	W 7.0
71	Dipper juglet	DJ1	70-7830	Light buff ware, white grits.	H 8.0	W 5.0
72	Dipper juglet	DJ1	70-7831	Brownish-red ware.	H 8.5+	W 6.0
73	Dipper juglet	DJ2	70-7833	Brownish-buff ware.	H 12.5	W 6.5
74	Dipper juglet	DJ2	70-7832	Reddish-brown ware.	H 12.0	W 6.5
75	Dipper juglet	DJ2	70-7834	Reddish-brown ware.	H 13.0	W 7.5
76	Dipper juglet	DJ2	70-7835	Reddish-brown ware, white grits.	H 13.5	W 6.5
77	Dipper juglet	DJ2	70-7838	Reddish-brown ware.	H 12.5	W 5.0
78	Dipper juglet	DJ2	70-7836	Reddish-brown ware, white grits.	H 10.5	W 6.0
79	Dipper juglet	DJ2	70-7839	Grayish-buff ware, white grits.	Fr	
80	Dipper juglet	DJ2	70-7841	Pinkish-buff ware.	Fr	
81	Dipper juglet	DJ2	70-7840	Reddish-gray ware, white grits.	Fr	
82	Dipper juglet	DJ2	70-7842	Pinkish-buff ware, white grits.	Fr	
83*	Cooking pot	C3	70-7887	Reddish-brown ware, white grits.	Fr	
84	Juglet	CP6	70-7843	Reddish-brown ware, worn.	H 7+	W 5.5
85*	Juglet	CP9	70-7847	Buff ware. Matt, black-painted decoration.	Fr	
86*	Juglet	CP9	70-7848	Yellowish-buff ware.	H 8.5	W 6.5

Small Finds

No.	Object		IAA No.	Description	Dimensions (cm)	
87*	Ring		48-5	Bronze. Ends overlapping, probably part of fibula.	D 1.5	
88*	Ring		48-9/1	Iron, badly corroded.	D 1.5	
89	Bracelet		48-4	Bronze. Fragment.	L 4.5	

Catalogue of Finds, Tomb Z I, Eastern Chamber (contd., Fig. 3.1)

No.	Object	Type	IAA No.	Description	Dimensions (cm)	
90	Bracelet		48-7	Bronze. Fragment.	D 6.0	
91	Fibula		48-3	Bronze. Fragment.	L 4+	
92*	Fibula		48-6	Bronze. Pin wound spirally; bow broken.	L 9.5	
93	Fibula		48-8	Iron. Pin missing; badly corroded.	L 8.5+	
94*	Bead		48-9	Glass. Cylindrical; dark brown with white trailed decoration.	D 1.2	
95*	Bead		48-10	Blue glass. Oblate globular.	D 1.3	
96	Bead		48-10/1	Carnelian. Oblate globular.	D 0.8	
97	2 beads		48-10/2	Faience. Cylindrical; broken.	L 0.6+, 0.4+	
98*	5 beads		48-11	Glass. Oblate globular.	D 0.3–0.6	
99	Amulet		48-9/3	Pebble. Flat, elongated.	L 4.5	W 1.7

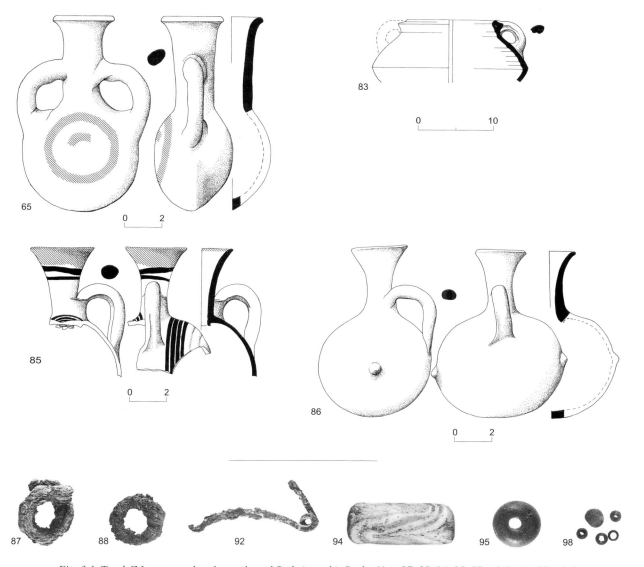

Fig. 3.1. Tomb Z I, eastern chamber, selected finds (contd.). Scale: Nos. 87, 88, 94, 95, 98— 1:1; No. 92—1:3.

Catalogue of Finds, Tomb Z I, Western Chamber
(For pottery types see Chapter 5. Fr = fragment; * = illustrated in Fig. 3.2)

No.	Object	Type	IAA No.	Description	Dimensions (cm)		References
Pottery							
1	Bowl	B1 I	70-7950	Coarse orange-brown ware, white and black grits.	Fr		
2	Bowl	B1 I	70-7953	Coarse orange-brown ware.	Fr		
3	Bowl	B1 I	70-7952	Coarse reddish-brown ware. White slip inside, with red-painted band below rim.	H 6.0		
4	Bowl	B2 III	70-7947	Grayish-yellow ware, white grits.	H 2.0	D 18.5	
5*	Bowl	B2 IV	70-7949	Reddish-brown ware, gray core.	Fr		
6	Bowl	B5 IV	70-7948	Coarse reddish-brown ware, white grits.	H 2.0	D 13.5	
7	Bowl	B8 IV	70-7955	Pinkish-buff ware.	Fr		
8*	Bowl	B9 III	70-7954	Brownish-gray ware, white grits. Red- and black-painted decoration inside, red-painted band around rim outside.	Fr		
9	Storage jar	SJ3	70-7957	Yellow-buff ware.	Fr		
10*	Jug	JG1 II	70-7910	Reddish-brown ware, white grits, red slip.	H 21.0	W 15.0	
11	Jug	JG2 I	70-7935	Orange-buff ware, red slip, burnished.	Fr		
12	Jug	JG2 I	70-7934	Orange-buff ware, red slip, burnished.	Fr		
13	Jug	JG2 I	70-7940	Orange-buff ware, red slip, burnished.	H 9+	W 10.5	
14	Jug	JG2 I	70-7933	Orange-buff ware, red slip, burnished.	H 16+	W 11+	
15	Jug	JG2 I	70-7939	Orange-buff ware, red slip, burnished.	Fr		
16	Jug	JG2 I	70-7937	Orange-buff ware, red slip, burnished.	Fr		
17	Jug	JG2 II	70-7936	Orange-buff ware, red slip, burnished.	H 16.0	W 9.0	
18	Jug	JG2 II	70-7938	Reddish-brown ware, white grits.	Fr		
19	Jug	JG5 I	70-7941	Orange-buff ware, red slip, burnished.	H 15+	W 11.5+	
20*	Jug	Misc.	70-7903/1	Yellowish-buff ware, well-levigated. Red-painted decoration.	H 14.5	W 8.0	
21	Jug	JG6 I	70-7909	Pinkish-buff ware, burnished.	W 11.0		
22*	Jug	JG6 III	70-7904	Buff ware. Black- and red-painted decoration on upper part of neck.	H 21.5+	W 10.5	
23*	Jug	JG6 IV	70-7903	Orange-buff ware. Red-painted decoration.	Fr		
24*	Jug	JG7 I	70-7905	Buff ware. Red- and black-painted decoration.	H 18.0	W 11.0	
25	Jug	JG7 IV	70-7911	Coarse reddish-brown ware, black and white grits.	Fr		
26*	Jug	JG8	70-7906	Brownish-buff ware, well-levigated, burnished. Red-painted bands on body.	H 18.0	W 11.5	
27	Pilgrim flask	PF1	70-7917	Reddish-buff ware. Black-painted decoration.	H 8.8	W 5.5	
28	Pilgrim flask	PF1	70-7918	Yellowish-buff ware. Black-painted decoration.	H 5.7+	W 5.5	
29	Pilgrim flask	PF1	70-7914	Yellowish-buff ware. Black-painted decoration.	H 9.5	W 5.0	
30	Pilgrim flask	PF1	70-7921	Reddish-brown ware. Black-painted decoration.	Fr		
31	Pilgrim flask	PF1	70-7922	Brownish-buff ware. Black-painted decoration.	H 5.5+	W 5.3	
32	Pilgrim flask	PF1	70-7919	Reddish-brown ware. Black-painted decoration.	H 10.0	W 6.2	
33	Pilgrim flask	PF1	70-7920	Brownish-buff ware, white grits.	·H 6+	W 5.0	
34	Dipper juglet	DJ1	70-7916	Coarse reddish-brown ware, white grits.	H 10.0	W 6.5	
35	Dipper juglet	DJ1	70-7928	Coarse grayish-brown ware.	H 9.5	W 5.4	
36	Dipper juglet	DJ1	70-7926	Coarse reddish-brown ware, white grits.	Fr		
37*	Dipper juglet	DJ1	70-7899	Buff ware.	H 9.0	W 5.5	
38	Dipper juglet	DJ2	70-7915	Coarse reddish-brown ware, white grits.	H 10.5	W 5.4	
39	Dipper juglet	DJ2	70-7927	Coarse reddish-brown ware, white grits.	H 12+	W 7.0	
40	Dipper juglet	DJ2	70-7931	Coarse reddish-brown ware, white grits.	H 11+	W 6.0	
41	Dipper juglet	DJ2	70-7923	Coarse reddish-brown ware, white grits.	H 7.0	W 4.5	
42*	Cooking pot	C3	70-7958	Coarse reddish-brown ware, gray core, white grits.	H 13+	D 23+	
43	Barrel-shaped juglet	CP9	70-7913	Fine buff ware. Traces of red paint on rim.	H 8.8	W 6.5	

Catalogue of Finds, Tomb Z I, Western Chamber (contd., Fig. 3.2)

No.	Object	Type	IAA No.	Description	Dimensions (cm)		References
44	Barrel-shaped juglet	CP9	70-7932	Fine buff ware.	Fr		
Small Finds							
45*	Figurine		70-7102	Terracotta. Horse-and-rider.	H 10.2	L 8.2	See Chap. 7: No. 14
46	Fragments of charred wood		48-2				

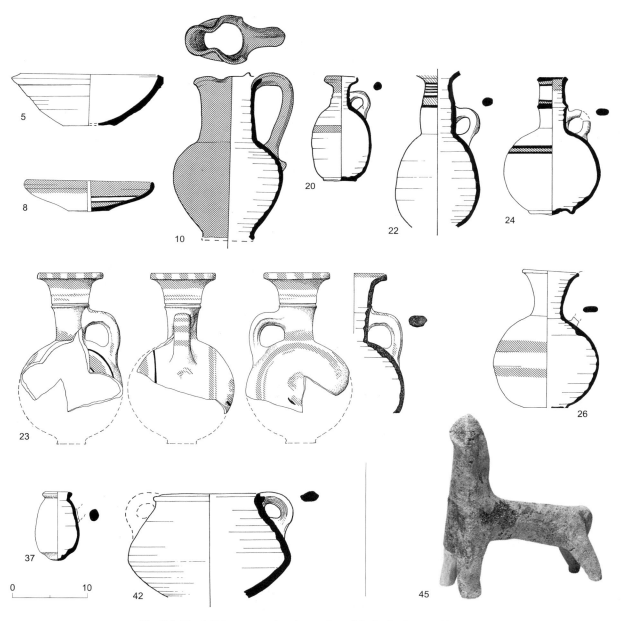

Fig. 3.2. Tomb Z I, western chamber, selected finds. Scale: No. 45—1:2.

Catalogue of Finds, Tomb Z I, Vestibule

(For pottery types see Chapter 5; * = illustrated in Fig. 3.3)

No.	Object	Type	IAA No.	Description	Dimensions (cm)	
Pottery						
1*	Bowl	B3 II	70-7896	Fine buff ware.	H 4.5	D 21.0
2*	Bowl	B4 VI	70-7895	Coarse reddish-brown ware, white grits.	H 6.5	D 12.5
3	Jug	JG6 I	70-7891	Orange-buff ware. Black- and red-painted decoration on upper part of neck.	H 16+	W 11.0
Small Finds						
4*	Armlet	48-1		Bronze.	D 11.5	

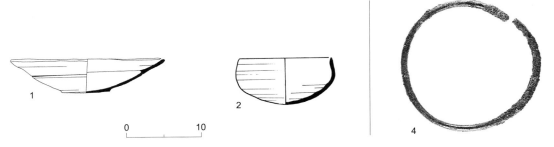

Fig. 3.3. Tomb Z I, vestibule, selected finds. Scale: No. 4—1:3.

Tomb Z II (Type 2; Plan 3.2)

The tomb consists of a shallow rectangular shaft and a large burial chamber. The shaft (0.88 × 1.30 m; depth

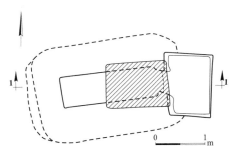

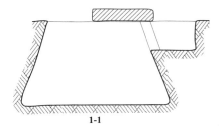

Plan 3.2. Tomb Z II, plan and section.

0.60 m) ends in an abrupt deep drop into the chamber. The chamber entrance (width 0.50 m; height 0.63 m) was originally closed with a rectangular stone slab (0.73 × 0.80 m; thickness 0.07 m), which was found lying in the shaft. The chamber is rectangular (2.00 × 2.88 m), with walls sloping sharply inward, giving it the form of a truncated pyramid. The burial chamber ceiling has a rectangular opening in the middle (0.63 × 2.00 m), covered with two large stone slabs; only one was recovered *in situ* (0.90 × 1.20 m; thickness 0.22 m).

Chronology: As the tomb was found looted and empty, no dating was possible.

Tomb Z III (Type 2; Plan 3.3; Fig. 3.4)

The tomb consists of a large burial chamber accessible via a rectangular shaft (width 1.13 m; depth 0.88 m). A shallow depression (*c.* 0.10 m deep, 0.63 m wide) is present in the center of the shaft floor. At 0.88 m below surface level a narrow opening (length 0.38 m; height 0.50 m) leads to the burial chamber.

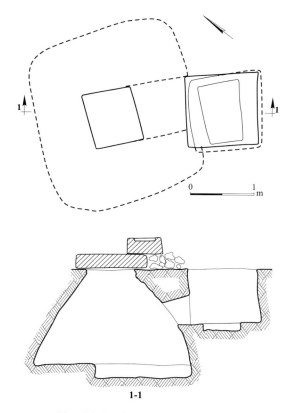

1-1

Plan 3.3. Tomb Z III, plan and section.

ber roof consists of a wide opening (width 0.75 m) covered with flat dressed stone slabs laid in two regular courses, one above the other. The stone slabs were laid on a bedding of lime mortar, sand and stone chips. One of the stones in the upper layer is trough-shaped, evidently in secondary use. A broken, pointed-base jar was discovered outside the tomb.

The tomb had been robbed and the burials were unearthed in a disturbed state. Burial remains lay on the floor near the entrance. Some bones were uncovered in the pit, but there was no way of ascertaining whether they had been placed there originally or whether they had shifted down from above. In the eastern part of the pit, just below the entrance, a group of pottery vessels was located next to the rock and lying against it. These included pointed-base jars, a holemouth jar, a complete bowl, the head of a pottery animal figurine and several other vessels. It seems likely that the pit had served as a repository.

Despite its disturbed state, the tomb yielded a considerable number of finds. It contained complete pottery vessels, as well as some small finds. Of particular interest is a pottery mask with a wrinkled face, the head of a pottery horse figurine and a clay model of a figure kneading dough.

The entrance to the burial chamber was found open. The chamber plan is roughly square (2.50 × 2.75 m; height 1.55 m), with walls sloping steeply inward, forming a truncated pyramid. The chamber floor is 0.75 m lower than the floor level of the shaft. In its center is a rectangular pit (0.88 × 1.75 m; 0.25 m deep). The cham-

Chronology: The bulk of the pottery dates to the 8th–7th centuries BCE, based mainly on types such as the red-burnished jugs (JG2 I, JG5 I, and JG5 II), which form one-third of the pottery assemblage. Some vessels, such as an urn (Type K1) and storage jars (Type SJ1), belong to the late Iron Age, 7th–6th century repertoire.

Catalogue of Finds, Tomb Z III
(For pottery types see Chapter 5. Fr = fragment; * = illustrated in Fig. 3.4)

No.	Object	Type	IAA No.	Description	Dimensions (cm)		References
Pottery							
1	Bowl	B3 III	69-7664	Reddish-brown ware.	Fr		
2*	Bowl	Hellenistic	69-7650	Yellowish-buff ware.	H 3.5	D 10.0	
3*	Krater (urn)	K1	69-7659	Orange-buff ware, white grits. Red slip.	H 38.0	W 30.0	
4*	Storage jar	SJ1	69-7661	Reddish-brown ware.	H 45.0	W 22.0	
5*	Storage jar		69-7662	Brownish-buff ware, white grits.	Fr		
6*	Holemouth jar	HJ1	44.248	Brownish-buff ware, burnished. Red- and black-painted decoration.	H 19.5	W 22.0	
7	Jug	JG2 I	69-7647	Orange-buff ware, dark red slip, burnished.	H 20.0	W 11.0	
8	Jug	JG2 I	69-7646	Orange-buff ware, red slip, burnished.	H 19.0	W 11.0	
9	Jug	JG2 I	69-7645	Orange-buff ware, dark red slip, burnished.		W 9.0	

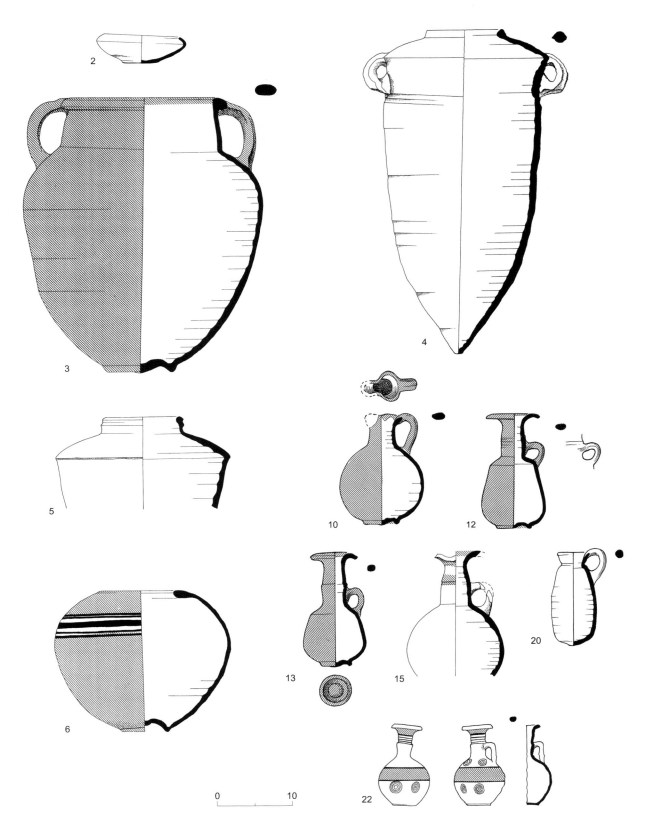

Fig. 3.4. Tomb Z III, selected finds.

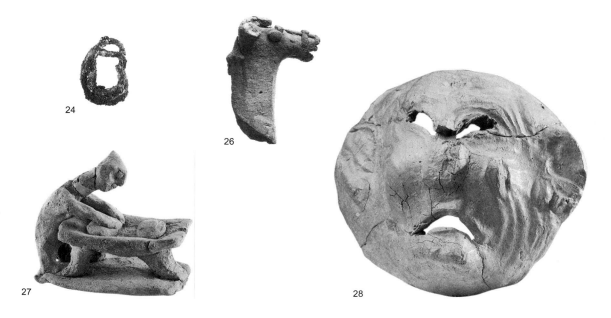

Fig. 3.4. Tomb Z III, selected finds (contd.). Scale: No. 24—1:1; Nos. 26–28, 1:2.

Catalogue of Finds, Tomb Z III (contd., Fig. 3.4)

No.	Object	Type	IAA No.	Description	Dimensions (cm)			References
10*	Jug	JG3 III	69-7649	Orange-buff ware, dark red slip, burnished.	H 15.0	W 10.5		
11	Jug	JG5 I	69-7648	Orange-buff ware, dark red slip, burnished.	H 18.5	W 9.0		
12*	Jug	JG5 I	69-7642	Orange-buff ware, dark red slip, burnished.		W 8.5		
13*	Jug	JG5 II	69-7643	Orange-buff ware, dark red slip, burnished.	H 15.0	W 8.5		
14	Jug	JG5 II	69-7644	Orange-buff ware, dark red slip, burnished.	H 18.0	W 11.5		
15*	Jug	JG6 II	69-7657	Brownish-buff ware, red-painted bands on upper part of neck, burnished.	H 15+	W 12+		
16	Jug	JG6 II	69-7658	Yellowish-buff ware.	Fr			
17	Dipper juglet	DJ1	69-7655	Reddish-brown ware, white grits.	H 8.5	W 5.5		
18	Dipper juglet	DJ2	69-7654	Reddish-brown ware, white grits.	H 12.0	W 6.0		
19	Dipper juglet	DJ2	69-7653	Reddish-brown ware, white grits.	H 13.0	W 6.0		
20*	Dipper juglet	DJ2	69-7651	Reddish-brown ware, white grits.	H 12.0	W 6.0		
21	Dipper juglet	DJ2	69-7652	Reddish-brown ware, white grits.	H 12.0	W 6.0		
22*	Juglet	CP7	69-7641	Pinkish-buff ware. Red- and black-painted decoration.	H 11.0	W 6.5		

Small Finds

No.	Object		IAA No.	Description	Dimensions (cm)			References
23	2 earrings		48-12	Bronze. Crescent-shaped; fragments.	D 2.1			
24*	2 earrings		48-13	Bronze. Crescent-shaped; attached.	L 1.9	W 1.2		
25	Tool		48-14	Iron. Fragment.	L 5.0	W 1.0		
26*	Animal figurine		48-15	Terracotta. Head of a horse.	L 7.0	W 4.8		See Chap. 7: No. 16
27*	Human figurine		44.51	Terracotta. Breadmaker.	H 7.0	L 7.5	W 5.5	See Chap. 7: No. 11
28*	Mask		44.52	Terracotta. Grotesque.	L 13.5	W 13.8		See Chap. 7: No. 23

Tomb Z IV (Type 2; Plan 3.4; Fig. 3.5)

This tomb consists of a single burial chamber approached by an irregularly-shaped oblong shaft. Three rock-cut steps descend into the chamber on the southern side. These steps probably became obsolete when the chamber was covered with stone slabs and was then entered through the shaft (1.13 × 1.55 m). At 0.88 m below surface level an opening (width 0.80 m) leads from the shaft to the burial chamber. The entrance to the chamber was found open, with the closing slab lying in the shaft.

The rectangular chamber (2.38 × 3.13 m; height 1.30 m) has a shallow oval pit in the center (depth 0.13 m). The chamber walls slope slightly inward. The roof is a wide rectangular opening (1.88 × 2.43 m), which originally was probably covered with stone slabs, none of which were found.

The tomb was found looted with only a few pottery vessels left intact.

Chronology: The few vessels uncovered in this tomb can be dated to the 8th century BCE.

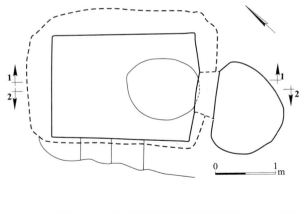

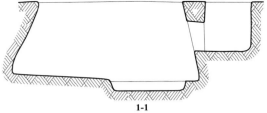

1-1

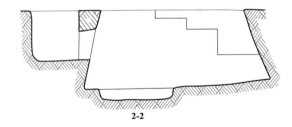

2-2

Plan 3.4. Tomb Z IV, plan and section.

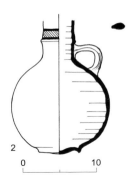

Fig. 3.5. Tomb Z IV, jug.

Catalogue of Finds, Tomb Z IV

(For pottery types see Chapter 5. * = illustrated in Fig. 3.5)

No.	Object	Type	IAA No.	Description	Dimensions (cm)	
Pottery						
1	Jug	JG6 I	70-8492	Reddish-brown ware, burnished. Black- and red-painted decoration.	H 20.5	W 11.0
2*	Jug	JG6 I	70-7992	Reddish-brown ware, burnished. Black- and red-painted decoration.	H 19.5+	W 12.0
3	Jug	JG6 I	70-8498	Brownish-red ware, burnished. Remnants of black paint on neck.	H 13.5+	W 11.0
4	Dipper juglet	DJ2	70-8497	Brownish-red ware, white grits.	H 12.0	W 5.6
5	Dipper juglet	DJ2	70-8495	Yellowish-buff ware.	H 10.6	W 6.0

Tomb Z V (Type 1; Plan 3.5; Fig. 3.6)

The tomb has a single burial chamber approached by a square shaft (1.00 × 1.13 m; depth 1.25 m). The shaft is deeper than the usual shafts in this cemetery and has two rock-cut steps. An opening (length 0.25 m) leads from the shaft to the chamber, the entrance (width 0.63 m) to which was found open. A large stone slab, probably used to close the entrance, lay in the upper part of the shaft's fill.

The chamber is rectangular in plan (2.38 × 2.75 m; height 2.63 m). The wall opposite the shaft slopes sharply inward, ending in a rock-cut roof.

The tomb had been opened previously and only one complete pottery jug and some small finds were recovered.

Chronology: The only pottery vessel found in this tomb dates to the late 9th–8th centuries BCE; this and the fragmentary small finds recovered are insufficient for an exact dating.

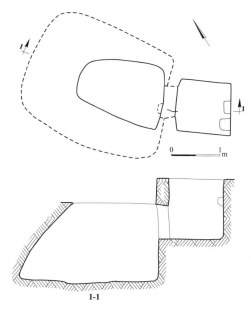

Plan 3.5. Tomb Z V, plan and section.

Catalogue of Finds, Tomb Z V
(For pottery types see Chapter 5. * = illustrated in Fig. 3.6)

No.	Object	Type	IAA No.	Description	Dimensions (cm)	
Pottery						
1	Jug	JG2 I	71-8429	Orange-buff ware, dark red slip, burnished.	H 12.0	W 10.0
Small Finds						
2	Fibula pin		48-17	Bronze. Fragment.	L 3.0	
3*	2 beads		48-24	Ivory. Fragments.	D 1.0	
4	Handle		48-21	Ivory. Fragment in shape of a vertebra.	L 3.5	W 1.8
5*	Pomegranate		48-22	Ivory. Half.	L 1.5	W 1.4
6	5 pieces of inlay		48-26	Ivory. Incised.	L 3.0–4.0	W 2.0–2.5
7.	Dagger sheath(?)		48-16	Iron. Broken, traces of bronze nails.	L 4.0–6.0	W 1.0–4.0
8	2 prisms		48-18	Bronze.	L 0.5	W 0.5
9	Game piece		48-25	Faience. Conical; top broken.	D 1.5	H 1+

3

5

Fig. 3.6. Tomb Z V, selected finds. Scale: No. 3—1:1; No. 5—1.5:1.

Tomb Z VI (Type 2; Plan 3.6; Fig. 3.7)

The tomb has a single burial chamber approached by a shallow rectangular shaft (0.95 × 1.13 m; depth 0.63 m), with a rock-hewn step in one corner. An opening (width 0.50 m) leads from the shaft to the burial chamber. The entrance to the chamber was open and no closing slab was recovered. The rectangular chamber (1.72 × 2.88 m;

height 1.60 m) has slightly inward-sloping walls. The wide, rectangular opening (1.00 × 2.43 m) at the top of the chamber was covered with five long, thick stone slabs. The tomb had been opened previously and no burials could be traced. The finds consisted of some pottery vessels and a bronze bowl, as well as a group of small finds: beads, amulets, etc.

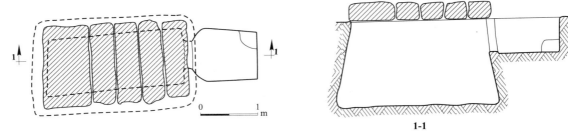

Plan 3.6. Tomb Z VI, plan and section.

Chronology: The pottery vessels show that the tomb was in use during the late 10th–9th centuries BCE based mainly on Types PF1, JG6 I and the *askos* (Type M3). The bowls (Type B3 I) indicate continuity into the 8th–7th centuries.

Catalogue of Finds, Tomb Z VI
(For pottery types see Chapter 5. Fr = fragment; * = illustrated in Fig. 3.7)

No.	Object	Type	IAA No.	Description	Dimensions (cm)		References
Pottery							
1*	Bowl	B2 III	70-8005	Reddish-brown ware.	H 4.5	D 19.0	
2*	Bowl	B3 I	70-8004	Brownish-yellow ware.	H 3.0	D 24.0	
3	Bowl	B3 I	70-8006	Yellowish-buff ware. Incisions around base.	Fr		
4	Bowl	B3 I	70-8006	Reddish-brown ware.	Fr		
5*	Bowl	B7 II	70-8003	Grayish-buff ware. Red slip, burnished.	H 4.5	D 26.0	
6*	Jug	JG6 I	70-7992	Yellow-pinkish ware, white grits, burnished. Black- and red-painted decoration.	H 18.5	W 12.0	
7	Pilgrim flask	PF1	70-7995	Reddish-brown coarse ware.	H 6+	W 6.0	
8*	Cooking pot	C1	70-8007	Reddish-brown ware, gray core, white grits.	Fr		
9*	*Askos*	M3	67-43	Reddish-brown ware, white grits. Red slip, burnished.	H 8.5	W 14.0	
Small Finds							
10*	Ring		48-66	Red gold. Mount.	D 1.0		
11	Bracelets and pins		48-31	Bronze. Fragments.			
12	Fibula pin		48-34	Bronze.	L 7.0		
13*	Bead		48-65	Gold leaf, dark fill inside (bitumen?). Biconical ribbed, collars at both ends.	L 0.5	D 0.7	Gjerstad 1948: Fig. 35:10
14	Bead		48-44	Greenish faience. Fluted, melon-shaped.		D 0.5	
15*	2 beads		48-46	Bluish faience. Barrel-shaped, melon-shaped ribbed.	L 0.5, 0.8	D 0.3, 0.5	
16*	Bead		48-45	Bluish faience. Barrel-shaped, ribbed.	L 0.9	D 0.5	
17*	Bead		48-58	Greenish faience. Melon-shaped.		D 0.5	
18*	Bead		48-47	Bluish faience. Cylindrical.	L 0.3		
19	Bead		48-39	Black glass. Oblate globular, fragment.			
20*	Bead		48-48	Black glass. Oblate globular.		D 0.8	
21*	4 beads		48-51	Black glass. Oblate globular.		D 0.3–0.5	
22*	Bead		48-57	Brown glass. Oblate globular.		D 0.8	
23*	3 beads		48-59	Carnelian. Oblate globular.		D 0.6–0.8	
24*	Bead		48-64	Carnelian. Oblate globular.		D 0.5	
25*	2 beads		48-60	Carnelian. Cylindrical, barrel-shaped.	L 1.2, 1.3		
26*	Bead		48-62	Amethyst. Oblate globular.		D 0.6	
27*	Bead		48-43	Alabaster. Cylindrical.	L 1.3		

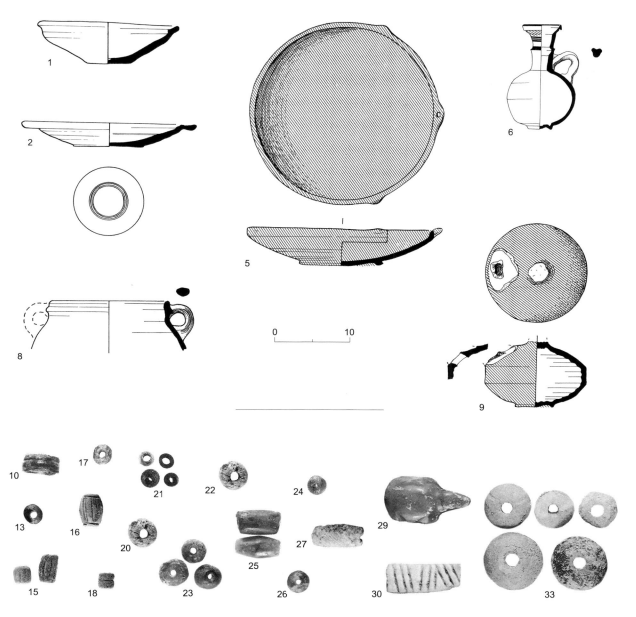

Fig. 3.7. Tomb Z VI, selected finds. Scale, small finds— 1:1.

Catalogue of Finds, Tomb Z VI (contd., Fig. 3.7)

No.	Object	Type	IAA No.	Description	Dimensions (cm)		References
28	Pendant		48-61	Carnelian. Lotus-shaped.	L 1.9	W 0.8	
29*	Pendant		48-63	Carnelian with white spots. Turtle-shaped.	L 2.3	W 1.3	Petrie 1914: Pl. XLI: 239b
30*	Inlay		48-37	Bone. Rectangular, decorated with incisions.	L 2.0	W 0.8	
31	Bowl		48-29	Bronze. Fragment.			
32	Knife		48-30	Iron. Broken.	L 12+	W 2.0	
33*	5 spindle whorls		48-36	Bone. Flat bottom and domed or rounded top.	D 1.0–1.6		Pritchard 1988: Fig. 22

Tomb Z VII (Fig. 3.8)

No plan or description available.

Catalogue of Finds, Tomb Z VII

(* = illustrated in Fig. 3.8)

No.	Object	IAA No.	Description	Dimensions (cm)	
Small Finds					
1	Bracelet	48-69	Bronze. Fragment.	L 4.0	
2	Pin	48-68	Bronze. Broken.	L 4.5	
3*	Bead	48-70	Carnelian. Biconical.	L 1.2	D 0.5
4*	Bead	48-71	Marble. Prism-shaped.	L 1.5	W 1.0

3   4

Fig. 3.8. Tomb Z VII, selected finds. Scale—1:1.

Chronology: No pottery vessels reported; the few small finds do not allow a clear dating.

Tomb Z VIII

No description or plan available.

Tomb Z IX (Type 1; Plan 3.7)

The tomb has a roughly rectangular straight shaft (0.75 × 1.00 m; depth 0.88–1.00 m) without a stairway.

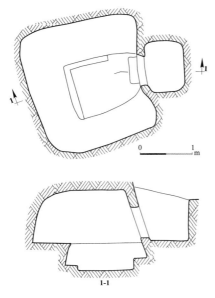

1-1

Plan 3.7. Tomb Z IX, plan and section.

An opening (length 0.12 m) at the bottom leads into the burial chamber. This roughly rectangular chamber (2.25 m × 2.50 m; height 1.13) has a rectangular trough (1.12 × 1.50 m; depth 0.50 m) in the center. Its edges (width 0.13 m) are higher on two sides than at the center, forming a bench along these sides. A rock-cut step (height 0.33 m) facilitated the descent from the passage into the trough. The walls of the chamber slope slightly inward toward a rock-cut roof.

Chronology: It appears that the tomb was looted mainly in antiquity, since the fill of the shaft consists of hardened sand and was found full of tree roots. No finds were reported and dating is therefore impossible.

Tomb Z X (Type 1; Plan 3.8; Fig. 3.9)

The tomb consists of a burial chamber approached by a small, roughly rectangular shaft (0.88 × 1.00 m; depth 0.88 m). An opening (length 0.25 m), found open, leads to the burial chamber. Three steps descend from the opening down to the oval pit (1.75 × 2.00 m; depth 0.63 m) dug into the chamber floor. The almost square chamber (2.38 × 2.50 m; height 1.5 m) has high benches (0.63 m) along two sides. The walls are fairly vertical, meeting a rock-cut ceiling.

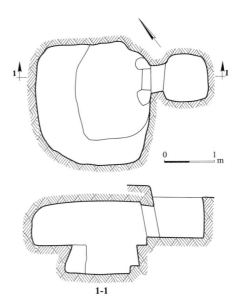

1-1

Plan 3.8. Tomb Z X, plan and section.

Although the tomb was found open—it had probably been looted—it contained many pottery vessels, mostly broken, and a group of small finds.

Catalogue of Finds, Tomb Z X

(For pottery types see Chapter 5. Fr = fragment; * = illustrated in Fig. 3.9)

No.	Object	Type	IAA No.	Description	Dimensions (cm)	
Pottery						
1*	Bowl	B1 I	70-7746	Reddish-brown ware.	H 5.5	W 19.0
2*	Bowl	B2 III	70-7745	Reddish-brown ware, white grits.	H 4.5	
3*	Bowl	B3 III	70-7743	Reddish-yellow ware.	H 3.5	D 23.0
4*	Bowl	B3 IV	70-7744	Coarse reddish-brown ware, white grits.	H 4.0	D 20.0
5*	Storage jar	SJ5	70-8531	Coarse reddish-brown ware.	H 55.0	W 35.0
6	Jug	JG2 II	70-7762	Orange-buff ware, red slip, burnished.	H 17+	
7*	Jug	JG2 II	70-7763	Orange-buff ware, red slip, burnished.	Fr	
8	Jug	JG2 II	70-7766	Reddish-brown ware, white grits. No slip or burnish.	Fr	
9*	Jug	JG3 I	70-7160	Coarse reddish-brown ware, white grits.	H 21.5	W 12.0
10	Jug	JG5 I	X 39	Orange-buff ware, red slip, burnished.	Fr	
11	Jug	JG5 I	70-7770	Orange-buff ware, red slip, burnished.	H 14+	W 9.5
12	Jug	JG5 I	70-7771	Orange-buff ware, red slip, burnished.	Fr	
13*	Jug	Misc.	70-7761	Orange-buff ware, red slip, burnished.	W 8.5	
14	Jug	JG5 I	70-7767	Orange-buff ware, red slip, burnished.	Fr	
15	Jug	JG5 I	70-7773	Orange-buff ware, red slip, burnished.	Fr	
16*	Jug	Misc.	70-7752	Pinkish-buff ware, red slip, burnished.	H 21.0	W 9.0
17*	Jug	JG5 II	70-7774	Orange-buff ware, red slip, burnished.	H 18.5	W 10.0
18*	Jug	JG5 III	70-7765	Pinkish-buff ware, red slip, burnished.	Fr	
19	Jug	JG5 IV	70-7769	Pinkish-buff ware, red slip, burnished.	Fr	
20*	Jug	JG6 I	70-7753	Brownish-gray ware, white grits. Red- and black-painted decoration.	H 21.0	W 11.0
21	Pilgrim flask	PF1	70-7747	Coarse reddish-gray ware.	H 7+	W 7.0
22	Pilgrim flask	PF1	70-7748	Coarse reddish-brown ware, white and black grits.	H 7.5+	W 7.0
23	Pilgrim flask	PF1	70-7749	Coarse reddish-brown ware, black grits.	H 5.5+	W 5.0
24	Dipper juglet	DJ1	70-7754	Reddish-brown ware, white grits.	H 11.5	W 5.2
25	Dipper juglet	DJ1	70-7951	Pinkish-buff ware.	Fr	
26	Dipper juglet	DJ2	70-7755	Light buff ware.	H 12.0	W 6.0
27	Dipper juglet	DJ2	70-7758	Coarse reddish-brown ware, white grits.	Fr	
28*	Juglet	CP5	70-7724	Grayish-buff ware, white slip. Black-painted decoration.	Fr	
29*	Barrel juglet	CP9	70-7716	Light buff ware, buff slip, burnished. Matt, black- and red-painted decoration.	H 9.0	W 6.5
Small Finds						
30	Earrings and pins		48-82	Bronze. Fragments.		
31*	Ring		48-75	Silver and green jasper. With scaraboid.	D 2.6	
32	Bead		48-78	Bluish glass. Oblate globular, broken.	D 0.4	
33*	Bead		48-79/1	Dark basalt(?). Cylindrical.	L 1.5	D 0.8
34*	Bead		48-79	Black steatite. Cylindrical.	L 1.8	D 1.0
35*	Bead		48-80	Blue faience. Cylindrical, ribbed.	L 1.0	D 0.5
36	9 beads		48-84	Bluish glass. Oblate globular, broken.		
37*	Bead		48-74	Bone. Rectangular plaque/spacer. One side depicts a Horus eye, the other a crouching sphinx.	W 1.2	L 0.9
38*	Spindle whorl		48-76	Bone. Broken.	L 0.8	D 1.4
39*	Spindle whorl		48-77	Bone. Flat base, rounded on other side.	D 1.4	

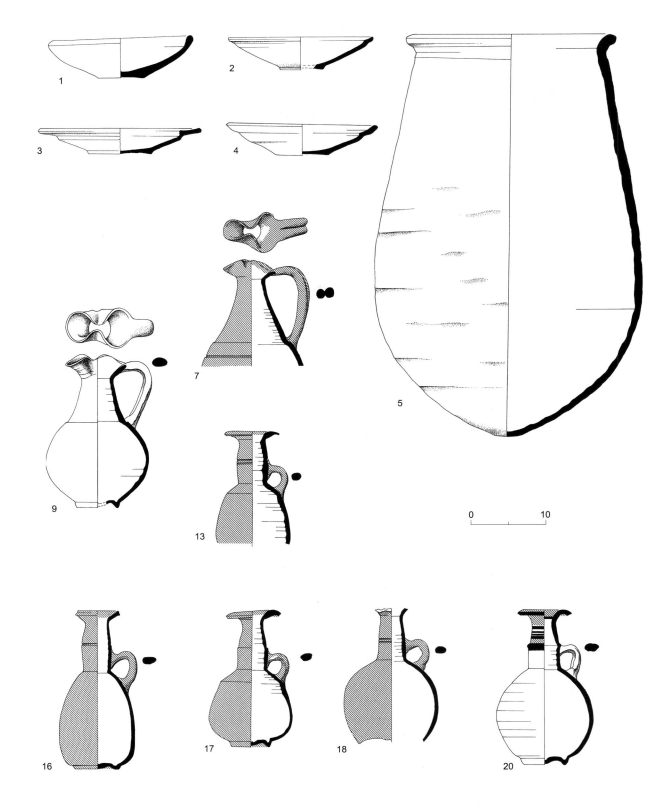

Fig. 3.9. Tomb Z X, selected finds.

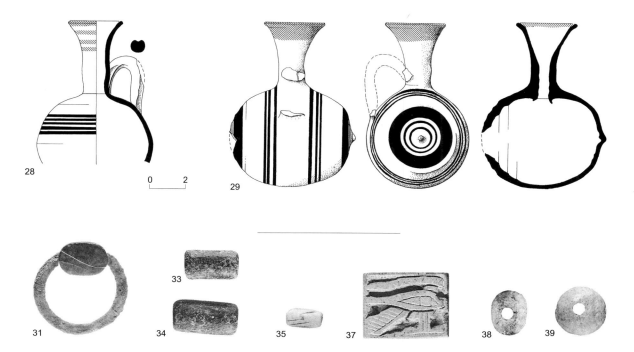

Fig. 3.9. Tomb Z X, selected finds (contd.). Scale: Nos. 31, 33, 34, 35, 38, 39—1:1; No. 37—2:1.

Chronology: This is one of the cemetery's earlier tombs. The earliest pottery types (PF1, CP5 and CP9) are dated to the 10th–9th centuries BCE. The largest group of vessels, forming 50% of the assemblage, are the red-burnished jugs (JG5 I, JG2 II, etc.) dating from the 8th century BCE.

Tomb Z XI (Fig. 3.10)
No description or plan available.

Chronology: The tomb contained one of the earliest and richest assemblages excavated. Most of the vessels date to the 10th–9th centuries BCE (Types B9 II, PF1,

Catalogue of Finds, Tomb Z XI
(For pottery types see Chapter 5. Fr = fragment; * = illustrated in Fig. 3.10)

No.	Object	Type	IAA No.	Description	Dimensions (cm)		References
Pottery							
1	Bowl	B1 I	70-7135	Reddish-brown ware.	H 4.5	D 17.0	
2	Bowl	B1 I	70-7734	Reddish-brown ware, white grits.	Fr		
3	Bowl	B2 III	70-7736	Reddish-gray ware, white grits.	Fr		
4	Bowl	B4 V	70-7740	Reddish-brown ware, white grits. Black-painted concentric circles on interior.	H 5.0	D 12.0	
5*	Bowl	B6 I	70-7731	Reddish-buff ware.	H 5.0	D 21.0	
6	Bowl	B6 II	70-7741	Coarse reddish-brown ware, white grits.	Fr		
7*	Bowl	B6 II	70-7738	Reddish-brown ware, white grits. Base missing.	D 26.0		
8	Bowl	B8 I	70-7739	Buff ware. Red slip inside and over the rim. Burnished all over.	H 3.5	D 16.0	
9*	Bowl	B9 II	70-7733	Yellow-buff ware. Black- and red-painted bands.	H 6.5	D 23.0	
10*	Bowl	B9 II	70-7732	Pinkish-buff ware, white grits. Black- and red-painted bands on interior.	H 7.5	D 24.0	

Catalogue of Finds, Tomb Z XI (contd., Fig. 3.10)

No.	Object	Type	IAA No.	Description	Dimensions (cm)		References
11	Jug	JG 6V	70-7728	Light reddish-brown ware, white grits.	H 17+	W 12.5	
12	Jug	JG 6V	70-7729	Light reddish-brown ware.	W 16.0		
13	Pilgrim flask	PF1	70-7708	Reddish-buff ware, gray core. Black-painted concentric circles.	H 10.0	W 5.5	
14	Pilgrim flask	PF1	70-7705	Reddish-buff ware, white grits. Black-painted concentric circles on body.	H 9.5+	W 5.5	
15	Pilgrim flask	PF1	70-7706	Reddish-buff ware. Black-painted concentric circles on body.	H 9.5+	W 5.5	
16	Pilgrim flask	PF1	70-7709	Reddish-buff ware. Black-painted concentric circles on body.	Fr		
17	Pilgrim flask	PF1	70-7710	Reddish-buff ware. Gray core. Black-painted concentric circles on body.	Fr		
18	Pilgrim flask	PF1	70-7723	Reddish-buff ware, gray core. Black-painted concentric circles on body.	Fr		
19	Pilgrim flask	PF1	70-7707	Reddish-buff ware, gray core. Black-painted concentric circles on body.	Fr		
20	Pilgrim flask	PF1	70-7712	Coarse reddish-brown ware, white grits.	H 9.0	W 5.0	
21*	Dipper juglet	DJ4	70-7930	Pinkish-buff ware, white grits.	H 10+	W 6.5	
22	Juglet	CP6	70-7923	Fine reddish-brown ware. Black-painted decoration.	H 6.5+	W 4.5	
23	Barrel-shaped juglet	CP9	70-7722	Fine reddish ware, buff slip. Matt, black-painted decoration.		W 6.5	
24	Barrel-shaped juglet	CP9	70-7717	Fine reddish-buff ware, white slip. Black-painted decoration.	Fr		
25	Barrel-shaped juglet	CP9	70-7720	Fine buff ware, white slip. Black- and red-painted decoration.	Fr		
26	Barrel-shaped juglet	CP9	70-7721	Buff ware. Black- and red-painted decoration.	Fr		
27	Barrel-shaped juglet	CP9	70-7718	Buff ware, light slip. Black- and red-painted decoration.	Fr		
28*	Barrel-shaped juglet	CP10	70-7715	Brownish-buff ware, red slip. Black-painted decoration.	Fr		
29*	Pilgrim flask	CP11	70-7714	Fine buff ware. Matt, black- and red-painted decoration.	Fr		

Small Finds

No.	Object	Type	IAA No.	Description	Dimensions (cm)		References
30	Fibula pin		48-105	Bronze.	L 3.0		
31*	Eye-bead		48-90	Blue glass.		D 0.7	
32*	Bead		48-96	Brown glass. Cylindrical, two horizontal grooves in middle.	L 1.0	D 0.8	
33*	3 beads		48-102	Carnelian. Oblate globular, roughly worked.		D 0.8–1.1	
34*	Bead		48-103	Carnelian. Biconical, flat on one side.	L 1.6		
35*	Bead		48-99	Greenish faience. Oblate globular, fluted.		D 0.7	
36*	Bead		48-89	Bluish faience. Oblate globular, fluted.		D 0.7	
37*	3 beads		48-98	Whitish faience. Disk-shaped.		D 0.3–0.5	
38*	Fishhook		48-100	Bronze.	H 3.0		
39*	Stamp seal		48-88	Bone. Conical.	D 0.8	H 1.0	
40*	Bead/spindle whorl		48-93	Bone. Truncated.	H 1.0	D 1.1	
41*	Spindle whorl		48-94	Bone. Dome-shaped.	H 0.6	D 2.3	
42*	Spindle whorl		48-99/1	Bone. Truncated, broken.	H 1.0		
43*	Scarab		48-82	Steatite.	$9.9 \times 7.2 \times 5.1$ (mm)		See App. 2:1; Keel 1997: 20: No. 1
44*	Pomegranate		48-91	Ivory.	H 1.5		

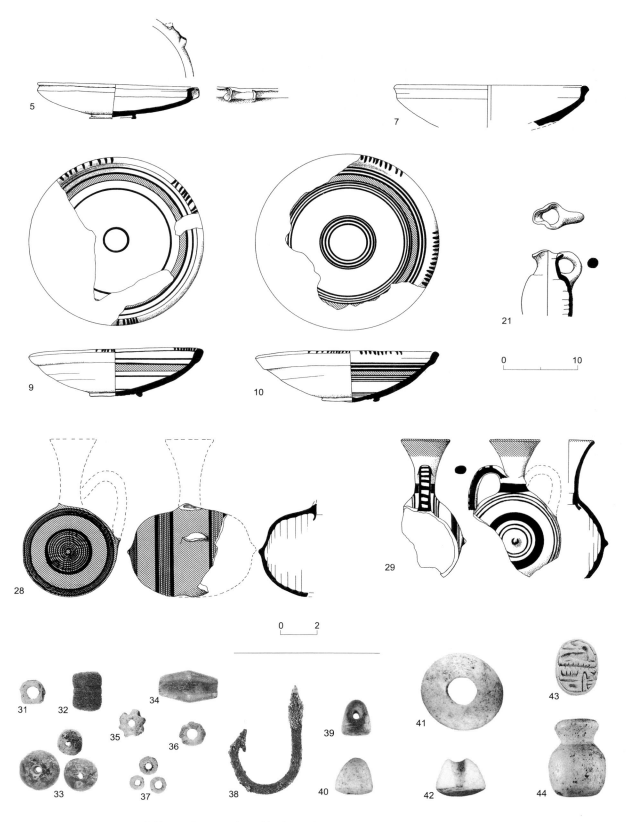

Fig. 3.10. Tomb Z XI, selected finds. Scale: Nos. 31–42—1:1; Nos. 43, 44—1.5:1.

CP9, etc.), with some continuing into the 8th century BCE (Type DJ4). A single scarab from this tomb was dated to the second half of the 10th–8th centuries BCE (see Appendix 2:1; Keel 1997:20: No. 1).

Tomb Z XII
No plan, description or finds reported.

Tomb Z XIII (Type 2; Plan 3.9; Fig. 3.11)
The tomb consists of a large burial chamber approached by a rectangular shaft (depth 1.63 m; width 1.38 m at the bottom), with three rock-cut steps. An opening (length 0.50 m; width 0.75 m at entrance, widening to 0.88 m) leads to the burial chamber. The rectangular chamber (1.75 × 2.00 m) has a small, shallow (0.10 m) depression just inside the doorway. The chamber walls are vertical,

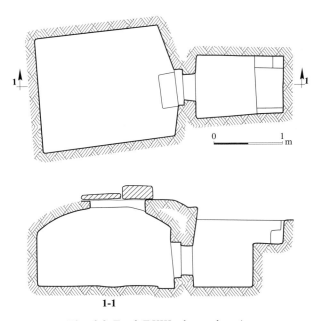

Plan 3.9. Tomb Z XIII, plan and section.

rising to a domed ceiling with a rectangular opening (length 1.25 m) in the center. The opening was closed with two large stone slabs (length *c.* 0.75 m) found *in situ* (one apparently broken by tomb robbers).

The tomb was found looted, except for two oil lamps.

Chronology: The lamps, which date from the Persian period, are an insufficient basis for dating this tomb.

Catalogue of Finds, Tomb Z XIII
(For pottery types see Chapter 5. * = illustrated in Fig. 3.11)

No.	Object	Type	IAA No.	Description	Dimensions (cm)	
Pottery						
1*	Lamp	L1	70-8510	Light buff ware.	H 2.5	D 13.0
2*	Lamp	L2	70-8511	Reddish-brown ware.	H 5.5	D 18.2

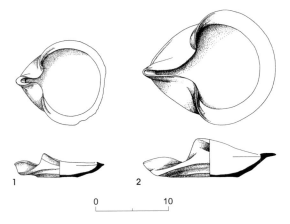

Fig. 3.11. Tomb Z XIII, lamps.

Tomb Z XIV (Type 3; Plan 3.10)
This is a trough tomb consisting of a roughly rectangular shallow pit (1.25 × 2.50 m; depth 1.25) hewn into the rock. It was found open but was probably originally covered with stone slabs, which were removed by looters.

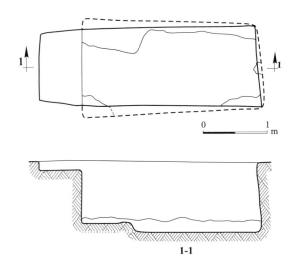

Plan 3.10. Tomb Z XIV, plan and section.

Chronology: Only one bowl from the late 9th century BCE was reported; it does not allow a clear dating of the tomb.

Catalogue of Finds, Tomb Z XIV

(For pottery type see Chapter 5. Not illustrated)

No.	Object	Type	IAA No.	Description	Dimensions (cm)
Pottery					
1	Bowl	B1 I	70-8463	Reddish-brown ware, white grits.	H 5.0 D 18.0

Tomb Z XV

No plan, description or finds reported.

Tomb Z XVI (Type 2; Plan 3.11; Fig. 3.12)

The tomb consists of a medium-sized burial chamber approached by a rectangular shaft (depth 0.70 m; width 1.00 m). In one corner of the shaft are two rock-cut steps. A short opening (length 0.25 m) leads to the rectangular burial chamber (1.88 × 2.75 m; height 1.5 m), with a floor 0.75 m lower than the shaft floor. The chamber walls slope slightly inward, ending in a wide rectangular opening (1.38 × 2.38 m), probably originally covered with stone slabs which were not found.

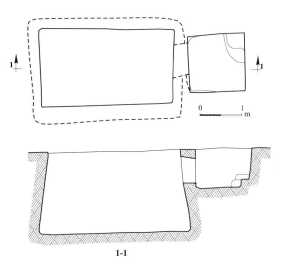

1-1

Plan 3.11. Tomb Z XVI, plan and section.

Catalogue of Finds, Tomb Z XVI

(For pottery types see Chapter 5. * = illustrated in Fig. 3.12)

No.	Object	Type	IAA No.	Description	Dimensions (cm)
Pottery					
1*	Bowl	B7 I	70-8467	Pinkish-buff ware, white and black grits.	H 5.5 D 28.0

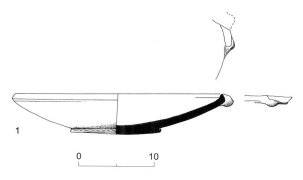

Fig. 3.12. Tomb Z XVI, bowl.

Chronology: The tomb had been looted. Only a single pottery bowl (B7 I) was reported, dated to the 9th century BCE.

Tomb Z XVII (Type 2; Plan 3.12; Fig. 3.13)

The tomb consists of a large burial chamber approached by a small shaft. The shallow shaft is roughly square (1.00 × 1.13 m; depth 0.88 m) and has a step in one corner. An opening (length *c.* 0.20 m), found open, leads to the burial chamber. The rectangular chamber (2.00 × 3.13 m) has a floor 0.63 m lower than the shaft floor (total height 1.5 m). The walls slope slightly inward, forming a truncated pyramid. The wide opening (1.30 × 1.75 m) in the chamber roof was covered with four flat rectangular stone slabs (*c.* 0.75 × 2.00 m) found *in situ*. The slab closest to the entrance was broken, and only one half remained, indicating that the tomb had been entered through the gap by looters.

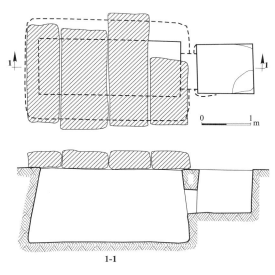

1-1

Plan 3.12. Tomb Z XVII, plan and section.

Catalogue of Finds, Tomb Z XVII

(For pottery types see Chapter 5. * = illustrated in Fig. 3.13)

No.	Object	Type	IAA No.	Description	Dimensions (cm)
Pottery					
1	Bowl	B3 III	70-8337	Reddish-yellow ware, white grits.	Fr
2	Bowl	B8 I	70-8336	Light buff fine ware. Red slip on interior, red and yellow slip alternating in bands on base.	Fr
3*	Jug	JG7 I	70-8325	Orange-buff ware. Red- and black-painted decoration.	H 20.5 W 12.0
Small Finds					
4	Knife and sheath		48-108	Iron. Fragment. Remnants of wood, nails and part of blade adhering.	L 5.0

Fig. 3.13. Tomb Z XVII, jug.

Chronology: Although the scant assemblage does not allow a clear dating, the presence of an 8th century BCE 'Samaria' bowl (Type B8 I) is noteworthy.

Tomb Z XVIII (Type 2; Plan 3.13; Fig. 3.14)

The tomb, similar in shape to Tombs Z VI and Z XVII, has a single burial chamber approached by a rectangular shaft (1.50 × 1.75 m; depth 1.38 m) without steps. The entrance into the burial chamber was blocked with a flat stone slab (length 1.10 m), which was found *in situ*, propped up by a large boulder. The chamber has an elongated rectangular plan (2.25 × 3.63 m; height 1.63 m). Its sloping walls form a truncated pyramid.

The long and narrow opening at the top of the chamber (1 × 3 m) was originally covered with stone slabs, which were probably removed when the chamber was entered through the roof, and the tomb looted.

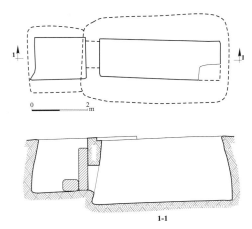

Plan 3.13. Tomb Z XVIII, plan and section.

Chronology: The pottery assemblage clearly indicates that the tomb was used in the 8th–7th centuries BCE, mainly according to Types JG2 I, JG5 I, DJ1. The two scarabs found in it seem to cover a wide span of time, 10th–7th centuries BCE (see Appendix 2:2, 3; Keel 1997:20: Nos. 2, 3).

Catalogue of Finds, Tomb Z XVIII

(For pottery types see Chapter 5. Fr = fragment; * = illustrated in Fig. 3.14)

No.	Object	Type	IAA No.	Description	Dimensions (cm)		References
Pottery							
1	Bowl	B1 I	70-7990	Reddish-brown ware.	Fr		
2*	Bowl	B5 IV	70-7988	Reddish-brown ware, white grits. White wash on the interior.	Fr		
3	Bowl	B5 IV	70-7989	Reddish-brown ware, white grits. White wash on the interior.	H 2.5	D 11.0	
4	Bowl	B8 I	70-7987	Buff ware, red slip, burnished.	Fr		
5*	Jug	JG2 I	67-78	Orange-buff ware, red slip, burnished.	H 18.5	W 10.5	
6	Jug	JG2 I	70-8468	Orange-buff ware, red slip, burnished.	H 22.0	W 11.5	
7	Jug	JG5 I	70-7977	Orange-buff ware, red slip, burnished.	Fr		

Catalogue of Finds, Tomb Z XVIII (contd., Fig. 3.14)

No.	Object	Type	IAA No.	Description	Dimensions (cm)		References
8	Jug	JG6 III	70-7982	Pinkish-buff ware, burnished. Black- and red-painted decoration.	Fr		
9*	Jug	JG6 V	70-7981	Buff ware, white grits.	H 18.5	W 12.0	
10	Dipper juglet	DJ1	70-7963	Light buff ware.	H 7.0	W 3.5	
11*	Dipper juglet	DJ1	70-7964	Light buff ware.	H 11.0	W 5.5	
12	Dipper juglet	DJ1	70-7965	Light buff ware.	Fr		
13	Dipper juglet	DJ1	70-7967	Reddish-brown ware, white grits.	Fr		
14	Dipper juglet	DJ2	70-7966	Reddish-brown ware, white grits.		W 6.5	
15	Lamp	L3	70-7962	Brownish-buff ware, white grits.	Fr		

Small Finds

No.	Object	Type	IAA No.	Description	Dimensions (cm)		References
16	Ring		48-114	Iron. Fragment.	L 2.8		
17	Bracelet		48-116	Bronze. Broken.	L 5.2		
18*	Bead		48-109	Carnelian. Oblate globular.	D 0.6		
19*	Pin		48-112	Ivory. Broken. Shaft tapers to a point.	L 11.3+		
20*	Plaque		48-115	Bronze. Five-sided. Thick (ingot?).	L 2.0	W 1.8	
21.	Long nail		48-113	Iron. Broken.	L 13+		
22*	Spindle whorl		48-111	Bone. Truncated.	D 1.2	H 0.6	
23*	Scarab		48-117/1	Soft composite material. Blue, surface partly gray.	15.2 × 9.6 × 6.9 (mm)		See App. 2:2; Keel: 1997: 20: No. 2
24*	Scarab		48-87	Enstatite.	13.0 × 9.3 × 6 (mm)		See App. 2:3; Keel: 1997: 20: No. 3

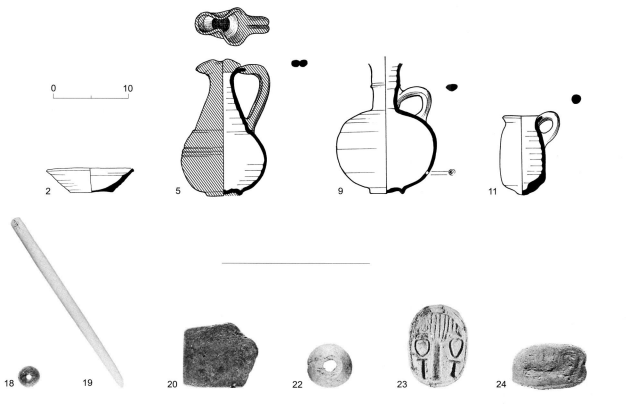

Fig. 3.14. Tomb Z XVIII, selected finds. Scale: Nos. 18, 20, 22—1:1; No. 19—1:2; Nos. 23, 24—1.5:1.

Tomb Z XIX (Type 2; Plan 3.14; Fig. 3.15)
This tomb is of a type common in this cemetery, consisting of a single burial chamber approached by a shaft. The square shaft (1.20 × 1.25 m; total depth 1.13 m) has two rock-cut steps along one wall, the upper one positioned between two adjoining sides. A short and narrow opening leads into the rectangular burial chamber (2.00 × 2.88 m). The walls slope slightly inward, forming a truncated pyramid. The walls end in a wide rectangular opening (1.25 × 2.50 m), which must originally have been covered with stone slabs.

The tomb was looted and no pottery remained; only a few bronze bracelets were left by the looters.

Chronology: The few objects left are non-diagnostic; dating of this tomb is therefore not possible.

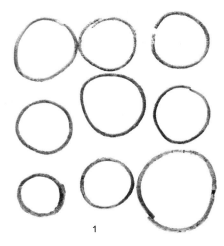

Fig. 3.15. Tomb Z XIX, bracelets. Scale: 1:3.

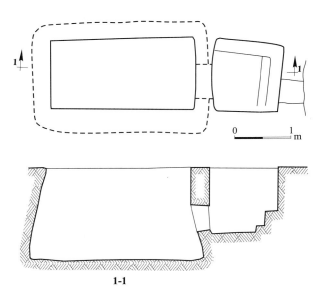

Plan 3.14. Tomb Z XIX, plan and section.

Tomb Z XX (Type 2; Plan 3.15; Fig. 3.16)
This tomb has a single burial chamber (1.30 × 2.20 m; width 1.30 m; height 1.60 m) and an almost square shaft (width 1.00 m; depth 1.25 m). The walls of the burial chamber are vertical, unlike the more common sloping walls. The ceiling was found open, without the covering stone slabs.

The tomb had been badly disturbed by looters, which obliterated any evidence of the number of burials. It contained a fairly rich and interesting assemblage of pottery, as well as a few small finds.

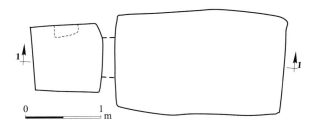

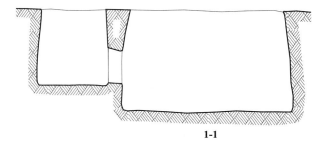

Plan 3.15. Tomb Z XX, plan and section.

Catalogue of Finds, Tomb Z XIX
(* = illustrated in Fig. 3.15)

No.	Object	IAA No.	Description	Dimensions (cm)
Small Finds				
1*	9 bracelets	48-118	Bronze. Some with ends meeting, others with overlapping ends.	D 3.5–6.2
2	Bracelet	48-119	Bronze. In two parts.	D 4.0

Chronology: This tomb is outstanding in its assemblage, with 20% of the vessels belonging to the Black-on-Red group. The general impression is of an early tomb, since many vessels date to the 10th–9th centuries BCE (Types PF1, JG6 I, CP1, CP8 and others). Continuity into the 8th century BCE is evidenced by a type such as DJ2.

Catalogue of Finds, Tomb Z XX
(For pottery types see Chapter 5. Fr = fragment; * = illustrated in Fig. 3.16)

No.	Object	Type	IAA No.	Description	Dimensions (cm)		References
Pottery							
1	Bowl	B1 I	69-7632	Reddish-brown ware, white and black grits.	Fr		
2*	Bowl	B1 I	69-7633	Reddish-brown ware, white and black grits.	H 4.0	D 17.0	
3	Bowl	B1 I	69-7634	Reddish-brown ware, white grits.	H 4.0	D 18.5	
4*	Bowl	B1 I	69-7635	Coarse pinkish-buff ware.	Fr		
5	Bowl	B1 I	69-7631	Reddish-brown ware, white and black grits.	H 5.5	D 18.5	
6*	Bowl	B5 I	69-7637	Reddish-brown ware, white grits.	H 2.5	D 11.7	
7*	Bowl	B5 II	69-7636	Coarse reddish-brown ware, white grits.	H 2.7	D 13.0	
8*	Bowl	B7 II	69-7638	Reddish-brown ware, red slip, burnished.	H 6.0	D 28.5	
9*	Bowl	B8 II	69-7230	Light buff very fine ware, burnished.	H 3.5	D 17.0	
10*	Jug	JG1 I	69-7612	Buff ware, thick red slip, burnished.	H 18.0	W 11.0	
11*	Jug	JG1 III	44.249	Grayish ware, thick black slip, burnished.	H 15.5	W 9.0	
12*	Jug	JG3 II	69-7610	Orange-buff ware, red slip, burnished.	H 18.5	W 11.5	
13*	Jug	Misc.	69-7611	Orange-buff ware, red slip, burnished.	H 16.0	W 10.0	
14*	Jug	JG3 I	69-7629	Coarse reddish-brown ware, grits.	H 22.0	W 13.5	
15*	Jug	JG6 I	69-7625	Pinkish-buff ware. Black- and red-painted decoration.	H 17.0	W 10.5	
16	Jug	JG6 I	69-7624	Light buff ware. Black- and red-painted decoration.	H 22.0	W 14.0	
17	Jug	JG6 I	69-7627	Pinkish-buff ware. Black- and red-painted decoration.	H 21.5	W 14.0	
18	Jug	JG6 I	69-7616	Brownish-buff ware. Black- and red-painted decoration.	H 18.5	W 11.0	
19	Jug	JG6 I	69-7626	Brownish-buff ware. Black- and red-painted decoration.	H 17.0	W 11.0	
20	Jug	JG6 I	69-7628	Coarse reddish-brown ware.	H 21.0	W 15.0	
21	Jug	JG6 I	44.253	Pinkish-brown ware. Black- and red-painted decoration.	H 20.5	W 13.5	
22*	Jug	JG7 III	69-7618	Reddish-orange ware.	H 21.0	W 14.0	
23*	Pilgrim flask	PF1	69-7594	Orange-gray ware, black grits.	H 11.0	W 7.2	
24	Pilgrim flask	PF1	69-7591	Reddish-orange ware, white grits.	H 11.0	W 7.0	
25	Pilgrim flask	PF1	69-7590	Orange ware.	H 11.5	W 7.0	
26	Pilgrim flask	PF1	69-7593	Orange-buff ware.	H 10.0	W 6.5	
27	Pilgrim flask	PF1	69-7595	Grayish-buff ware.	H 10.0	W 6.0	
28	Pilgrim flask	PF1	69-7584	Reddish-orange ware.	H 9.5	W 6.5	
29	Pilgrim flask	PF1	69-7620	Orange-buff ware, white grits.	H 11+	W 8.0	
30	Pilgrim flask	PF1	69-7621	Gray-buff ware.	H 8+	W 6.5	
31	Pilgrim flask	PF1	69-7596	Grayish-buff ware.	H 11	W 6.5	
32*	Pilgrim flask	PF1	69-7602	Grayish-buff ware.	H 7.5	W 5.0	
33	Pilgrim flask	PF1	69-7623	Orange-buff ware. Black-painted decoration.	H 9+	W 5.5	
34	Pilgrim flask	PF1	69-7622	Grayish-orange ware. Black-painted decoration.	H 7+	W 6.0	
35	Pilgrim flask	PF2	69-7600	Brownish-gray ware.	H 7.0	W 3.5	
36	Pilgrim flask	PF2	69-7597	Brownish-gray ware.	H 6.0	W 3.5	
37*	Pilgrim flask	PF2	69-7601	Brownish-gray ware.	H 6.0	W 3.0	

Catalogue of Finds, Tomb Z XX (contd., Fig. 3.16)

No.	Object	Type	IAA No.	Description	Dimensions (cm)		References
38	Pilgrim flask	PF2	69-7598	Brownish-gray ware.	H 7.0	W 3.5	
39	Pilgrim flask	PF2	69-7599	Brownish-gray ware.	H 6.5	W 3.5	
40	Pilgrim flask	PF2	69-7608	Brownish-gray ware.	H 6+	W 3+	
41*	Pilgrim flask	PF3	44.251	Gray ware, thick black slip, burnished.	H 7.5	W 5.0	
42*	Dipper juglet	DJ2	69-7619	Light buff ware.	H 12.5	W 6.0	
43	Dipper juglet	DJ2	69-7605	Reddish-orange ware.	H 13.0	W 6.5	
44	Dipper juglet	DJ2	69-7606	Brownish-buff ware, white grits.	H 13.0	W 6.5	
45	Dipper juglet	DJ2	69-7604	Reddish-brown ware, white grits.	H 12.5	W 6.5	
46	Dipper juglet	DJ2	69-7607	Brownish-gray ware, white and black grits.	H 13.0	W 7.5	
47	Jug	CP1	69-7613	Orange-buff ware, thick dark red slip, burnished. Black-painted decoration.	H 20.5	W 11.0	
48*	Jug	CP1	69-7614	Orange-buff ware, thick red dark slip, burnished. Black-painted decoration.	H 18+	W 12.0	
49*	Jug	CP2	69-7615	Light orange ware, orange-red slip, burnished. Black-painted decoration.	H 22.5	W 15.0	
50*	Jug	CP2	69-7617	Light orange ware, orange-red slip, burnished. Black-painted decoration.	H 21.0	W 14.0	
51	Jug	CP2	44.252	Light orange ware, thick orange-red slip, burnished. Black-painted decoration.	H 19.5	W 12.5	
52*	Juglet	CP5	69-7589	Fine grayish ware, white slip, burnished. Black-painted decoration.	H 10.0	W 6.5	
53*	Juglet	CP6	69-7586	Orange-buff ware, red slip, burnished. Black-painted decoration.	H 6.3	D 4.0	
54*	Juglet	CP6	69-7595	Reddish-orange ware, thick red slip, burnished. Black-painted decoration.	H 9.3	D 6.0	
55*	Juglet	CP6	69-7592	Reddish-orange ware, thick red slip, burnished. Black-painted decoration.	H 11.3	D 7.4	
56*	Juglet	CP6	69-7587	Orange-buff ware, slip and burnish. Black-painted decoration.	H 7.7	D 4.7	
57*	Juglet	CP8	69-7583	Red-orange ware, red slip, burnished. Black-painted decoration.	H 10.5	W 3.5	

Small Finds

No.	Object	Type	IAA No.	Description	Dimensions (cm)		References
58	Bead		48-128	Carnelian. Cylindrical.	L 1.6	W 0.7	
59*	Pomegranate		48-123	Bone. With 4 leaves.	H 1.7	W 1.3	Avigad 1989
60*	Pomegranate		48-124	Bone. With 4 leaves, perforated lengthwise.	H 2.0	W 1.5	
61	Rod		48-122	Bone. Probably of pomegranate.	L 1.9	W 0.5	
62	Tubular fitting		48-132	Bronze.	L 3+	D 1.2	
63	2 sheets		48-133	Bronze. Flattened. Perforated.	W 2.7		
64*	2 arrowheads		48-130	Iron. Stuck together.	L 10+; 5.5+		
65	5 arrowheads		48-131	Iron. Stuck together, with adhering remains of wood.			
66*	Spindle whorl		48-120	Bone.	H 2.0	D 2.3	
67	Spindle whorl		48-121	Bone. Fragment.	H 1.3	D 3.4	
68*	11 beads and fragments		48-126	Bone.		D 0.7–1.4	
69*	6 spindle whorls		48-127	Bone.	H 0.5–0.7	D 1.0–1.2	
70*	Stick		48-134	Hematite. Flat.	L 2.1	W 0.3	

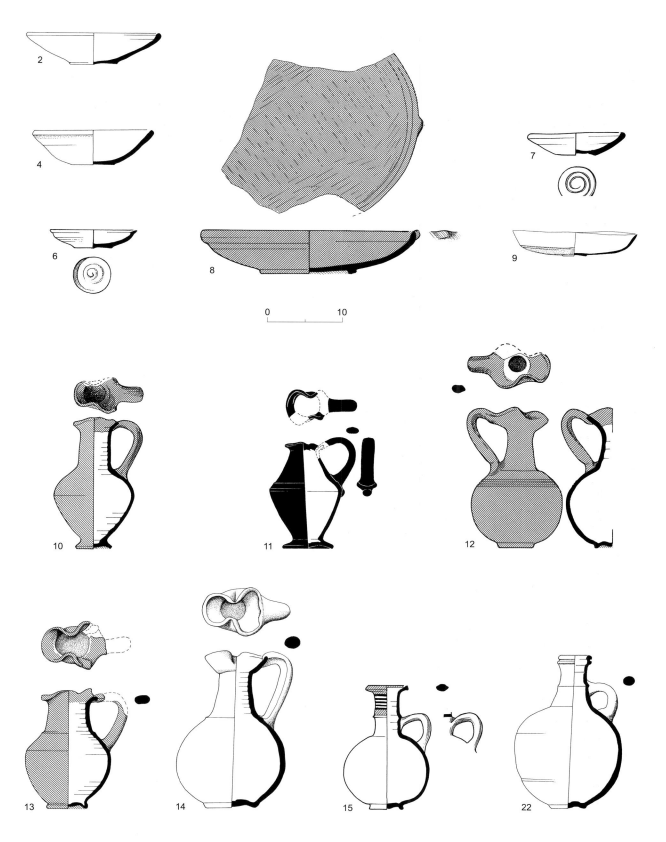

Fig. 3.16. Tomb Z XX, selected finds.

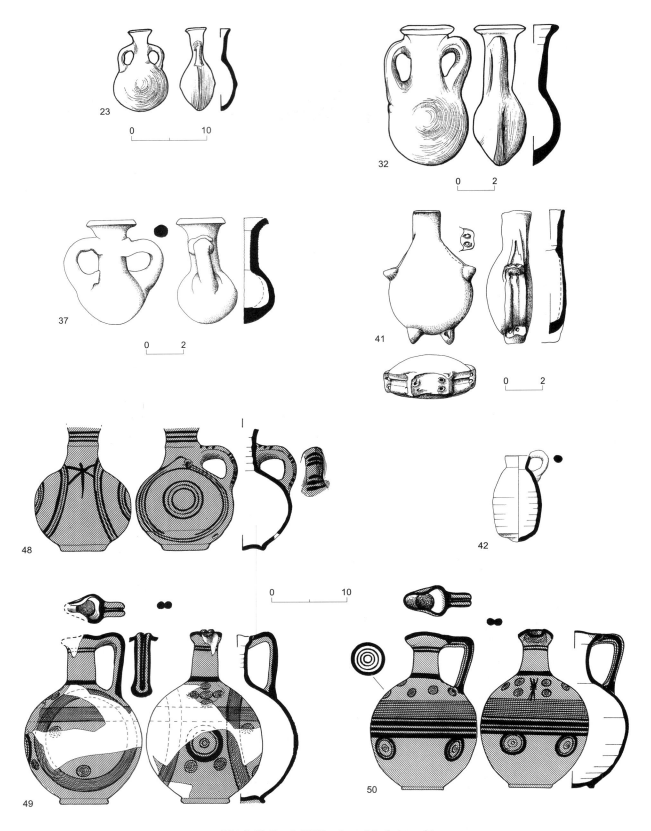

Fig. 3.16. Tomb Z XX, selected finds (contd.).

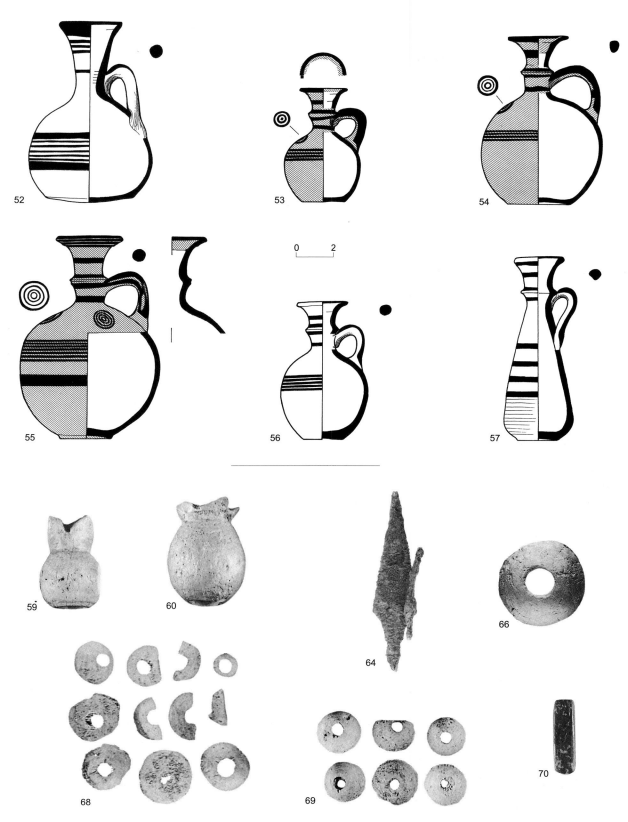

Fig. 3.16. Tomb Z XX, selected finds (contd.). Scale: Nos. 59, 60—1.5:1; No. 64—1:2; Nos. 66, 68–70—1:1.

Tomb Z XXI (Type 2; Plan 3.16)

A short *dromos* leads to a tomb, consisting of a shaft and a single burial chamber. The *dromos* slopes gradually from the ground level to the shaft. The rectangular shaft (0.88 × 1.13 m; depth 1.13 m) has a rock-cut step in one corner, below the *dromos*. A short opening (length 0.30 m) leads into the rectangular (2.10 × 3.00 m) burial chamber. The sloping walls form a truncated pyramid. A narrow opening (1.10 × 2.38 m) at the top was covered with flat stone slabs, discovered *in situ*. Although these were in place, the tomb had been looted through the shaft. Many pottery vessels were found, mainly of common Akhziv types.

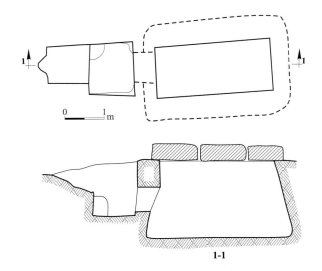

Chronology: This tomb may be dated well into the 8th century BCE by the presence of jugs (Types JG2 I, JG2 II and JG5 I) and dipper juglets (DJ2).

Plan 3.16. Tomb Z XXI, plan and section.

Catalogue of Finds, Tomb Z XXI
(For pottery types see Chapter 5. Fr = fragment; not illustrated.)

No.	Object	Type	IAA No.	Description	Dimensions (cm)	
Pottery						
1	Bowl	B2 IV	70-8479	Reddish-brown ware, white grits.	H 6.0	
2	Storage jar	SJ3	102	Yellow-buff ware.	H 50+	W 22.0
3	Jug	JG2 I	70-8389	Pinkish-buff ware, red slip, burnished.	Fr	
4	Jug	JG2 I	70-8387	Pinkish-buff ware, red slip, burnished.	Fr	
5	Jug	JG2 II	70-8383	Pinkish-buff ware, red slip, burnished.	W 12.0	
6	Jug	JG2 II	70-8381	Pinkish-buff ware, red slip, burnished.	W 11.5	
7	Jug	JG5 I	70-8388	Pinkish-buff ware, red slip, burnished.	Fr	
8	Jug	JG5 I	70-8382	Pinkish-buff ware, red slip, burnished.	Fr	
9	Dipper juglet	DJ2	70-8393	Coarse reddish-brown ware, white and black grits.	W 7.0	
10	Dipper juglet	DJ2	70-8394	Reddish-gray ware, white grits.	W 6.5	
11	Cooking pot	C4	70-8392	Fine light buff ware.	Fr	
12	Misc.		70-8391	Clay altar(?), buff ware.	Fr	
13	Misc.		70-8390	Drooping leaves, probably of a chalice, reddish-brown ware, black grits.	Fr	

CHAPTER 4

THE ER-RAS CEMETERY: TOMBS, POTTERY AND SMALL FINDS

Tomb ZR I (Type 1)
Shaft tomb with stairway. Unfinished chamber, due to the poor quality of the rock. No plan available.

Chronology: The excavator reported on some fragments of cooking pots and pointed-bottom jars, but no further details were given.

Tomb ZR II (Type 1; Fig. 4.1)
Shaft tomb with stairway. Blocking stone still *in situ* in the shaft of the disturbed tomb. No plan available. According to the excavator's diary, sherds of various periods were found in the tomb. Among the small finds

were fibulae, earrings, rings, bracelets, beads of various materials, etc.

Chronology: The tomb was found looted. A single jug of Type JG6 I dated to the late 10th–9th centuries BCE was recovered. The tomb contained a considerable number of small finds, including bronze bracelets, finger rings, iron nails, an iron arrowhead and glass beads. The relatively large number of glass fragments suggests the tomb was re-used in the Roman period. Of particular interest is a conoid seal bearing the symbol of Tanit, dated 800–650 BCE (see Appendix 2:11; Keel 1997:24: No. 11).

Catalogue of Finds, Tomb ZR II
(For pottery types see Chapter 5. * = illustrated in Fig. 4.1)

No.	Object	Type	IAA No.	Description	Dimensions (cm)		References
Pottery							
1	Jug	JG6 I	70-8494	Pinkish-buff ware. Red- and black-painted decoration.	H 17.5+	W 9.5	
Small Finds							
2*	Earring		48-148	Bronze. Crescent-shaped.	W 1.2	L 2.3	
3*	Earring or nose ring		48-147	Bronze. Blue glass stratified white and blue. With threaded stratified eye bead.	L 1.8		Gjerstad 1948: Fig. 31:1a
4*	Finger ring		48-180	Bronze. Flattened section, overlapping ends.	D 2.3		
5*	Finger ring		48-181	Bronze. Overlapping ends.	D 2.0		
6*	Finger ring		48-182	Bronze. Square in section, twisted.	D 2.2		
7	Bracelet		48-141	Bronze. Fragment.	L 5.0		
8	Bracelet		48-142	Bronze. Spiral grooves. Fragment.	L 4.0		
9	Bracelet		48-143	Bronze. Thin coil, flattened end. Fragment.	L 4.0		
10	Bracelet		48-146	Bronze. Decoration of wound wire. Fragment.	L 3.0		
11	Bracelet		48-175	Bronze. Flattened terminals. Fragmentary.	L 4.0		
12*	Bracelet		48-179	Bronze. Square in section. Twisted.	D 4.0		

Catalogue of Finds, Tomb ZR II (contd., Fig. 4.1)

No.	Object	Type	IAA No.	Description	Dimensions (cm)		References
13	Fibula pin		48-145	Bronze. Fragment.	L 2.5+		
14*	Bead		48-165	Black glass. Oblate globular.	D 0.9		
15*	Bead		48-153	Black glass. Oblate globular.	D 0.8		
16*	Bead		48-157	Black glass. Melon-shaped. Fragment.	D 0.4	L 0.5	
17	2 beads		48-163	Black and blue glass. Globular.	D 0.5, 0.4		
18*	Bead		48-159	Blue glass. Globular.	D 0.4		
19*	Bead		48-168	Blue glass with white bands. Prism-shaped. Pierced lengthwise.	L 0.8	W 0.6	
20*	Eye bead		48-158	Blue glass with white and blue. Oblate globular. Stratified.	D 0.5		
21*	Ring bead		48-160	Green glass.	D 0.4		
22	Bead		48-154	Brownish glass. Globular.	D 0.7		
23*	Bead		48-162	Green glass. Globular.	D 0.8		
24*	Bead		48-152	Greenish glass. Globular.	D 1.0		

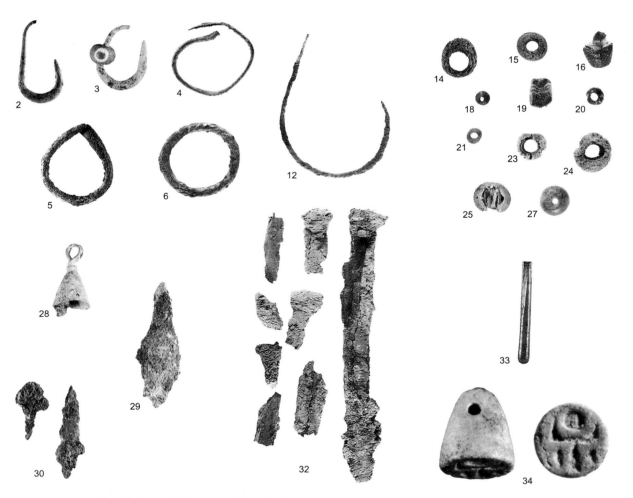

Fig. 4.1. Tomb ZR II, selected finds. Scale: Nos. 2–6, 14, 15, 18–21, 23–25, 27, 28, 33—1:1;
No. 16—2:1; Nos. 12, 29, 30, 32—3:4; No. 34—1.5:1.

Catalogue of Finds, Tomb ZR II (contd., Fig. 4.1)

No.	Object	Type	IAA No.	Description	Dimensions (cm)		References
25*	Bead		48-166	Translucent glass. Globular. Originally covered with gold or silver leaf.	D 1.0		
26	Bead		48-155.	White glass. Barrel-shaped.	L 1.0		
27*	Bead		48-167	Carnelian. Globular.	D 0.6		
28*	Bell		48-149	Bronze. Loop on top.	L 2.0		
29*	Tanged arrowhead		48-183	Iron. Broad leaf-shaped blade, badly corroded.	L 4.5	W 1.5	
30*	2 nails		48-136	Iron. Corroded.	L 2.0, 3.0		
31	Nail		48-137	Iron. Button-shaped head.	L 1.5		
32*	Nails		48-138	Iron. Button-shaped head. Broken.	L 10.0+		
33*	Stick		48-171	Blue glass. Round in section, thickened at one end and broken at the other. Kohl stick(?).	L 2.8		
34*	Seal		48-229	Faience. Conoid, with symbol of Tanit on base.	H 1.6	D 1.3	See App. 2:11; Keel 1997:24: No. 11

Tomb ZR III (Type 1; Plan 4.1; Fig. 4.2)

Shaft tomb without stairway but with two projecting knobs serving as footholds. The rock surface around the door entrance was smoothed, forming a kind of frame. Rectangular chamber. Only the sketch in the plan of the cemetery is available.

The finds consisted of a ceramic boat and sherds of pottery vessels, as well as earrings, bracelets, fibulae, beads, pendants and a scarab.

Chronology: The tomb had been looted. The fragment of a terracotta boat is dated to the 7th–6th centuries BCE. The scarab dates from the same period (see Appendix 2:12; Keel 1997:24: No. 12). The small finds span a long period of time, and therefore cannot be used to provide a precise date. The presence of a Hellenistic bowl indicates its reuse in a later period.

Catalogue of Finds, Tomb ZR III

(* = illustrated in Fig. 4.2)

No.	Object	IAA No.	Description	Dimensions (cm)		References
Small Finds						
1*	Earrings	48-205	Bronze. Crescent-shaped. Fragments.	D 1.0–2.2		
2*	Earring	48-197	Silver. Crescent-shaped.	L 1.8		
3	Earring or nose ring	48-199	Gold. Crescent-shaped.	L 0.8		
4*	Bracelet	48-193	Bronze. Overlapping ends.	D 5.0		
5*	Bracelets and rings	48-206	Bronze. Fragments.	L 0.7–2.8		
6*	Bracelets and armlets	48-203	Bronze. Fragments.	D 5.0–6.0		
7*	Fibula	48-202	Bronze. Bow-shaped. Pin missing.	L 5.0		
8*	Bead	48-187	Carnelian. Barrel-shaped.	L 1.8	D 0.5	
9*	6 beads	48-185	Carnelian. Globular.	D 0.3–0.4		
10*	3 beads	48-186	Carnelian. Globular.	D 0.5–0.8		
11*	Bead	48-188	Blue faience. Ribbed.	D 0.5		
12*	Bead	48-189	Greenish faience. Oblate globular.	D 0.4		

Catalogue of Finds, Tomb ZR III (contd., Fig. 4.2)

No.	Object	IAA No.	Description	Dimensions (cm)		References
13*	Bead	48-191	Quartz. Oblate globular.	D 0.8		
14*	Bead	48-192	Silver. Collared. Long barrel-shaped.	L 1.4		
15	Pendant	48-184	Blue faience. Frog-shaped. Perforated.	L 0.6		Petrie 1914: Pl. II: 181
16*	Pendant	48-196	Carnelian. Wedge-shaped.	L 1.7		Petrie 1930: Pl. XXXVII: 222
17	Inlays	48-198	Bone. Fragments.	L 2.0–4.0	W 1.0	
18*	Olive pits	48-194	Broken.	L 1.0, 0.8		
19*	Scarab	48-201	Soft composite material. White, traces of blue-green glaze.	17.5 x 12.8 × 6.9 (mm)		See App. 2:12; Keel 1997:24: No. 12
20*	Model boat	70-8491	Terracotta. Fragment.	L 13+	W 7.8	See Chap. 7: No. 16

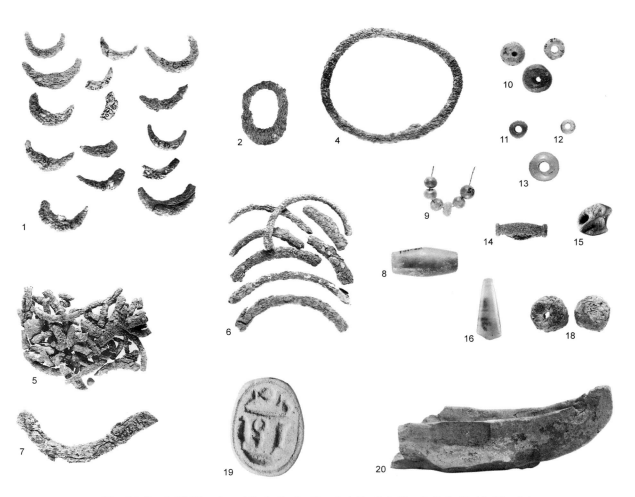

Fig. 4.2. Tomb ZR III, selected finds. Scale: Nos. 1, 4, 7—3:4; Nos. 2, 5, 8–14, 16, 18—1:1;
Nos. 6, 20—1:2; Nos. 15, 19—1.5:1.

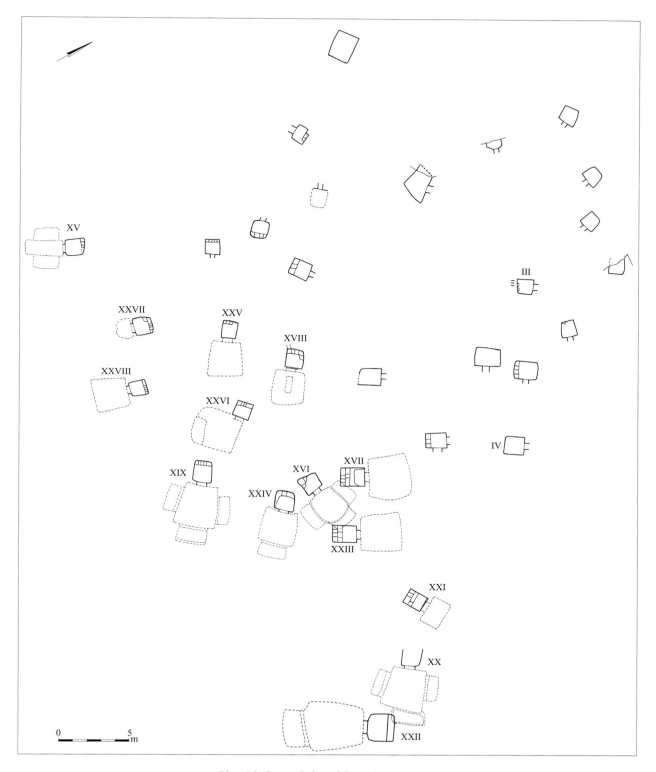

Plan 4.1. General plan of the er-Ras cemetery.

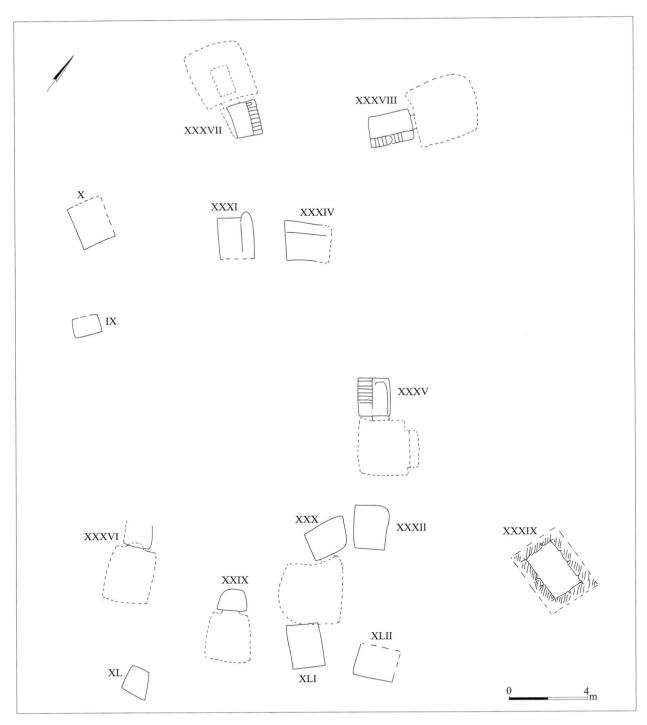

Plan 4.1a. General plan of the er-Ras cemetery.

Tomb ZR IV (Type 1; Plan 4.1; Fig. 4.3)
Shaft tomb with stairway, and a 180° turn halfway down. Deep shaft with two benches at floor level. Framed doorway, rectangular chamber. Only the sketch in the plan of the cemetery is available.

Among the finds were a few fragments of pottery vessels, as well as earrings, armlets, bracelets, etc.

Chronology: The tomb contained fragments of vessels spanning two centuries. A single sherd of a flask (Type PF1) suggests that the original use of the tomb was no later than the late 10th–9th centuries BCE. The red-slipped jugs of Type JG2 II are dated to the late 8th–7th centuries BCE.

Catalogue of Finds, Tomb ZR IV

(For pottery types see Chapter 5. Fr = fragment; * = illustrated in Fig. 4.3)

No.	Object	Type	IAA No.	Description	Dimensions (cm)		
Pottery							
1	Jug	JG2 II	70-8497	Orange-buff ware, thick red slip, burnished.	Fr		
2	Jug	JG2 II	70-8496	Orange-buff ware, thick red slip, burnished.	Fr		
3*	Jug	JG7 V	70-8498	Brownish-buff ware. Red- and black-painted decoration.	Fr		
4	Pilgrim flask	PF1	70-8499	Reddish-buff ware, gray core.	Fr		
Small Finds							
5*	Earring		48-210	Silver. Crescent-shaped.	L 2.2	W 1.4	
6*	Earring		48-213	Bronze. Crescent-shaped.	L 2.0	W 1.3	
7	Ring		48-214	Bronze. Fragment.			
8*	Armlet		48-215	Bronze. Overlapping ends.	D 11.7		
9*	Armlet		48-216	Bronze. Gap between ends.	D 13.0		
10	Bracelet		48-209	Bronze. Fragment.			
11	Cube		48-212	Bronze. Fragment of basket-shaped earring(?).	L 0.8	W 0.8	H 0.8

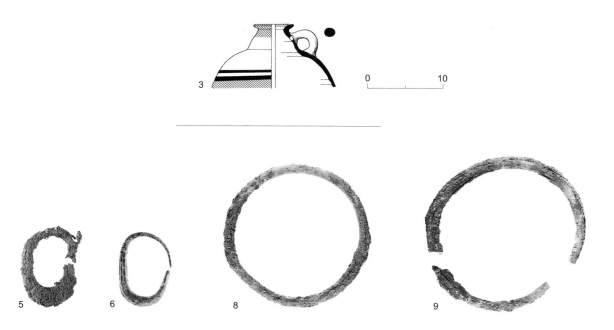

Fig. 4.3. Tomb ZR IV, selected finds. Scale: Nos. 5, 6—1:1; Nos. 8, 9—1:3.

Tomb ZR V (Type 1; Fig. 4.4)
Shaft tomb with stairway, leading to two rectangular chambers, framed doorway. No plan available.

Chronology: The tomb was found looted. It contained a few pottery vessels, mainly juglets of Type DJ1, dated to the 8th–7th centuries BCE. The head of a terracotta figurine dated to the 7th–6th centuries BCE escaped the notice of the looters.

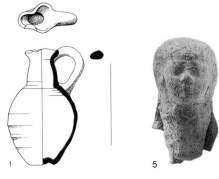

Fig. 4.4. Tomb ZR V, selected finds. Scale: No. 5—1:2.

Catalogue of Finds, Tomb ZR V

(For pottery types see Chapter 5. Fr = fragment; * = illustrated in Fig. 4.4)

No.	Object	Type	IAA No.	Description	Dimensions (cm)		References
Pottery							
1*	Jug	JG2 IV	70-8317	Coarse reddish-brown ware, white grits.	H 16.0	W 8.5	
2	Dipper juglet	DJ1	70-8321	Orange-buff ware, white grits.	Fr		
3	Dipper juglet	DJ1	70-8322	Reddish-brown ware, white grits.	H 10.0	W 5.5	
4	Dipper juglet	DJ1	70-8323	Reddish-brown ware, white grits.	H 8.5	W 5.0	
Small Finds							
5*	Figurine		70-8319	Terracotta. Head of female or young male. Moldmade. Traces of red paint on ears and collar.	H 7.0	W 4.0	See Chap. 7: No. 9

Tomb ZR VI (Type 1.1; Fig. 4.5)
Shaft tomb with stairway, originating outside the deep shaft and turning inside. The entrance was blocked with a slab specially cut to fit the opening. Rectangular chamber with benches and a niche in the wall opposite the entrance. No plan available.

Chronology: The tomb contained a small assemblage of pottery vessels, as well as some small finds. To judge by its pottery, especially bowl Type B5 V known from Tell Keisan as well as from Punic sites, and jug Type JG7 V which is of Phoenician character, this tomb cannot predate the 8th century BCE.

Of special interest among the small finds is a bronze amulet case, probably of the 7th–6th centuries BCE. Frequently this type of amulet case bears zoomorphic ornamentation such as a falcon's head (Petrie 1914: Pl. XIX: 133d; Barnett and Mendelson 1987: Pl. 87:7/33; Moscati 1988:692: Nos. 639–643). Another special find is an amphora-shaped glass bead; its parallels date from the 5th–4th century BCE (Johns 1938:145, Fig. 5:6a). Most of the finds in this tomb date to the 8th–6th centuries BCE.

Catalogue of Finds, Tomb ZR VI

(For pottery types see Chapter 5. Fr = fragment; * = illustrated in Fig. 4.5)

No.	Object	Type	IAA No.	Description	Dimensions (cm)		References
Pottery							
1*	Bowl	B5 V		Orange-buff ware. Red-painted decoration.	H 5.5	D 14.5	
2*	Storage jar	SJ1	70-8520	Reddish-brown ware.	H 36.0	W 21.0	

Catalogue of Finds, Tomb ZR VI (contd., Fig. 4.5)

No.	Object	Type	IAA No.	Description	Dimensions (cm)		References
3	Storage jar	SJ1	70-8519	Reddish-brown ware. Squared-off rim. Short pointed base.	H 44.0	W 24.0	
4*	Storage jar	SJ2		Orange-buff ware.	H 47.0	W 25.0	
5	Jug	JG7 V	44.254	Orange-buff ware, burnished. Red-painted decoration.	H 15.0	W 11.5	
6	Dipper juglet	DJ1		Pinkish-buff ware.	H 6.9	W 4.2	
7*	Jug	JG7 V	44.254	Brownish-buff ware.	H 16.2		
Small Finds							
8*	Finger ring		48-218	Silver.	D 2.3		
9*	Bead		48-219	Blue glass. Biconical, disk-shaped.	D 0.8		
10*	Bead		48-221	Green glass. Amphora-shaped.	L 1.3		
11	Pendant		48-220	Carnelian. Lozenge-shaped. Perforated at top.	L 1.7		
12*	Pendant amulet case		48-217	Bronze. Topped by ornamentation. Corroded.	L 3.3	W 0.9	Petrie 1914: Pl. XIX: 133d; Barnett and Mendelson 1987: Pl. 87:7/33; Moscati 1988:692: Nos. 639–643
13*	Stele		42.251	Sandstone.	78 × 36 × 35		See App. 1: No. 1

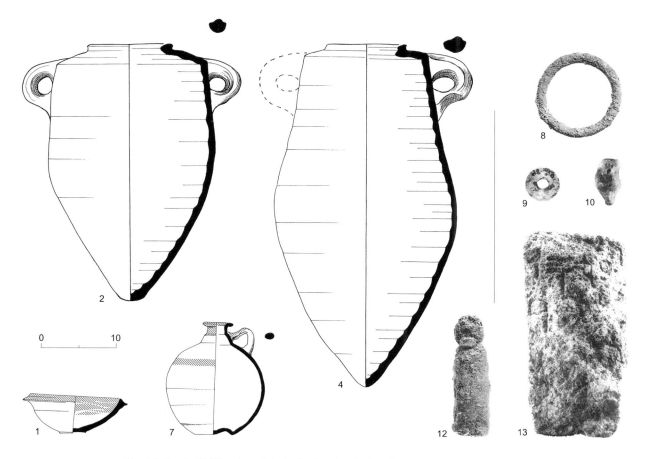

Fig. 4.5. Tomb ZR VI, selected finds. Scale: Nos. 8–10, 12—1:1; No. 13—not to scale.

Tomb ZR VII (Type 1)

Shaft tomb with stairway. Framed doorway. Rectangular chamber with benches. No plan available.

Catalogue of Finds, Tomb ZR VII
(Not illustrated)

No.	Object	IAA No.	Description	Dimensions (cm)
Small Finds				
1	Nail	48-222	Iron. Button-shaped head.	L 7+

Chronology: As the tomb was found virtually empty, dating is not possible. Although lacking a plan, the description in the excavator's diaries fits the Phoenician-type tombs in this cemetery.

Tomb ZR VIII (Type 1; Fig. 4.6)

Shaft tomb with stairway, and irregular slab outside shaft. Framed doorway, with blocking slab specially cut to fit the entrance. Rectangular chamber with benches. No plan available.

Chronology: Only a few pottery vessels, dated to the 8th–6th centuries BCE, were uncovered in this looted tomb. Two scarabs were found, one from the 7th–6th century BCE and another from the second half of the 10th–9th century BCE (see Appendix 2:13, 14; Keel 1997:24: No. 13; 26: No. 14).

Catalogue of Finds, Tomb ZR VIII
(For pottery types see Chapter 5. * = illustrated in Fig. 4.6)

No.	Object	Type	IAA No.	Description	Dimensions (cm)		References
Pottery							
1*	Bowl	B2 III	70-8509	Coarse reddish-brown ware.	H 5.0	D 20.0	
2*	Bowl	B3 II	70-8508	Coarse reddish-brown ware.	H 4.2	D 17.5	
3*	Storage jar	SJ 1	70-8453	Reddish-buff ware.	H 41.0	D 27.0	
4	Storage jar	SJ 2	70-8453/1	Orange-buff ware.	H 48.0	D 23.0	
Small Finds							
5*	Finger ring		48-227	Bronze. Overlapping ends.	D 2.5		
6*	Bead		48-228	Carnelian. Oblate globular.	D 0.6		
7*	Scarab		48-224	Steatite. White.	14.6 × 11.0 × 7.1 (mm)		See App. 2:13; Keel 1997:24: No. 13
8	Scarab		48-225	Soft composite material. Blue.	16.6 × 10.5 × 7.0 (mm)		See App. 2:14; Keel 1997:26: No. 14

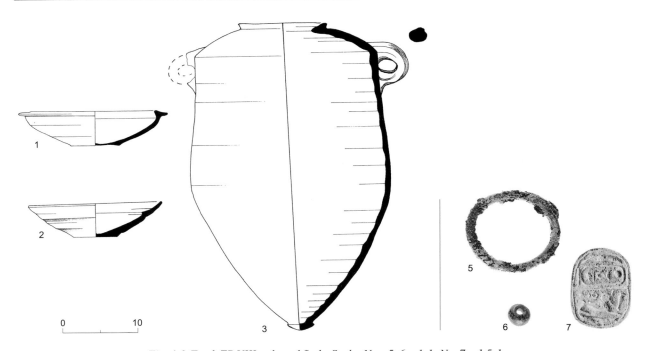

Fig. 4.6. Tomb ZR VIII, selected finds. Scale: Nos. 5, 6—1:1; No. 7—1.5:1.

Tomb ZR IX (Type 1; Plan 4.1a; Fig. 4.7)
Shaft tomb without stairway. Large, rough blocking slab. Square chamber. Only the sketch in the plan of the cemetery is available.

The rich finds included trefoil and mushroom-rim jugs of red slip and bichrome ware, as well as a wide variety of small finds: scarabs, a scaraboid seal, plaques, beads, pendants, earrings, finger rings, weights, fibulae and amulets.

Chronology: This tomb yielded a rich and varied assemblage of pottery and small finds. The earliest pottery vessels of Type JG6 I are dated to the late 10th–9th centuries BCE. Vessels such as bottle J7 cannot be earlier than the 7th century. The twelve scarabs found in the tomb date between the 13th and 6th centuries BCE (see Appendix 2:15–26; Keel 1997:26: Nos. 15–18; 28: Nos. 19–23; 30: Nos. 24–26), indicating a long span of use.

Catalogue of Finds, Tomb ZR IX

(For pottery types see Chapter 5. Fr = fragment; * = illustrated in Fig. 4.7)

No.	Object	Type	IAA No.	Description	Dimensions (cm)		References
Pottery							
1*	Bowl	B6 I	70-8032	Reddish-brown ware, white grits.	H 4.0	D 27.5	
2*	Jug	JG2 I	70-8024	Orange-buff ware, red slip, burnished.	H 24.0	W 12.0	
3	Jug	JG2 I	70-8013	Orange-buff ware, red slip, burnished.	H 12+	W 14.5	
4	Jug	JG3 III	70-8016	Coarse reddish-brown ware, white grits.	H 22.5	W 15.0	
5*	Jug	JG3 III	70-8030	Coarse reddish-brown ware, white grits.	H 18.0	W 11.5	
6*	Jug	JG4 II	70-8027	Orange-buff ware, red slip, burnished.	H 12.0	W 11.0	
7	Jug	JG4 II	70-8486	Orange-buff ware, red slip, burnished.	Fr		
8*	Jug	JG5 II	70-8026	Orange-buff ware, red slip, burnished. Black lines on upper neck and rim.	H 22.0	W 12.0	
9*	Jug	JG6 II	70-8029	Pinkish-buff ware.	H 11+	W 14.0	
10*	Jug	JG6 I	70-8017	Yellow-buff ware, burnished. Black- and red-painted decoration.	H 24.0	W 13.0	
11	Jug	JG6 I	70-8010	Pinkish-buff ware. Black- and red-painted decoration. Knob under handle.	H 18.5	W 12.0	
12*	Jug	JG7 IV	70-8025	Greenish-buff ware.	H 16.5	W 12.0	
13	Jug	JG7 IV	44.255	Reddish-brown coarse ware, rich in white grits.	H 18.5	W 12.5	
14*	Jug	JG9	70-8028	Reddish-brown ware, white grits.	H 14.5	W 10.5	
15*	Dipper juglet	DJ1	70-8012	Reddish-brown ware, white grits.	H 11.5	W 6.0	
16	Dipper juglet	DJ1	70-8015	Reddish-brown ware, white grits.	H 11.0	W 5.5	
17	Dipper juglet	DJ1	70-8036	Reddish-brown ware, white grits.	H 6.5+	W 4.5	
18*	Dipper juglet	DJ2	70-8014	Reddish-brown ware, white grits.	H 11.5	W 6.0	
19*	Dipper juglet	DJ3	70-8031	Light buff ware.	H 12.0	W 6.0	
20*	Juglet	J4	70-8019	Grayish coarse ware.	Fr		
21*	Bottle	J7	70-8011	Light buff ware.	H 10.5	W 10.0	
22*	Bowl (lid?)	M2	70-8033	Pinkish-buff ware, white grits, red slip.	H 4.5	D 24.0	
23*	Miniature amphoriskos	Misc.	70-8035	Coarse reddish-brown ware, white grits.	H 2.5	W 3.0	
Small Finds							
24	2 earrings		48-342	Silver. Crescent-shaped. Overlapping ends.	D 1.1, 1.2		

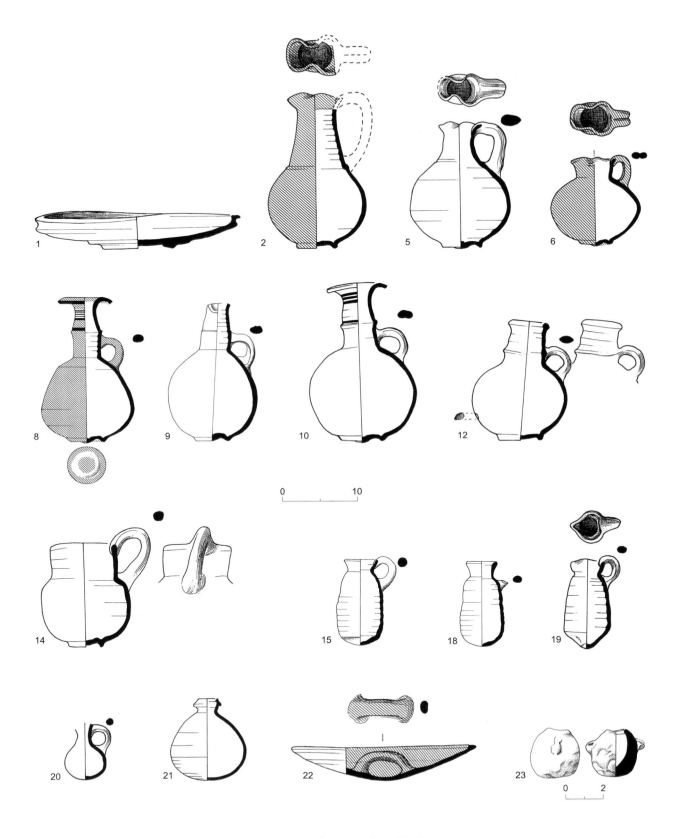

Fig. 4.7. Tomb ZR IX, selected finds.

Catalogue of Finds, Tomb ZR IX (contd., Fig. 4.7)

No.	Object	Type	IAA No.	Description	Dimensions (cm)	References
25*	Earring		48-343	Silver. Crescent-shaped. Broken.	D 1.3	
26*	9 earrings		48-329	Bronze. Crescent-shaped. Broken.	D 1.1–1.8	
27*	3 earrings		48-331	Bronze. Crescent-shaped. Broken.	D 1.8–2.0	
28*	8 earrings		48-330	Bronze. Crescent-shaped. Broken.	D 1.0–1.5	
29*	2 earrings		48-339	Bronze. Crescent-shaped. Broken.	D 1.3	
30	Earring		48-338	Bronze. Crescent-shaped. Fragment.	D 1.1	
31*	Earring		48-341	Bronze. Crescent-shaped. Oval.	L 2.2	Petrie 1930: Pl. XLII: 309
32*	2 earrings		48-332	Bronze. Crescent-shaped. Oval.	L 2.3, 1.9	
33*	Earring		48-333	Bronze. Crescent-shaped. Oval.	L 2.0	
34*	2 earrings		48-264	Bronze. Crescent-shaped. Overlapping ends, one end thickened.	D 1.5	
35*	2 earrings		48-346	Silver. Crescent-shaped. One with wound wire.	D 1.0	
36*	Finger ring		48-349	Silver.	D 2.2	
37*	Finger ring		48-334	Bronze. Overlapping ends. Oval in section.	D 1.8	
38*	Finger ring		48-336	Bronze. Gap between ends. Flattened in section.	D 2.2	
39	3 finger rings		48-335	Bronze. Fragments.		
40	Finger ring		48-340	Bronze. With flattened oval bezel. Broken.		
41*	Swivel ring		48-344	Silver. Tapering ends with wound wire.	D 2.5	Barnett and Mendelson 1987: Pl. 97: 12/10–12
42*	Swivel ring		48-326	Silver.	D 2.4	
43*	Bracelet		48-232	Bronze. With overlapping ends. Remnants of fabric.	D 5.0	
44*	Bracelet		48-328	Bronze. With gap between ends, oval in section. Broken.	D 6.0	
45*	Arched knee fibula		48-325	Bronze. With beaded moldings, flattened and decorated with cross at one end and with hook at other end. Pin missing.	L 4.1	Cf. 48-348; Stronach 1959:190
46*	Fibula pin		48-348	Bronze. Broken, may belong to fibula No. 45 (IAA No. 48-325).	L 3.0	
47*	Bead		48-239	Carnelian. Globular.	D 1.3	
48*	Bead		48-238	Carnelian. Globular. Silver tube in perforation.	D 0.8	
49*	Bead		48-310	Carnelian. Globular.	D 0.3	
50*	Bead		48-309	Carnelian. Biconical. Lentil-shaped.	D 0.7	
51*	Bead		48-271	Carnelian. Long cylindrical.	L 1.8	
52*	Bead		48-272	Carnelian. Long barrel-shaped.	L 2.2	
53*	Bead		48-273	Carnelian. Barrel-shaped. Broken.	L 1.4+	
54*	Bead		48-267	Carnelian. Biconical, disk-shaped.	D 1.2	
55*	2 beads		48-269	Carnelian. Oblate globular.	D 1.0, 1.2	
56*	Bead		48-240	Carnelian. Globular.	D 0.8	
57*	Bead		48-241	Carnelian. Barrel-shaped.	L 1.6	
58*	Bead		48-242	Carnelian. Biconical, disk-shaped.	D 1.2	
59*	Bead		48-243	Carnelian. Barrel-shaped.	L 0.9	
60*	Bead		48-244	Carnelian. Biconical, disk-shaped.	D 0.8	
61*	Bead		48-283	Carnelian. Irregular biconical.	D 1.0	
62*	8 beads		48-284	Carnelian. Biconical, disk-shaped.	D 0.7–0.8	

Catalogue of Finds, Tomb ZR IX (contd., Fig. 4.7)

No.	Object	Type	IAA No.	Description	Dimensions (cm)		References
63*	3 beads		48-285	Carnelian. Disk-shaped.	D 0.5–0.9		
64*	Bead		48-286	Carnelian. Long barrel-shaped.	L 1.5		
65*	5 beads		48-257	Greenish faience. Barrel-shaped.	L 0.7–1.1		
66*	6 beads		48-258	Greenish faience. Cylindrical.	L 0.9–1.2		
67	4 beads		48-260	Greenish faience and bronze. Cylindrical.	L 1.0		
68*	2 beads		48-260/1	Bronze. Cylindrical with tiny globular beads attached to one end.	L 1.0		
69	4 beads		48-319	Faience. Cylindrical.	L 0.6–0.9		
70*	Bead		48-233	Greenish faience. Globular.	D 2.0	H 1.4	
71*	Bead		48-245	Greenish faience. Globular.	D 0.8		
72*	Bead		48-246	Greenish faience. Globular.	D 0.6		
73*	Bead		48-247	Greenish faience. Biconical.	D 0.6		
74*	2 beads		48-248	Whitish faience. Globular.	D 0.6		
75*	5 beads		48-278	Greenish faience. Globular.	D 0.3–0.5		
76*	Bead		48-279	Greenish faience. Globular.	D 0.7		
77*	Bead		48-280	Yellowish-blue faience. Ring-shaped.	D 0.8		
78*	Bead		48-281	Yellowish faience. Globular.	D 0.3		
79*	2 beads		48-282	Yellowish faience. Barrel-shaped.	L 1.0, 1.2		
80*	Bead		48-313	Whitish faience. Globular.	D 0.4		
81*	Bead		48-314	Greenish faience. Globular.	D 0.6		
82*	Bead		48-315	Blue faience. Oblate globular.	D 0.7		
83*	Bead		48-292	Dark glass. Oblate globular.	D 0.5		
84*	Bead		48-291	Dark glass. Ring-shaped.	D 1.0		
85*	Bead		48-252	Light-colored glass. Biconical. Broken.	D 0.5		
86	Bead		48-274	Dark glass. Globular.	D 0.7		
87*	Bead		48-250	Dark glass. Globular.	D 0.8		
88	Bead		48-276	Dark glass. Globular.	D 0.5		
89	Bead		48-251	Blue glass. Cylindrical.	L 1.3		
90*	Bead		48-288	Dark glass. Globular. Wide horizontal groove in center.	D 0.9		
91*	Bead		48-317	Dark glass. Barrel-shaped. Broken.	D 0.6		
92*	2 beads		48-312	Blue glass. Globular.	D 0.4		
93*	Bead		48-311	Blue glass. Oblate globular.	D 0.6		
94	Eye bead		48-249	Blue glass with white and blue. Stratified.	D 0.5		
95	2 beads		48-261	Bronze. Globular.	D 0.4		
96*	Bead		48-270	Quartz. Melon-shaped.	D 1.4		
97*	Bead		48-275	Grayish-green glass. Cylindrical ribbed.	L 0.4		
98*	Bead		48-256	Glass. Barrel-shaped. Broken.	D 0.9		
99	Bead		48-255	White stone. Globular.	D 1.0		
100	Bead		48-289	Hematite. Biconical.	L 0.6		
101*	Bead		48-290	Hematite. Flattened cylindrical.	L 1.2		
102*	Bead		48-237	Red and yellow jasper. Lozenge-shaped.	L 2.2		
103*	Pendant		48-277	Faience(?) Glass(?). Elongated. Perforated at top.	L 2.1		
104*	Pendant		48-305	Green stone, jasper(?). Lozenge-shaped.	L 1.5		
105*	Pateke amulet		48-296	Faience. Carved in the round, seal on bottom with unclear hieroglyphs.	H 1.0		

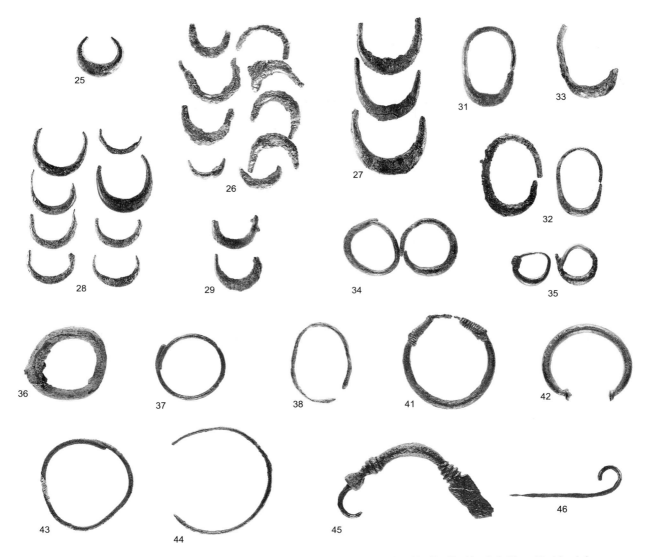

Fig. 4.7. Tomb ZR IX, selected finds (contd.). Scale: Nos. 25–29, 31–38, 41, 42, 45, 46—1:1; Nos. 43, 44—1:2.

Catalogue of Finds, Tomb ZR IX (contd., Fig. 4.7)

No.	Object	Type	IAA No.	Description	Dimensions (cm)		References
106	Weight		48-293	Black stone. Conoid.	H 0.6		Wt 1.3376 gm
107*	Weight		48-299	Hematite. Globular.	D 1.2		Wt 3.9812 gm
108*	Weight		48-300	Hematite. Domed.	L 2.0	H 1.0	Wt 5.8140 gm
109	Weight		48-301	Hematite. Trapezoidal.	D 1.0		Wt 2.2513 gm
110*	Loomweight(?)		48-347	Terracotta. Conical. Perforated in middle.	D 1.9	H 1.5	
111	Weight		48-345	Hard limestone. Round. Flattened on both sides.	D 2.5	H 1.0	Wt 11.0540 gm
112	Weight		48-352	Red limestone. Globular.	D 2.3		Wt 11.4972 gm
113*	Hair ornament (?)		48-342	Silver. Coiled wire.	D 1.4		
114*	Pendant holder		48-302	Silver.	D 0.6	H 0.6	Gjerstad 1948: Fig. 35:26

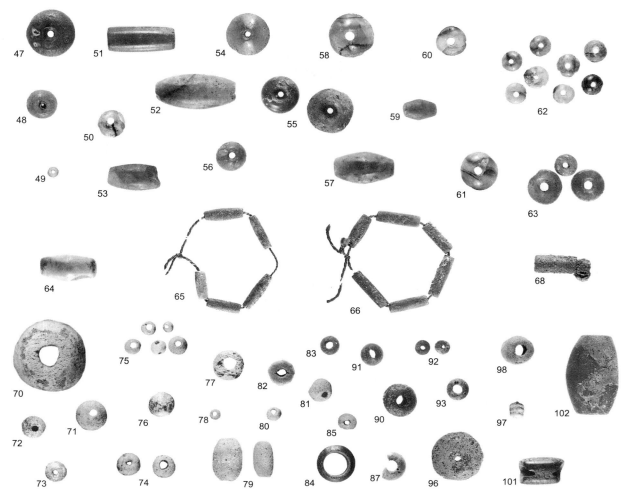

Fig. 4.7. Tomb ZR IX, selected finds (contd.). Scale—1:1.

Catalogue of Finds, Tomb ZR IX (contd., Fig. 4.7)

No.	Object	Type	IAA No.	Description	Dimensions (cm)	References
115*	2 hair ornaments		48-268	Silver.	D 1.5, 1.8	
116	Lumps		48-354	Bitumen.		
117*	Cylinder seal		48-320	Hematite(?). Horse crouching on hind legs behind a tree. Behind the horse an unclear incision and another animal crouching on hind legs, looking backward.	L 1.1 D 0.6	
118*	Round seal		48-234	Steatite. Gray, surface appearance white.	$11.6 \times 10.6 \times 5.6$ (mm)	See App. 2:15; Keel 1997:26: No. 15
119*	Scarab		48-236	Steatite. White.	$14.9 \times 11.0 \times 6.2$ (mm)	See App. 2:16; Keel 1997:26: No. 16
120*	Scarab		48-265	Steatite.	$14.6 \times 11.2 \times 4.2$ (mm)	See App. 2:17; Keel 1997:26: No. 17
121*	Scarab		48-266	Steatite.	$11.0 \times 7.2 \times 7.8$ (mm)	See App. 2:18; Keel 1997:26: No. 18

Fig. 4.7. Tomb ZR IX, selected finds (contd.). Scale: Nos. 103, 104, 107, 108, 110, 115—1:1; Nos. 105, 117—2:1;
Nos. 113, 114, 118–121, 123–127, 129—1.5:1.

Catalogue of Finds, Tomb ZR IX (contd., Fig. 4.7)

No.	Object	Type	IAA No.	Description	Dimensions (cm)	References
122	Scarab		48-266A	Enstatite.	11.5 × 7.9 × 5.4 (mm)	See App. 2:19; Keel 1997:28: No. 19
123*	Scarab		48-295	Steatite or very soft white composite material.	14.7 × 10.8 × 7.1 (mm)	See App. 2:20; Keel 1997:28: No. 20
124*	Scarab		48-307	Steatite. White.	15.0 × 12.0 × 8.0 (mm)	See App. 2:21, n. 1
125*	Scarab		48-308	Soft composite material.	14.7 × 10.2 × 7.0 (mm)	See App. 2:22; Keel 1997:28: No. 22
126*	Scarab		48-321	Steatite. Whitish with very dark veining.	14.7 × 11.1 × 6.6 (mm)	See App. 2:23; Keel 1997:28: No. 23
127*	Scarab		48-322	Steatite. Badly weathered.	12.8 × 9.2 × 5.5 (mm)	See App. 2:24; Keel 1997:30: No. 24
128	Conoid		48-347	Fired clay. Red.	H 16.5–18.2	See App. 2:25; Keel 1997:30: No. 25
129*	Scarab		48-351	Steatite. White.	17.2 × 11.6 × 7.6 (mm)	See App. 2:26; Keel 1997:30: No. 26

Tomb ZR X (Type 1.1; Plan 4.1a; Fig. 4.8)
Shaft tomb with stairway. Doorway blocked by stone slab. Chamber with benches and niche hewn into the wall opposite the entrance. Only the sketch in the plan of the cemetery is available.

Chronology: Only a few pottery vessels, mainly storage jars from the 7th–6th century BCE, were uncovered in this tomb. The scarabs are dated between the 7th and 6th centuries BCE (see Appendix 2:27–30; Keel 1997:30: Nos. 27–30).

Catalogue of Finds, Tomb ZR X
(For pottery types see Chapter 5. * = illustrated in Fig. 4.8)

No	Object	Type	IAA No.	Description	Dimensions (cm)		References
Pottery							
1*	Storage jar	SJ1		Reddish-buff ware.	H 38	W 25	
2*	Storage jar	SJ2		Reddish-brown ware.	H 54	W 24	
3	Storage jar	SJ2		Orange-buff ware.	H 46	W 24	
Small Finds							
4*	Finger ring		48-358	Bronze. Ends meeting.	D 2.3		
5*	Finger ring		48-357	Bronze. Round in section, ends broken.	D 2.2		
6*	Bead		48-359	Carnelian, white strip in center. Barrel-shaped.	L 0.8		
7*	Bead		48-363	Carnelian. Globular, ribbed lengthwise.	D 0.5		
8*	5 beads		48-360	Carnelian. Oblate globular.	D 0.4–0.7		
9*	3 beads		48-361	Carnelian. Biconical, disk-shaped.	D 0.8		
10*	Bead		48-362	Carnelian. Biconical.	D 0.6		
11*	2 beads		48-376	Bluish glass. Cylindrical.	L 0.9		
12*	Eye bead		48-372	Bluish glass, stratified blue and white. Oblate globular.	D 1.0		
13*	Eye bead		48-373	Glass, stratified white and blue. Oblate globular.	D 0.7		
14*	Bead		48-374	Quartz. Short barrel-shaped.	D 0.6		
15*	Bead		48-368/a	Greenish faience. Short cylindrical.	D 0.7		
16*	7 beads		48-368/b	Greenish faience. Ring-shaped.	D 0.2–0.3		
17*	4 beads		48-366	Greenish faience. Globular.	D 0.3–0.4		
18*	6 beads		48-367	Whitish faience. Globular.	D 0.5–0.6		
19	2 beads		48-365	Bluish faience. Barrel-shaped.	L 0.9–1.0		
20*	Bead		48-370	Greenish faience. Globular.	D 0.7		
21*	2 beads		48-364	Red stone. Biconical.	D 0.5, 0.8		
22*	6 beads		48-382	Blue glass. Lotus-flower-shaped.	L 0.9	W 1.2	Beck 1928: Fig. 24: B5 e; Vercoutter 1945: Pl. XXV; Spaer 2001: 62–64, Fig. 35
23	Bead		48-377	Silver. Cylindrical spiral, collared.	L 1.5		
24*	Lion amulet		48-384	Greenish faience. Suspension loop in back.	L 1.2	H 1.0	Petrie 1914: Pl. XXXVIII: 219 g; Herrmann 1994:540–544
25*	Shu amulet		48-380	Faience. Depicting the deity Shu: bent knees and upraised arms, perforated behind head and arms.	L 1.4	W 0.9	Petrie 1914: Pl. XXX: 167e; Herrmann 1994: 229–235
26*	Khnum amulet		48-388	Bluish faience. Crouching ram.	W 1.9	H 1.2	Petrie 1914: Pl. XXVIII:212
27*	Scarab		48-381	Bone?	16.1 × 11.6 × 7.9 (mm)		See App. 2:27; Keel 1997: 30: No. 27
28*	Scarab		48-385	Grainy composite material. Light blue.	13.5 × 9.9 × 7 (mm)		See App. 2:28; Keel 1997: 30: No. 28
29*	Scarab		48-386	Grainy composite material. Remains of light blue glaze.	14.2 × 10.3 × 6.4 (mm)		See App. 2:29; Keel 1997: 30: No. 29
30*	Scarab		48-387	Composite material.	16.6 × 12.0 × 7.3 (mm)		See App. 2:30; Keel 1997: 32: No. 30

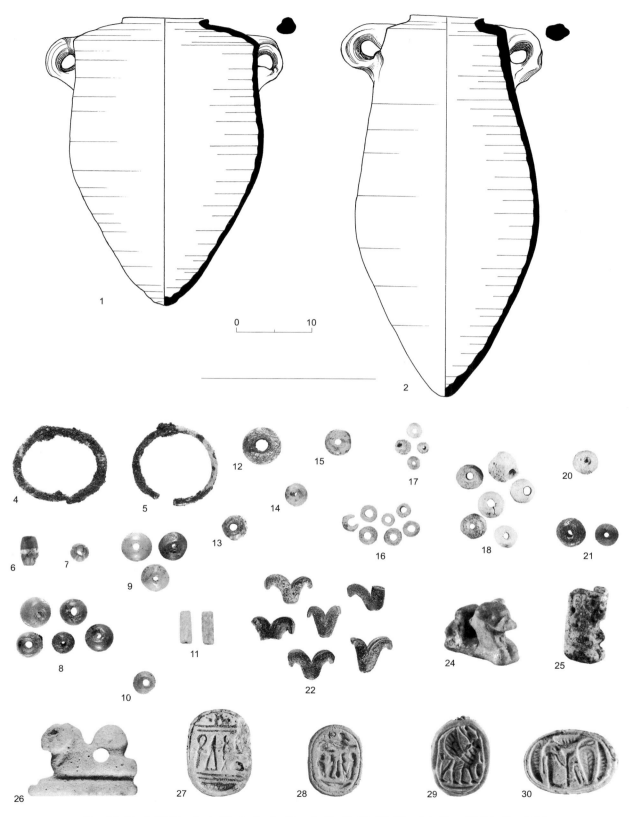

Fig. 4.8. Tomb ZR X, selected finds. Scale: Nos. 4–15, 17, 18, 20–22—1:1; Nos. 16, 24–30—1.5:1.

Tomb ZR XI (Type 1; Fig. 4.9)
Shaft tomb with stairway. Doorway blocked by stone slab. Rectangular chamber with trench in center. No plan available. Jugs, juglets and earrings were found in the tomb.

Chronology: The pottery of this tomb does not predate the 8th century BCE. This dating is based mainly on the presence of red-slipped jugs of Types JG2 I, III.

Catalogue of Finds, Tomb ZR XI
(For pottery types see Chapter 5. * = illustrated in Fig. 4.9)

No.	Object	Type	IAA No.	Description	Dimensions (cm)	
Pottery						
1	Storage jar	SJ1	70-7699	Reddish-buff ware.	H 43.0	W 21.0
2*	Jug	JG2 I	70-7698	Coarse-reddish brown ware, white grits, red slip, burnished.	H 19.5	W 10.5
3*	Jug	JG2 III	70-7688	Orange-yellow ware, red wash except base. Black-painted decoration.	H 17.5	W 9.0
4*	Jug	JG2 V	70-7697	Coarse reddish-brown ware, white grits.	H 21.0	W 12.0
5	Jug	JG5 I	44.256	Orange-buff ware, red slip, burnished.	H 18.5	W 10.0
6	Jug	JG5 IV	70-7696	Orange-buff ware. Red-painted decoration.	H 21.5+	W 10.5
7*	Dipper juglet	DJI	70-7692	Reddish-brown ware, white grits.	H 8.0	W 5.3
8	Dipper juglet	DJ1	70-7693	Light buff ware.	H 9.0	W 4.7
9	Dipper juglet	DJ1	70-7691	Reddish-brown ware, white grits.	H 9.0	W 5.9
10	Dipper juglet	DJ1	70-7690	Reddish-brown ware, white grits.	H 8.7	W 5.3
11	Dipper juglet	DJ1	70-7700	Pinkish-buff ware.	H 9.0	W 5.3
12	Dipper juglet	DJ1	70-7701	Orange-brown ware, white grits.	H 8.8	W 5.2
Small Finds						
13*	2 earrings		48-391	Bronze. Crescent-shaped. Fragments.	W 1.9	
14*	3 earrings		48-392	Bronze. Crescent-shaped, broken.	W 1.7–1.9	
15	2 bracelets		48-390	Bronze. Fragments.		

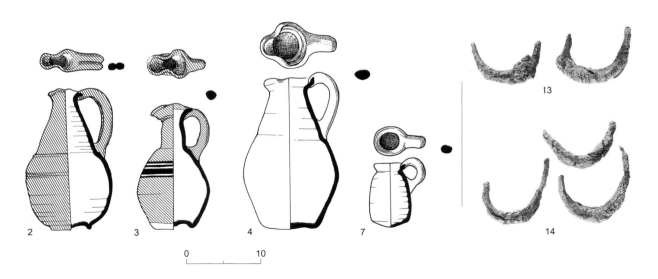

Fig. 4.9. Tomb ZR XI, selected finds. Scale: Nos. 13, 14—1:1.

Tomb ZR XII (Type 1.1; Fig. 4.10)

Shaft tomb with stairway. Doorway blocked by stone slab. Rectangular chamber with trench in center. Two niches hewn into the northern and western walls. Three irregular holes in the roof, probably for pouring liquids into the tomb after the entrance was blocked. No plan available.

The tomb yielded jugs, juglets and bowls, as well as female figurines, including a tambourine player (see Chapter 7: No. 3), earrings, scarabs, etc.

Chronology: The tomb contains a varied assemblage of pottery vessels. The earliest are of Type JG2 II, dated to the 8th–7th centuries BCE. Many of the vessels, such as SJ2 and the miniature forms, do not predate the 6th–5th centuries BCE, thus indicating a long span of use for the tomb. A single scarab of the XXVIth Dynasty (664–525 BCE; see Appendix 2:33; Keel 1997:32: No. 33) was also found. Noteworthy among the small finds are a basket-shaped earring, a type well-known from the 7th–6th century BCE Punic world, and the figurine of a tambourine (frame-drum) player, of the same period.

Catalogue of Finds, Tomb ZR XII

(For pottery types see Chapter 5. * = illustrated in Fig. 4.10)

No.	Object	Type	IAA No.	Description	Dimensions (cm)		References
Pottery							
1*	Bowl	B5 V	70-8047	Orange-buff ware. Red slip on rim.	H 4.5	D 13.0	
2	Storage jar	SJ2	70-8517	Reddish-buff ware.	H 53.0	W 27.0	
3	Jug	JG2 II	70-8051	Orange-buff ware, red slip, burnished.	Fr		
4*	Jug	JG2 II	70-8038	Coarse reddish-brown ware, white grits, red slip, burnished.	H 19.0	W 11.0	
5*	Jug	JG5 V	70-8039	Reddish-brown ware, gray core, white grits.	H 19.5	W 10.5	
6	Dipper juglet	DJ1	70-8044	Coarse light buff ware.	H 8.5	W 5.2	
7	Dipper juglet	DJ1	70-8045	Reddish-brown ware, white grits.	H 8.5	W 5.2	
8	Dipper juglet	DJ1	70-8049	Grayish-buff ware.	H 8.2	W 5.2	
9	Dipper juglet	DJ1	70-8050	Reddish-brown ware, white grits.	H 8.5	W 5.3	
10*	Juglet	J2	70-8041	Orange-buff ware, white wash. Red-painted decoration.	H 9.5	W 6.5	
11*	Miniature amphora	MV5	70-8042	Yellowish-buff fairly thin ware.	H 8.0	W 7.0	
12*	Miniature amphora	MV6	70-8040	Greenish-buff ware.	H 9.5	W 6.0	
13*	Lamp	L4	70-8046	Brownish-buff ware.	H 1.5	D 7.0	
Small Finds							
14*	2 earrings		48-394	Bronze. Crescent-shaped. Broken.	W 1.3, 1.5		
15*	Earring		48-399	Silver. Crescent-shaped. Traces of attachment on bottom. Broken.	W 1.4		
16*	Earring		48-395	Silver. Crescent-shaped. Broken.	W 1.5		
17*	Earring		48-393	Silver. Basket-shaped pendant with four granules on top. Fragment.	L 1+		Barnett and Mendelson 1987: Pl. 80: 4/16
18	Pin		48-396	Bronze. Broken.	L 4.5		
19*	Scarab		48-398	Blue faience. Plain.	L 1.2		
20*	Scarab		48-397	Soft composite material. Light yellow.	14.7 × 10.0 × 7.6 (mm)		See App. 2:33; Keel 1997:32: No. 33
21*	Tamburine (frame-drum) player		70-8043	Terracotta.	H 19+	D 6+	See Chap. 7: No. 3; Braun 1999: Pl. IV/1-2
22*	Musician playing a wind instrument(?)		70-8048	Terracotta.	H 15+	W 5+	See Chap. 7: No. 7

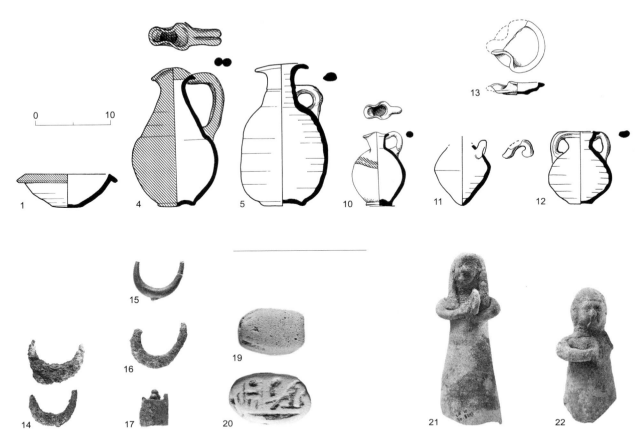

Fig. 4.10. Tomb ZR XII, selected finds. Scale: Nos. 14–17—1:1; Nos. 19, 20—1.5:1; Nos. 21, 22—1:4.

Tomb ZR XIII (Type 1; Fig. 4.11)
Entered through Tomb ZR IX. Shaft tomb, shaft and doorway not cleared. Rectangular chamber with trench in center. No plan available.

Chronology: The tomb was found almost empty of pottery vessels, except for a single storage jar of Type SJ2,

dated to the 6th–5th centuries BCE. A fair number of small finds were uncovered, most of which are known to have been in use for a long period of time, and thus are not diagnostic. Two scarabs which cover a wide span of time are dated between 1000 BCE and the mid 7th century BCE, mistakenly attributed to ZR X by Keel (see Appendix 2:31, 32; Keel 1997:32: Nos. 31, 32).

Catalogue of Finds, Tomb ZR XIII
(For pottery types see Chapter 5. * = illustrated in Fig. 4.11)

No.	Object	Type	IAA No.	Description	Dimensions (cm)		References
Pottery							
1	Storage jar	SJ2	6	Reddish-buff ware.	H 43+	W 24	
Small Finds							
2*	2 earrings		48-453	Bronze. Crescent-shaped. Broken.	W 1.9		
3*	Earring		48-454	Bronze. Crescent-shaped. Broken.	W 1.5		

Catalogue of Finds, Tomb ZR XIII (contd., Fig. 4.11)

No.	Object	Type	IAA No.	Description	Dimensions (cm)			References
4	Earring		48-455	Bronze. Crescent-shaped. Fragment.				
5*	Bracelet		48-446	Bronze. Overlapping ends. Round in section.	D 5.0			
6*	Knee fibula		48-444	Bronze. Pin missing.	L 4.8			
7	Fibula pin		48-451	Bronze. With double loop at one end.	L 4.5			
8*	Bead		48-440	Bluish faience. Lotus-flower-shaped.	L 1.0	W 1.5		Beck 1928: Fig. 24: B.I.e; Spaer 2001: 62–64, Fig. 35
9*	Bead		48-418	Agate. Barrel-shaped.	L 1.6			
10*	Bead		48-426	Agate. Long flattened.	L 1.5			
11*	Bead		48-420	Garnet(?). Cylindrical.	D 1.0			
12*	Bead		48-423	Carnelian. Globular.	D 1.2			
13*	Bead		48-424	Carnelian. Barrel-shaped.	L 2.0			
14*	Bead		48-425	Carnelian. Biconical.	L 0.9			
15*	Bead		48-427	Carnelian. Biconical.	D 0.8			
16*	Bead		48-428	Carnelian. Lozenge-shaped.	L 1.6+			
17*	Bead		48-406	Greenish faience. Ribbed melon-shaped.	D 0.6			
18*	Bead		48-412	Greenish faience. Melon-shaped.	D 0.8			
19*	4 beads		48-465	Faience. Melon-shaped.	D 0.5–1.0			
20*	Bead		48-409	Bluish faience. Cubical.	L 0.7	H 0.6		
21*	Bead		48-414	Greenish faience. Barrel-shaped.	L 1.0+			
22	Bead		48-415	Grayish-green faience. Barrel-shaped.	L 1.4			
23*	Bead		48-464	Greenish faience. Oblate globular.	D 0.6			
24*	Bead		48-466	Faience. Oblate globular.	D 0.5			
25*	11 beads		48-463	Faience. Globular.	D 0.3			
26*	Bead		48-405	Bluish faience. Globular.	D 0.5			
27*	Bead		48-411	Faience. Pentagonal.	D 0.9			
28*	Bead		48-468	Glass. Lentil-shaped.	D 0.5			
29*	Bead		48-421.	Dark glass. Short biconical.	D 0.9			
30*	2 beads		48-407	Glass. Globular.	D 0.7, 0.8			
31	Bead		48-467	Bronze. Oblate globular.	D 0.3			
32*	2 eye beads		48-417	Brown glass. Stratified. Eyes missing.	D 0.5			
33*	Bead		48-413	Whitish faience(?). Glass(?). Oblate globular.	D 1.0			
34*	Bead		48-410	Glass. Barrel-shaped. Grooved in middle.	D 1.0			
35	Bead		48-419	Turquoise(?). Chalcedony(?). Globular.	D 1.0			
36*	Wadj papyrus scepter amulet		48-439a	Bluish faience. Suspension hole at top.	L 1.1	W 0.4		Barnett and Mendelson 1987: Pl. 74:1
37*	Thoueris amulet		48-431	Greenish faience.	L 1.5	W 5.0	D 6.0	Petrie 1914: Pl. XI: 236; Herrmann 1994: 496–509
38*	Thoth(?) amulet		48-435	Greenish faience.	L 1.4	W 0.5	D 0.6	
39*	Thoth(?) amulet		48-434	Greenish faience.	L 1.4	W 0.5	D 0.6	
40*	Horus-hawk amulet		48-404	Greenish faience. With loop at back for suspension.	W 0.9	H 1.1		Barnett and Mendelson 1987: Pl. 121: 24/25
41*	Pateke amulet		48-436	Faience.	L 1.3	W 0.7	D 0.5	Herrmann 1994: 419–473

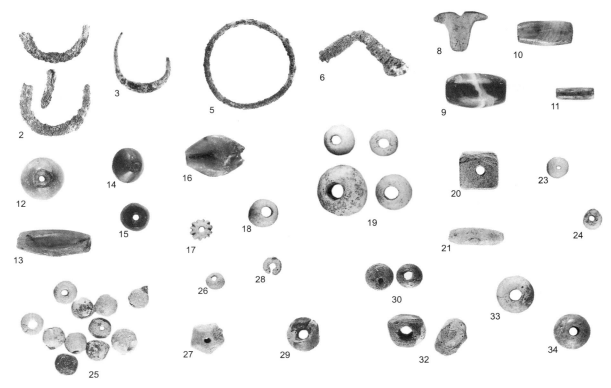

Fig. 4.11. Tomb ZR XIII, selected finds. Scale: Nos. 2, 3, 8–19, 23, 24, 26–30, 33, 34—1:1; Nos. 5, 6—1:2;
Nos. 20, 21—1.5:1; Nos. 25, 32—2:1.

Catalogue of Finds, Tomb ZR XIII (contd., Fig. 4.11)

No.	Object	Type	IAA No.	Description	Dimensions (cm)			References
42*	Pateke amulet		48-443	Faience. Collar on neck.	L 3.6	W 1.5	D 0.9	
43*	Udjat amulet		48-403	Faience.	L 1.1	H 1.3	D 0.4	
44*	Udjat amulet		48-428	Faience. Openwork.	L 0.9	W 1.0	D 0.3	
45*	Udjat amulet		48-437	Greenish faience.	L 0.7	W 0.7	D 0.3	
46*	Grazing sow amulet		48-431	Greenish faience. Suspension loop on back.	L 3.2			Gjerstad 1948: Fig. 18:23; Barnett and Mendelson 1987: Pl. 84: 6:47, 48; Herrmann 1994: 552–555
47*	Weight		48-461.	Hematite. Scaraboid.	L 2.4	Wt 6.0922 gm		
48	Kohl stick		48-447	Bronze. Broken.	L 9.0+			
49	5 kohl sticks		48-450	Bronze. Fragments.				
50	Nail		48-448	Iron. Square in section. Broken.	L 10.0+			
51	Nail		48-445	Iron. Badly corroded.	L 5.2			
52*	Arrowhead		48-449	Bronze. Winged with tubular socket. Irano-Scythian style.	L 4.5			Stern 1982:155
53	Unworked stone		48-459	Carnelian(?). Agate(?).				
54	Unworked stone		48-462	Slate(?).	L 1.9			
55*	Spindle whorl		48-460	Green steatite.	D 2.4			

Fig. 4.11. Tomb ZR XIII, selected finds (contd.). Scale: Nos. 36–46, 58, 59—1.5:1; Nos. 47, 52, 55, 56—1:1; No. 60—1:4.

Catalogue of Finds, Tomb ZR XIII (contd., Fig. 4.11)

No.	Object	Type	IAA No.	Description	Dimensions (cm)		References
56*	Inlay		48-441	Rock crystal. Plano-convex.	D 2.1	Th 0.4	
57	Bead		46-416	Glass. Globular.	D 0.7		
58*	Rectangular plaque		48-402	Limestone? White.	$10.8 \times 8.6 \times 4.2$ (mm)		See App. 2:31; Keel 1997:32: No. 31
59*	Scaraboid		48-422	Glass. Bluish.	$14.4 \times 11.4 \times 7.4$ (mm)		See App. 2:32; Keel 1997:32: No. 32
60*	Tambourine (frame-drum) player		44.54	Terracotta.	H 21.9	W 8.2	See Chap. 7: No. 2; Braun 1999: Pl. IV/1-2

Tomb ZR XIV (Type 1.1; Fig. 4.12)
Shaft tomb with stairway. Entrance blocked with stone slab. Rectangular chamber with central trench and niche hewn into the wall to the right of the entrance. No plan available.

Chronology: The pottery vessels found in this tomb range between the 8th century BCE, based on the red-slipped jugs of Type JG2 I, and the 7th–6th centuries BCE, to which many of the other vessels belong. A single alabastron of the 6th century BCE was uncovered in the tomb. A terracotta cat figurine dated to the 7th century BCE is of particular interest.

Catalogue of Finds, Tomb ZR XIV

(For pottery types see Chapter 5. Fr = fragment; * = illustrated in Fig. 4.12)

No.	Object	Type	IAA No.	Description	Dimensions (cm)		References
Pottery							
1	Jug	JG2 I	70-8295	Reddish-brown ware, red slip, burnished.	Fr		
2	Jug	JG2 I	70-8287	Orange-buff ware, red slip, burnished.	Fr		
3	Jug	JG2 I	70-8296	Orange-buff ware, red slip, burnished.	Fr		
4*	Jug	JG4 I	70-8285	Coarse pinkish-brown ware, white grits.	H 16.5	W 12.0	
5	Jug	JG5 IV	70-8288	Light buff ware, burnished. Red-painted decoration.	W 10.0		
6	Jug	JG5 IV	70-8292	Light buff ware. Red-painted decoration.	H 17+	W 10.0	
7	Jug	JG5 IV	70-8291	Reddish-brown ware.	H 17.5+	W 9.0	
8	Jug	JG6 III	70-8297	Orange-buff ware. Red-painted decoration.	Fr		

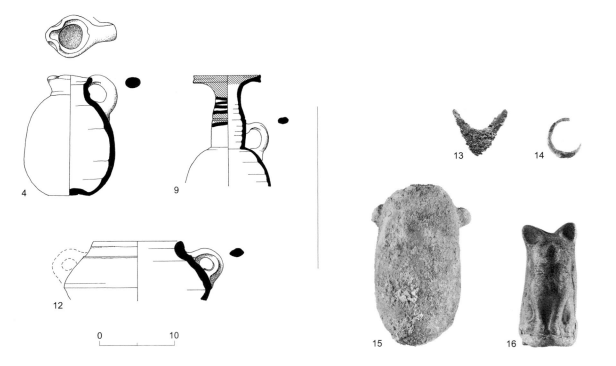

Fig. 4.12. Tomb ZR XIV, selected finds. Scale: Nos. 13, 14—1:1; No. 15—1:3; No. 16—1:2.

Catalogue of Finds, Tomb ZR XIV (contd., Fig. 4.12)

No.	Object	Type	IAA No.	Description	Dimensions (cm)		References
9*	Jug	JG6 III	70-8293	Fine light buff ware, burnished. Red- and black-painted decoration.	Fr		
10	Dipper juglet	DJ1	70-8290	Light buff ware.	H 11.5	W 6.5	
11	Dipper juglet	DJ1	70-8289	Light buff ware.	H 12.0	W 7.0	
12*	Cooking pot	C2	70-8294	Coarse reddish-brown ware, white grits.	Fr		
Small Finds							
13*	Earring		48-469	Silver. Crescent-shaped, with oblate attachment, made from an elliptical ring of thick wire, round in section. A silver ball is soldered onto the base of the ring.	D 1.5		
14*	Earring		48-470	Bronze. Crescent-shaped. Fragment.	W 1.1		
15*	Alabastron		70-8286	Alabaster. With vertical knob handles.	H 13.0	W 6.5	
16*	Cat figurine		44.55	Terracotta.	H 7.0	W 4.8	See Chap. 7: No. 17

Tomb ZR XV (Type 1.1; Plans 4.1, 4.2)

The tomb consists of a shaft leading to a rectangular chamber with two niches. The shaft is roughly rectangular (1.13 × 1.38 m), with a rock-cut stairway on its north side. The doorway on the opposite side has an inset frame for the blocking slab. On each side of the the rectangular chamber (1.00 × 2.88 m) is a rectangular niche (0.75 × 1.75 m) cut into the rock down to the floor level, leaving a rock-cut partition wall 0.87 m high in front of the niche. The main chamber is 1.75 m high, while the niches are slightly lower (1.60 m). The niches form deep troughs, used as burial places. It appears that there were two bodies in each niche, but no funerary gifts were found buried with them. Four holes, irregular in shape and blocked with pebbles and earth, were observed in the rock-cut ceiling of the chamber leading to the surface. Similar holes were noticed in other tombs in the er-Ras cemetery and were thought to be votive channels through which liquid (food offerings) for the dead could be poured. The northwestern hole, the one close to the entrance, has a corresponding hole cut in the floor exactly below, meant for collecting the liquid poured through the upper hole. The upper hole is roughly funnel-shaped, and its lower third was closed by a kind of stopper, flat on top and cone-shaped below. The stopper did not seal the opening tightly, but left enough space on the sides for the liquid offerings to be poured through.

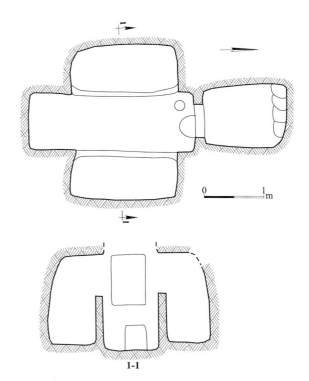

1-1

Plan 4.2. Tomb ZR XV, plan and section.

Chronology: The tomb was looted and found empty; dating is therefore not possible.

Tomb ZR XVI (Type 1.1; Plans 4.1, 4.3; Fig. 4.13)
The tomb consists of a shaft with a stairway and a burial chamber with three niches. The roughly square shaft (1.15 × 1.25 m; depth 1.83 m) has two rock-cut steps at one corner to facilitate the descent. An opening (length 0.25 m) leads to the roughly rectangular (2.00 × 2.40 m) burial chamber. Its walls slope slightly toward the rock-cut ceiling (height 1.88 m). Three shallow rectangular niches (*c.* 0.75 × 1.88 m, *c.* 0.10 m deep) were hewn along three of the walls, excluding the entrance wall. These were most likely used for burial.

Chronology: The tomb was found looted and only a few pottery vessels escaped the robbers. These belong to Types M3 and PF1 and are dated to the 10th–9th centuries BCE. Of particular interest is the tombstone inscribed 'Ama Han-nosek' (see Appendix 1:4).

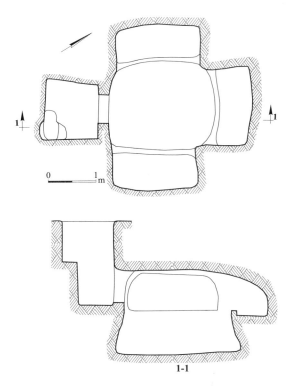

Plan 4.3. Tomb ZR XVI, plan and section.

Fig. 4.13. Tomb ZR XVI, selected finds.
Scale: Nos. 3, 4—1:1; No. 6—not to scale.

Catalogue of Finds, Tomb ZR XVI
(For pottery types see Chapter 5. * = illustrated in Fig. 4.13)

No.	Object	Type	IAA No.	Description	Dimensions (cm)		References
Pottery							
1	Pilgrim flask	PF1	70-8465	Orange-buff ware, gray core. Black-painted decoration.	H 9+	W 5.5	
2	Askos	M3	70-8466	Reddish-brown ware, thick red slip, burnished.	H 10+	W 15.0	
Small Finds							
3*	Finger ring		48-474	Bronze. Round in section, thick in center, ends not meeting.	D 2.5		
4*	Finger ring		48-475	Bronze. Thin and square in section, ends flattened and overlapping.	D 2.1		
5	Finger ring		48-476	Silver. Fragment.			
6*	Stele		44.323	Stone. Incised inscription הנסק/לעמא 'Ama-Han-nosek'.	76 × 38 × 22		See App.1: No. 4

Tomb ZR XVII (Type 1; Plans 4.1, 4.4; Fig. 4.14)
The tomb consists of a shaft with a stairway leading to a single burial chamber. A rectangular rock-cut opening (1.25 × 1.75 m; depth 2.13 m) on the surface level leads into the shaft. The stairway in the shaft consists of two flights of steps cut along the northern wall, requiring a 180° turn about halfway down the shaft.

An opening (length 0.25 m) was originally closed by a blocking slab supported on the left side by a boulder. The burial chamber is roughly square (3.00 × 3.15 m; height 1.60 m), although its walls are neither vertical nor exactly parallel. The walls slope toward the rock-cut ceiling, forming a truncated pyramid.

At the entrance to the chamber there is a rectangular trough (0.38 × 1.10 m; depth 0.25 m) and near the eastern wall a round hole (diam. 0.38 m) was hewn into the floor.

Two rock-cut square bone receptacles (a, b; 0.35 × 0.38 m, depth 0.38 m), covered with stone lids, were exposed next to the northern wall. These ossuaries have a flat ledge on which the stone lid was placed. The lids were smoothed and neatly fitted to the level of the floor, perhaps so as to conceal their existence.

One of the bone receptacles was found full of earth mixed with broken human bones. These were probably the bones of an adult, although no skull was discovered. The other receptacle was empty of earth, with only fragments of a small skull and part of a jaw, at the bottom.

The bone receptacles are an exceptional feature in the er-Ras cemetery, and there must have been a special reason for their existence. The usual burial practice at er-Ras was to move aside the existing bones from previous burials to make room for new ones.

The excavator suggested that the reason for hewing the bone receptacles was not connected to the social status of the deceased but rather the physical condition of the remains. There was a special need to keep the bodies together, similar to the practice of keeping ashes together as a separate entity.

This tomb was fairly rich in its pottery assemblage; it also contained some jewelry.

Chronology: This tomb stands out not only due to its unique architectural features but also because of some of its unusual finds. It contained an urn cover, a type fairly common at Carthage, as well as an east Greek skyphos and a rare iron knee-fibula. Evidence of the early use of this tomb is provided by the presence of the barrel-shaped juglet Type CP9. The tomb's continuous use is

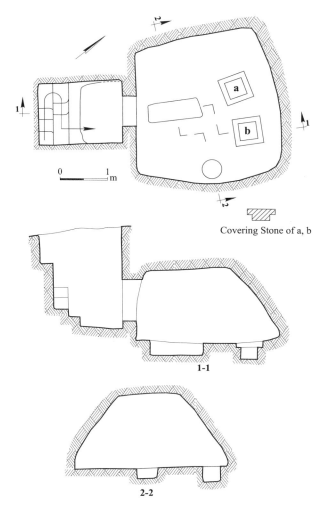

Covering Stone of a, b

Plan 4.4. Tomb ZR XVII, plan and section.

attested by the presence of jugs Type JG6 I, dated to the late 10th–9th centuries BCE. However, the bulk of the pottery belongs to the 9th–8th centuries BCE, including red-slipped jugs, a 'Samaria' bowl and others. The presence of the skyphos, the krater K1, and the storage jar SJ1 indicates that the tomb may have been used in the late 7th–6th centuries BCE. A single scarab was found, reminiscent in style of the XIIIth–XVth Dynasties (1760–1530 BCE), but more likely of the XIXth–XXth Dynasties (1292–1075 BCE), or later. A single bowl of the Hellenistic period (Fig. 4.14:6) may point to the tomb's latest phase. Despite the long time span observed in this tomb, the relatively small number of objects suggests that it had been looted (see Appendix 2:34; Keel 1997:32: No. 34).

Catalogue of Finds, Tomb ZR XVII
(For pottery types see Chapter 5. Fr = fragment; * = illustrated in Fig. 4.14)

No.	Object	Type	IAA No.	Description	Dimensions (cm)		References
Pottery							
1	Bowl	B1 I	70-8340	Reddish-brown ware, white grits.	H 3.5		
2	Bowl	B1 I	70-8339	Reddish-brown ware, white grits.	H 3.5	D 13.0	
3*	Bowl	B4 V	70-8315	Reddish-brown ware, gray core.	H 7.0	D 12.0	
4	Bowl	B8 I	70-8312	Fine light buff ware. Red slip inside, on exterior and narrow red band around base, burnished all over.	H 3.5	D 20.0	
5*	Bowl	B8 V	70-8338	Orange-buff ware, red slip, burnished.	H 2.5	D 19.0	
6*	Bowl		70-8314	Gray ware, burnished. Hellenistic.	Fr		
7	Krater	K1	70-8309	Coarse reddish-brown ware.	Fr		
8	Storage jar	SJ1	70-8299	Reddish-brown ware.	Fr		
9	Jug	JG2 I	70-8302	Orange-buff ware, red slip, burnished.	Fr		
10	Jug	JG2 I	70-8326	Orange-buff ware, red slip, burnished.	H 21+	W 14+	
11*	Jug	JG3 I	70-8303	Brownish-buff ware, white grits, red slip, burnished.	Fr		
12	Jug	JG5 I	70-8308	Orange-buff ware, red slip, burnished.	W 12+		
13*	Jug	Misc.	70-8310	Orange-buff ware, red slip, burnished.	H 12+	W 9.0	
14	Jug	JG5 IV	70-8301	Pinkish-buff ware. Red-painted decoration.	H 19+	W 10.0	
15	Jug	JG6 I	70-8304	Orange-buff ware. Red- and black-painted decoration.	Fr		
16	Jug	JG6 I	70-8316	Orange-buff ware. Red- and black-painted decoration.	Fr		
17	Dipper juglet	DJ1	70-8306	Pinkish-buff ware.	H 8.5	W 5.3	
18	Dipper juglet	DJ1	70-8560	Pinkish-buff ware.	H 9.0	W 5.5	
19*	Cover	CO1	70-8313	Pinkish-buff ware, red slip, burnished.	H 2.0	D 18.0	
20	Barrel-shaped juglet	CP9	70-8328	Fine buff ware. Black- and red-painted decoration.	H 8.5	W 10.0	
21*	Skyphos	M4	44.257	Pale orange ware, brownish-black paint on both sides, except for narrow band on shoulder.	H 7.0	D 10.0	
Small Finds							
22	Earring		48-477	Bronze. Crescent-shaped. Broken.			
23	Bracelet		48-478	Bronze. Double stranded. Fragment.			
24	Knee fibula		48-487	Iron. Pin missing. Badly corroded.	L 5.5		
25*	Bead		48-485	Agate. Long seven-faceted. Cylindrical.	L 1.5	D 0.8	
26	3 nails		48-479	Iron. Fragments.	L 1.5–2.0		
27*	Earring pendant(?)		48-480	Silver. Two stranded twisted wire with loop at one end.	L 2.5		Barnett and Mendelson 1987: Pl. 119: 23/6, 23/7
28*	Scarab		48-483	Steatite. Remains of greenish glaze.	21.8 × 15.1 × 8.4 (mm)		See App. 2:34; Keel 1997:32: No. 34

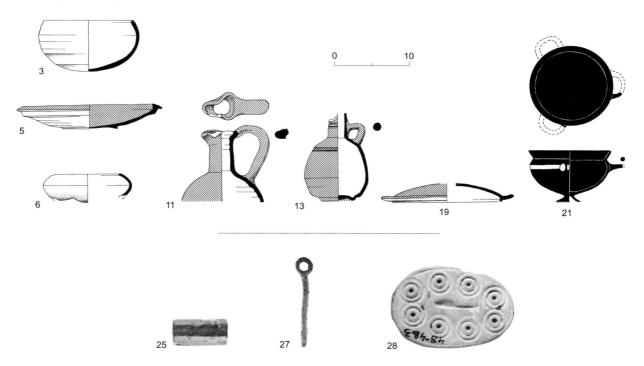

Fig. 4.14. Tomb ZR XVII, selected finds. Scale: Nos. 25, 27—1:1; No. 28—1.5:1.

Tomb ZR XVIII (Type 1; Plan 4.1)
According to the excavator's description and the sketch in the plan of the cemetery, this tomb is of Type 1 without any distinguishing features. It was re-used in the Roman period.

Chronology: The tomb was found empty; dating is therefore impossible.

Tomb ZR XIX (Type 1.1; Plans 4.1, 4.5; Fig. 4.15)
The tomb is similar in construction to other tombs in this cemetery, consisting of a shaft leading to a single burial chamber, in this case containing three niches.

The rectangular shaft (1.15 × 1.38 m; depth 1.75 m) has rock-cut steps along the wall opposite the entrance, facilitating the descent. An opening (length 0.25 m) leads into the burial chamber, followed by two rock-cut steps at the entrance.

The domed burial chamber is roughly rectangular in shape (2.50 × 3.00 m; height 1.85 m). The eastern and western walls each contain a niche, the bottom of which is higher than the floor level. The niche in the wall opposite the entrance was hewn down to floor level (0.75 × 2.00 m; depth 0.75 m), leaving a rock partition

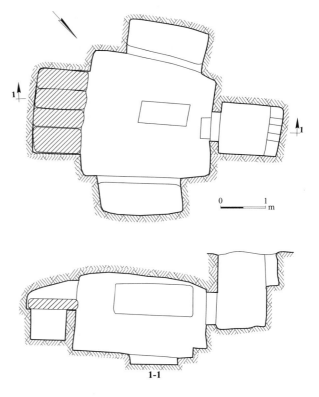

Plan 4.5. Tomb ZR XIX, plan and section.

and forming a deep trough-shaped receptacle. The crudely hewn and roughly rectangular rock-cut trough at the back of the niche was found covered with four stone slabs (*c.* 0.50 × 1.13 m; thickness; 0.22–0.24 m). Remains of human bones, very poorly preserved and in apparent disarray, were scattered on top of the slabs. Originally, there was one burial above each slab. It appears that the burials were not disturbed, as evidenced by the fine glass bottles found around them.

The skulls of the first and third burials were missing. Large white stone boulders had been placed at the conjectured location of the skulls. The bodies may have belonged to people who were beheaded or the victims of accidents, the boulder symbolizing the missing head.

The other two niches are symmetrical, each having a rock partition separating it from the chamber. In that west of the entrance (0.75 × 2.00 m), two skeletons were laid *tête-bêche*, with a few glass bottles and a complete cooking pot. The opposite niche is also narrow and long (0.75 × 1.88 m); it contained a layer of sand. Two skeletons were laid on the sand, with their hands to the right. Among the bones were Roman glass bottles.

The interior of the chamber was stacked with masses of human bones mixed with sand, deposited there with glass bottles at different times. There was a central rectangular trough (0.50 × 1.10 m) in the middle of the chamber, in which a few sherds from the time of the original burial were found.

Initially, it was thought that this tomb was untouched, since the closing slab was found leaning against the door. Once excavated, however, it became clear that the tomb had been re-used in the Roman period.

The pottery found in this tomb dates mainly from the Roman period (not included in this report). Among the small finds are a Roman mirror and fragments of Roman glass, as well as some jewelry and amulets known from other Iron Age contexts.

Chronology: The tomb contained no pottery vessels dating from its initial construction phase. The few finds datable to the Roman period indicate the tomb's re-use at that time. A single scarab dated to the XXIInd Dynasty (944–713 BCE; see Appendix 2:35; Keel 1997:34: No. 35) is attributed to the earlier use of the tomb.

Catalogue of Finds, Tomb ZR XIX
(* = illustrated in Fig. 4.15)

No.	Object	IAA No.	Description	Dimensions (cm)		References
Small Finds						
1*	Earring	48-498	Bronze. Crescent-shaped. Broken.	W 1.9		
2	Earring	48-489	Bronze. Crescent-shaped. Broken.	L 2.2		
3*	Bracelet	48-492	Silver. Round in section, with thickened ends. A double strand joins the two ends.	D 4.2		
4	Armlet	48-497	Bronze. Broken.	D 12.0		
5*	Bead	48-499	Carnelian. Globular.	D 0.6		
6*	*Anh̬* amulet	48-494	Silver.	L 3.0	W 1.5	Petrie 1914: Pl. III: 30b
7*	Mirror	48-490	Bronze. Perforated along the edges. Broken. Decoration of concentric circles on outer face. Characteristic of the Roman period.	D 10.0		
8*	Handle	48-495	Bronze. Cross-shaped. Probably from a mirror.	L 9.0		
9	2 disks	48-496	Bronze. Flat.	D 4.8		
10*	Scarab	48-501	Enstatite (gray-white coating).	12.2 × 9.4 × 5.8 (mm)		See App. 2:35; Keel 1997:34: No. 35
11*	Spindle and whorl	48-491	Ivory. Broken.	L 6.7		

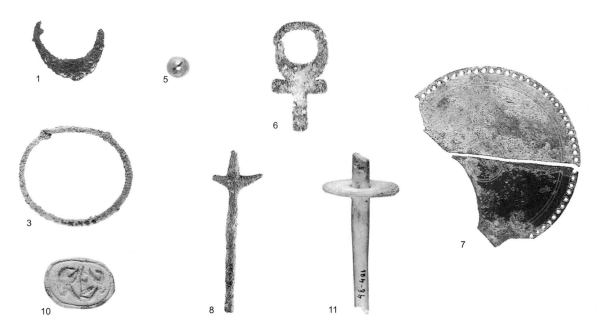

Fig. 4.15. Tomb ZR XIX, selected finds. Scale: Nos. 1, 5, 6—1:1; No. 3—3:4; Nos. 7, 8—1:2; No. 10—1.5:1; No. 11—2:3.

Tomb ZR XX (Type 1.1; Plans 4.1, 4.6)

The tomb consists of a shaft leading to a burial chamber with three niches. The roughly rectangular shaft (1.25 × 1.38 m; depth 1.75 m) has a rock-hewn stairway in the western wall.

Judging from the plan, most of this wall was washed away. The doorway (length 0.25 m) leading to the burial chamber has a slightly recessed and well-smoothed frame on three sides. It was carefully sealed by a closely fitting masonry block. The excavator maintained that there was "a second blocking behind the one at the entrance to the chamber. It consisted of two dressed stones laid one on top of the other, and further behind were four flat dressed slabs standing on edge, one behind the other and thus forming a close packing of stones which filled the upper part of the tomb proper. This had the form of a rectangular cist covered with six stone blocks." However, this blocking does not exist on the plan.

The burial chamber is large and spacious (*c.* 2.75 × 3.00 m; height *c.* 1.65 m) with a rock-cut ceiling. Three niches open out from the chamber: the one to the left of the entrance is narrow and long (0.75 m × 1.88 m) and has a slightly raised edge. That to the right of the entrance is also narrow and long (0.88 × 1.63 m) with a raised edge

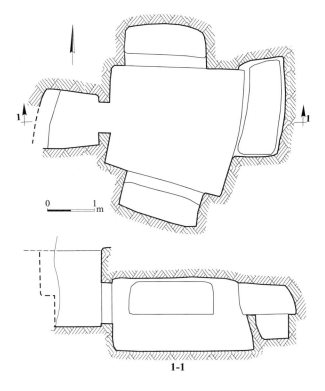

Plan 4.6. Tomb ZR XX, plan and section.

of 0.20 m. That opposite the entrance is larger than the two others (0.75 × 2.25 m) and was divided from the main burial chamber by a rock-cut partition, 0.80 m high. The excavator reported numerous mason's marks of various shapes on the walls.

Chronology: The tomb was found empty and dating is therefore not possible.

Tomb ZR XXI (Type 1; Plans 4.1, 4.7; Fig. 4.16)
The tomb consists of a shaft with a stairway and a single burial chamber. The shaft (1.10 × 1.38 m; depth 1.85 m) has three rock-cut steps. An opening (length 0.40 m) blocked by two courses of closely fitted and well-squared masonry leads to the burial chamber. The burial chamber was roughly rectangular (1.35 × 2.00 m; height 1.50 m). An exceptionally large trough (1.00 × 2.00 m; depth 0.60 m) occupies the entire space of the chamber floor. It was covered by six stone slabs in one or two rows (Ben-Dor's diary is self-contradictory). The walls of the chamber slope toward the rock-cut ceiling, forming a truncated pyramid.

Masons' marks:

On lower stone behind the first row of blocking stones

On top stone of the right wall, in front

On the wall, bottom row, first stone from the right

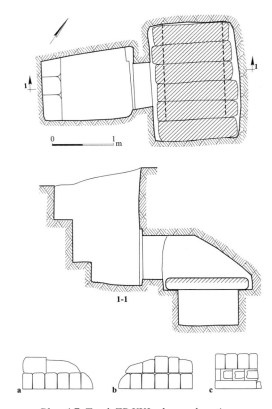

Plan 4.7. Tomb ZR XXI, plan and sections.

The tomb contained the skeletons of three adults with their faces to the east. No pottery accompanied the bodies, only four earrings and a bead.

Chronology: The tomb was found looted. It contained a few small finds including a fragment of a basket-shaped earring dated to the 7th–5th centuries BCE (Fig. 4.16:1; Barnett and Mendelson 1987: Pl. 78:3/12, 3/13).

Catalogue of Finds, Tomb ZR XXI
(* = illustrated in Fig. 4.16)

No.	Object	IAA No.	Description	Dimensions (cm)	References
Small Finds					
1*	Earring	48-504	Bronze. Crescent-shaped. With loop from which a basket-shaped pendant is suspended.	H 1.2–1.6 W 0.5–1.2	Barnett and Mendelson 1987: Pl. 78: 3/12–3/13
2*	Earring	48-506	Silver. Crescent-shaped.	L 1.5	
3*	Earring	48-505	Bronze. Crescent-shaped.	L 1.8	
4*	Earring	48-507	Bronze. Crescent-shaped, broken.	W 1.2	
5*	Bead	48-503	Greenish faience. Cylindrical.	L 0.5	

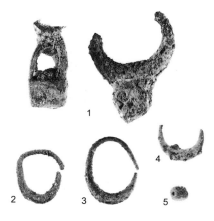

Fig. 4.16. Tomb ZR XXI, selected finds.
Scale: No. 1—2:1; Nos. 2–5—1:1.

Tomb ZR XXII (Type 1.1; Plans 4.1, 4.8)
This tomb is unique on account of its superstructure, although it does not differ in plan from many other tombs in the same cemetery. It consists of a shaft leading to a single burial chamber with one niche in the wall opposite the entrance. The roughly square shaft (1.30 × 1.38 m; depth *c.* 2.50 m) was entered by a rock-cut step in the northeastern wall. The bottom of the shaft and most of the chamber were covered with sand.

The shaft continued above surface as a square well, built of three courses of fine ashlar masonry (height 1.0 m); three large stone slabs sealed the mouth of the

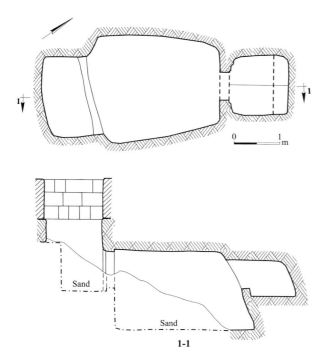

Plan 4.8. Tomb ZR XXII, plan and section.

well. The excavator assumed that the upper part of the well and its roof were intended to serve as a monument that could be seen from a distance. The chamber is rectangular in plan (2.25 × 2.75 m). The wall opposite the entrance slopes inward toward the roof. The ceiling is rock cut, with a total height of 1.75 m. The northern part of the chamber is covered with sand, over 1.0 m deep.

A niche 0.75 m deep was hewn in the back of the chamber, opposite the entrance. Its floor is higher than

the chamber floor and its ceiling was cut *c.* 0.13 m below the chamber ceiling. It is rectangular in plan (1.00 × 1.75 m), and a low (0.25 m high) partition separates it from the main burial chamber.

The tomb was looted shortly before the excavation, according to the information received; no sherds or other objects seem to have been found in the debris.

The niche contained the bones of a single burial. The fact that so much care was invested in the construction of this tomb seems to indicate that someone of high rank was buried there.

Chronology: The tomb was found looted, and its dating is therefore impossible.

Tomb ZR XXIII (Probably Type 1; Plan 4.1; Fig. 4.17)
The sketch in the plan of the cemetery shows that this tomb had the usual shaft and a chamber in the shape of a truncated pyramid. The burials were placed on the floor around the walls; only small finds were recovered. According to the excavator's diary it was found undisturbed.

Chronology: The few small finds that were retrieved are of a common type in use over a long span of time, and therefore do not allow for clear dating.

Catalogue of Finds, Tomb ZR XXIII
(* = illustrated in Fig. 4.17)

No.	Object	IAA No.	Description	Dimensions (cm)
Small Finds				
1*	Earring	48-509	Bronze. Crescent-shaped.	L 2.3
2*	Bracelet	48-508	Bronze. Round in section, ends overlapping.	D 3.2

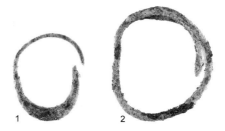

Fig. 4.17. Tomb ZR XXIII, selected finds. Scale—1:1.

Tomb ZR XXIV (Type 1.1; Plan 4.1; Fig. 4.18)
The excavator described this tomb as being undisturbed, and of the usual type. The blocking slab was found in position. It has a shaft, a burial chamber with a single niche and a trough near the entrance to the chamber. Only the sketch in the plan of the cemetery is available.

Chronology: The looters of this tomb overlooked a few objects, mainly small finds. Of particular interest is an ampulla juglet (Type J5) dated to the 7th century BCE and a single scarab dated to the 7th century BCE (Appendix 2:36; Keel 1997:34: No. 36).

Catalogue of Finds, Tomb ZR XXIV
(For pottery types see Chapter 5. * = illustrated in Fig. 4.18)

No.	Object	Type	IAA No.	Description	Dimensions (cm)		References
Pottery							
1	Storage jar	SJ1	46.79(?)	Reddish-brown ware.	H 50.0	W 20.0	
2*	Juglet	J5	70-8367	Thick coarse reddish-brown ware.	H 8.5	W 5.5	
3*	Cover	CO2	70-8588	Coarse reddish-brown ware.	H 2.0	D 16.7	
Small Finds							
4*	Scarab		48-512	Soft composite material. Yellowish, remains of olive-green glaze.	15.0 × 11.0 × 7.5 (mm)		See App. 2:36; Keel 1997:34: No. 36
5*	3 earrings		48-515	Bronze. Crescent-shaped.	L 2.1–2.5		
6*	5 earrings		48-516	Bronze. Crescent-shaped. Fragments.	W 1.0–2.0		
7.*	Armlet		48-510	Bronze. Ends meeting.	D 11.3		
8	Nail		48-511	Iron. Badly corroded. Fragments.			
9*	2 needles		48-513	Bronze. Broken.	L 7.2, 9.0		
10*	Bead		48-514	Carnelian. Oblate globular.	D 0.8		

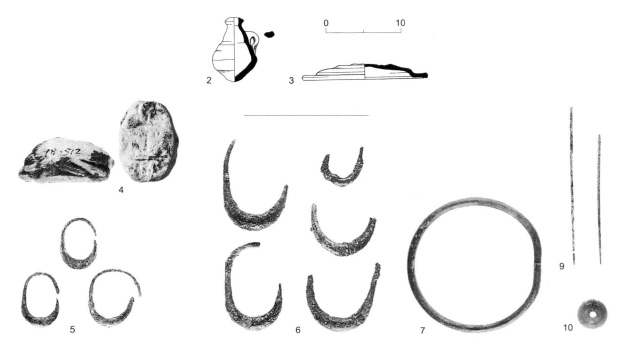

Fig. 4.18. Tomb ZR XXIV, selected finds. Scale : No. 4—1.5:1; No. 5—3:4; Nos. 6, 10—1:1; No. 7—1:3; No. 9—1:2.

Tomb ZR XXV (Type 1; Plan 4.1)
Tomb of the simplest type; narrow shaft with stairway and a chamber with sloping walls. Only the sketch in the plan of the cemetery is available.

Chronology: The tomb was found looted; dating is therefore impossible.

Tomb ZR XXVI (Type 1.1; Plans 4.1, 4.9; Fig. 4.19)
This tomb is of the type common in this cemetery, consisting of a shaft leading to a single burial chamber with an adjoining niche. A few details of construction differ from those found in similar tombs in the cemetery.

The roughly square shaft (1.13 × 1.25 m; depth 1.75 m) has a rock-cut stairway in the western wall. An opening (length 0.25 m) followed by two steps leads into the rectangular burial chamber (2.80 × 3.15 m; height 1.75 m), with a rock-cut roof and walls sloping in the shape of a truncated pyramid. The rectangular trough (0.50 × 1.50 m; depth 0.25 m) in the center of the chamber is common to this type of tomb; however, in this case it is parallel to the entrance wall and not perpendicular to it. A rock-cut bench runs along the southern chamber wall. A niche in the northern wall was left unfinished. The excavator assumed that the tomb builders were not satisfied with the quality of the rock and therefore decided to place the most important deceased person on the raised bench instead of in the niche.

Chronology: The tomb was found almost empty and the few remaining objects do not provide a sufficient basis

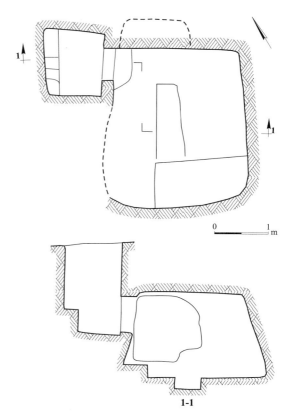

Plan 4.9. Tomb ZR XXVI, plan and section.

for dating. Of significance is a 'Samaria' bowl Type B8 III dating to the 9th century BCE, as well as a clay wheel and a handmade headless female figurine (see Chapter 7: No. 8).

Catalogue of Finds, Tomb ZR XXVI
(For pottery types see Chapter 5. Fr = fragment; * = illustrated in Fig. 4.19)

No.	Object	Type	IAA No.	Description	Dimensions (cm)		References
Pottery							
1	Bowl	B3 II	70-8380	Coarse reddish-brown ware.	Fr		
2*	Bowl	B8 III	70-8377	Fine brownish-buff ware, red slip. Wheel-burnished all over.	H 4.0	D 13.0	
3*	Jug	Misc.	70-8435	Yellow-buff ware.	H 13.5+	W 6.0	
4	Jug	JG6 III	70-8434	Orange-buff ware. Black- and red-painted decoration.	H 17.5+	W 8.5	
5*	Jug	JG7 II	70-8438	Pinkish-buff ware, gray core. Red-painted decoration.	H 19.5	W 12.0	
6*	Wheel	Misc.	70-8378	Brownish-buff ware.	D 9.0		
7*	Wheel	Misc.	70-8379	Brownish-buff ware.	D 8.0		

Catalogue of Finds, Tomb ZR XXVI (contd., Fig. 4.19)

No.	Object	Type	IAA No.	Description	Dimensions (cm)		References
Small Finds							
8*	13 earrings		48-518	Bronze. Crescent-shaped. Partly broken. One crescent-shaped earring threaded with silver wire.	W 1.2–2.0		
9*	Bead		48-519	Greenish faience. Oblate globular.	D 0.5		
10*	Female figurine		70-8436	Terracotta.	H 10.0+	W 8.0	See Chap. 7: No. 8

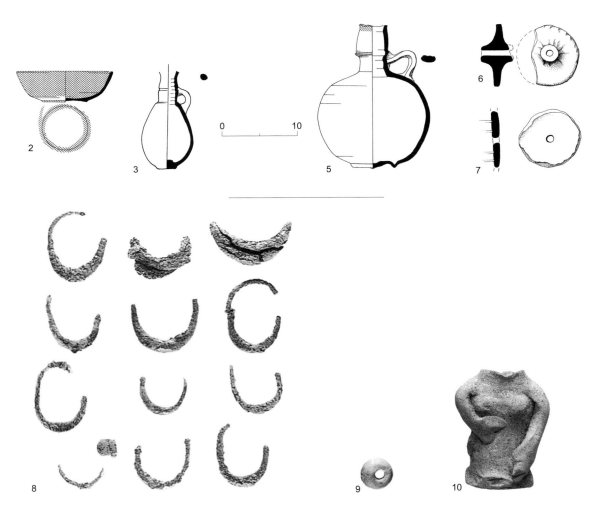

Fig. 4.19. Tomb ZR XXVI, selected finds. Scale: Nos. 8, 9—1:1; No. 10—1:3.

Tomb ZR XXVII (Type 1; Plans 4.1, 4.10)

'Unfinished' tomb with usual shaft leading to the small burial chamber, which was not completed. The shaft is square (*c.* 1.20 × 1.20 m; depth 2.0 m) and has steps to facilitate the descent. No closing slab was found in the shaft and the carefully worked doorway (length 0.35 m) leads to a small rock-cut space which was meant to serve as the burial chamber. One wall is vertical, while the other is convex (0.75 × 1.25 m), inclining toward the rock-cut ceiling with a maximum height of 0.90 m.

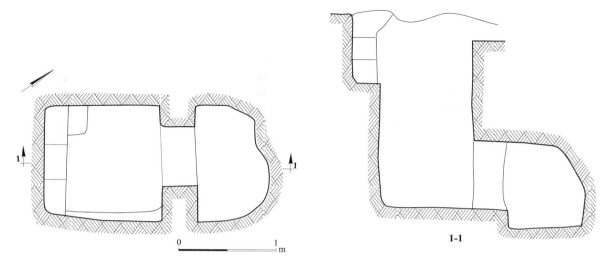

Plan 4.10. Tomb ZR XXVII, plan and section.

Chronology: The tomb was found looted, and a clear dating was therefore impossible.

Tomb ZR XXVIII (Type 1; Plan 4.1; Fig. 4.20)
Tomb with shaft and opening leading to tent-shaped burial chamber. Only the sketch in the plan of the cemetery is available. The tomb contained a few pottery vessels and some small finds, including finger rings, bracelets, beads, scarabs and pendants.

Chronology: The tomb was found disturbed and the few vessels recovered do not provide a sufficient basis for determining its period. An exception is the miniature jar Type MV4 dated to the Persian period. Figurines of a tambourine player and a pregnant woman dated to the 7th–6th centuries BCE were also found (see Chapter 7: Nos. 1, 6), as were three scarabs dated between the XXIInd and XXVIth Dynasties (945–525 BCE; see Appendix 2:37–39; Keel 1997:34: Nos. 37–39). The small finds from this tomb do not allow a more specific dating.

Catalogue of Finds, Tomb ZR XXVIII
(For pottery types see Chapter 5. Fr = fragment; * = illustrated in Fig. 4.20)

No.	Object	Type	IAA No.	Description	Dimensions (cm)		References
Pottery							
1	Dipper juglet	DJ1	70-8364	Coarse reddish-brown ware.	H 9.0	W 5.0	
2	Dipper juglet	DJ1	70-8359	Orange-brown ware, white grits.	H 8.5	W 5.0	
3	Dipper juglet	DJ1	70-8360	Reddish-brown ware.	H 8.5	W 5.0	
4*	Miniature jar	MV4	70-8361	Coarse reddish-brown ware.	H 10.0	W 7.5	
5	Cooking pot	C2	70-8365/1	Coarse reddish-brown ware, white grits.	Fr		
Small Finds							
6	9 earrings		48-520/1	Bronze. Crescent-shaped. Partly broken.	W 1.0–2.5		
7*	2 finger rings		48-525a	Bronze. Ends overlapping.	D 2.0–2.5		
8*	Finger ring		48-525b	Silver. Ends overlapping.	D 1.3		
9*	Finger ring		48-526	Bronze. Flat in section, ends slightly overlapping.	D 2.2		
10*	2 armlets		48-522	Bronze. Round in section, ends meeting.	D 11.0, 12.0		
11*	Bracelet		48-523	Bronze. Round in section, ends overlapping.	D 5.0		
12*	Bead		48-530	Bluish faience. Cubical.	H 0.7	W 0.7	

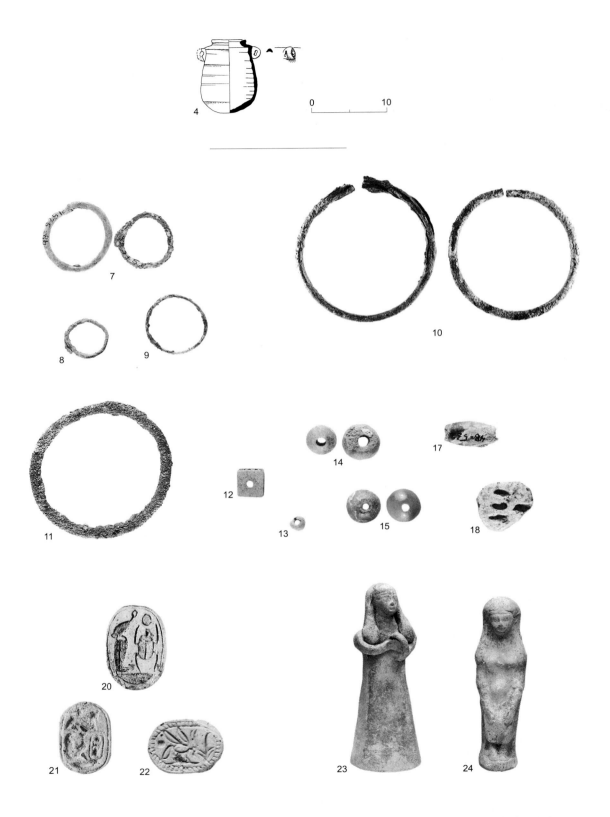

Fig. 4.20. Tomb ZR XXVIII, selected finds. Scale: Nos. 7–9, 11—3:4; No. 10—1:3; Nos. 12–15, 17—1:1;
Nos. 18, 20–22—1.5:1; Nos. 23, 24—1:4.

Catalogue of Finds, Tomb ZR XXVIII (contd., Fig. 4.20)

No.	Object	Type	IAA No.	Description	Dimensions (cm)		References
13*	Bead		48-531	Bluish faience. Globular.	D 0.4		
14*	2 beads		48-529	Chalcedony(?) Short. Biconical.	D 0.8, 1.0		
15*	2 beads		48-528	Carnelian. Biconical.	D 0.9		
16	Bead		48-533	Silver. Ring-shaped.	D 0.5		
17*	Bead		48-532	Agate. Barrel-shaped.	L 1.4		
18*	Udjat pendant		48-534	Greenish faience. Pierced (lengthwise), three perforations. Broken.	L 1.0		Pritchard 1988: Fig. 18:40
19	Nail		48-535	Iron. Fragment.	L 4.5		
20*	Scarab		48-520	Steatite.	15.2 × 10.5 × 6.9 (mm)		See App. 2:37; Keel 1997:34: No. 37
21*	Scarab		48-521	Steatite. White with hematite inclusions.	13.2 × 9.5 × 6.1 (mm)		See App. 2:38; Keel 1997:34: No. 38
22*	Scarab		48-521A	Steatite. White with hematite inclusions.	13.5 × 10.2 × 6.5 (mm)		See App. 2:39; Keel 1997:34: No. 39
23*	Tambourine (frame-drum) player		44.264	Terracotta.	H 20.6	D 8.0	See Chap. 7: No. 1; Braun 1999: Pl. IV/1-2
24*	Seated pregnant woman		44.263	Terracotta.	H 19.0	W 5.4	See Chap. 7: No. 6

Tomb ZR XXIX (Type 1; Plans 4.1a, 4.11; Fig. 4.21)
This tomb is of the simplest type, consisting of a single burial chamber and a shaft. The shallow shaft is roughly rectangular (1.00 × 1.30 m; depth 1.50 m) and has no stairway. The entrance (width 0.70 m; height 0.75 m) to the burial chamber was found open. The chamber is roughly square (2.13 × 2.25 m; height 1.75 m) with walls sloping slightly toward the ceiling, and without a niche or central trench.

Although the tomb was found looted and its contents severely disturbed and overturned, it contained a varied assemblage of pottery vessels, as well as a fairly large number of small finds, including jewelry, amulets and scarabs. Of particular interest are the terracotta mask depicting the face of a woman and the figurines of a double-pipe player and a woman bathing in a tub (see Chapter 7: Nos. 4, 10, 20).

Chronology: The bulk of the vessels in this tomb belongs to the 9th–8th centuries BCE, some of them continuing into the 7th century BCE. It should be noted that the tomb also yielded a number of 'Samaria' bowls, as well as Black-on-Red (CP2) and Bichrome wares (CP3). The scarabs found in the tomb are dated to the 8th century BCE (see Appendix 2:40, 41; Keel 1997:34: Nos. 40, 41).

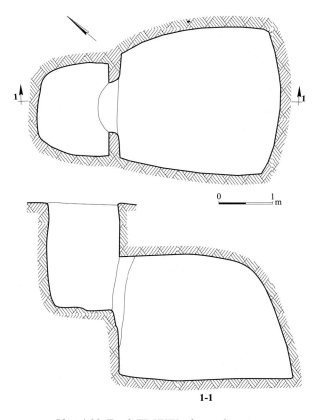

Plan 4.11. Tomb ZR XXIX, plan and section.

Catalogue of Finds, Tomb ZR XXIX
(For pottery types see Chapter 5. Fr = fragment; * = illustrated in Fig. 4.21)

No.	Object	Type	IAA No.	Description	Dimensions (cm)		References
Pottery							
1	Bowl	B1 I	70-8170	Coarse reddish-brown ware, white grits.	H 4.2	D 17.0	
2*	Bowl	B1 I	70-8169	Coarse reddish-brown ware, white grits.	H 4.5	D 17.5	
3*	Bowl	B1 II	70-8183	Coarse reddish-brown ware, white and black grits.	H 4.0	D 17.5	
4*	Bowl	B4 II	70-8171	Reddish-brown ware, red slip, wheel-burnished on outside.	H 10.0	D 16.0	
5*	Bowl	B4 III	70-8192	Grayish-brown ware, white grits.	H 5.5	D 11.5	
6*	Bowl	B4 IV	70-8193	Coarse light pinkish-buff ware.	H 8.5	D 11.5	
7*	Bowl	B5 II	70-8189	Coarse reddish-brown ware, white and black grits.	H 2.2	D 8.0	
8*	Bowl	B5 III	70-8186	Coarse reddish-brown ware, white and black grits.	H 3.0	D 12.0	
9*	Bowl	B5 IV	70-8187	Coarse reddish-brown ware, grits.	H 3.0	D 13 .0	
10*	Bowl	B8 I	70-8177	Light buff ware, red slip, burnished.	H 3.5	D 19.0	
11*	Bowl	B8 II	70-8477	Reddish-brown ware, white grits.	H 4.5	D 16.5	
12*	Jug	JG2 I	70-8156	Reddish-orange ware, dark red slip, burnished.	H 21.0	W 12.5	
13*	Jug	JG4 II	70-8178	Fine reddish-brown ware, red slip, burnished.	H 14.0	W 13.0	
14	Jug	JG4 II	70-8181	Fine reddish-brown ware, red slip, burnished.	Fr		
15	Jug	JG5 I	70-8159	Orange-buff ware, red slip, burnished.	Fr		
16*	Jug	JG5 II	70-8179	Orange-buff ware, red slip, burnished.	Fr		
17	Jug	JG5 I	70-8475	Orange-buff ware, red slip, burnished.	Fr		
18*	Jug	JG5 III	70-8158	Reddish-yellow ware, dark red slip, burnished.	H 11.5+	W 7.5	
19	Jug	JG6 I	70-8160	Reddish-buff ware. Black- and red-painted decoration.	H 17.5	W 11.0	
20*	Jug	JG6 I	70-8154	Light buff ware. Black- and red-painted decoration.	H 18.5	W 12.0	
21*	Jug	JG7 I	70-8153	Coarse reddish-brown ware, white grits.	H 15.5	W 12.0	
22*	Dipper juglet	DJ1	70-8470	Light pinkish-buff ware.	H 11.0	W 6.0	
23	Dipper juglet	DJ1	70-8472	Reddish-brown ware.	H 12.5	W 5.5	
24	Dipper juglet	DJ1	70-8473	Light buff ware.	H 13.0	W 5.0	
25*	Dipper juglet	DJ1	70-8476	Coarse grayish-brown ware, white grits.	H 12.0	W 6.0	
26*	Dipper juglet	DJ2	70-8471	Grayish-buff ware, white grits.	H 13.5	W 6.0	
27	Dipper juglet	DJ2	70-8474	Reddish-brown ware, white grits.	H 13.0	W 6.5	
28*	Juglet	J1	70-8164	Light buff ware. Red-painted decoration.	H 11.0	W 8.5	
29*	Juglet	J4	70-8172	Coarse grayish ware, black slip, burnished.	H 7+	W 5.0	
30*	Cooking pot	C4	70-8151	Fine reddish-buff ware. Soot stains on bottom.	H 10.0	D 11.8	
31*	Miniature jar	MV2	70-8165	Coarse reddish-brown ware, white grits.	H 11.5	W 7.5	

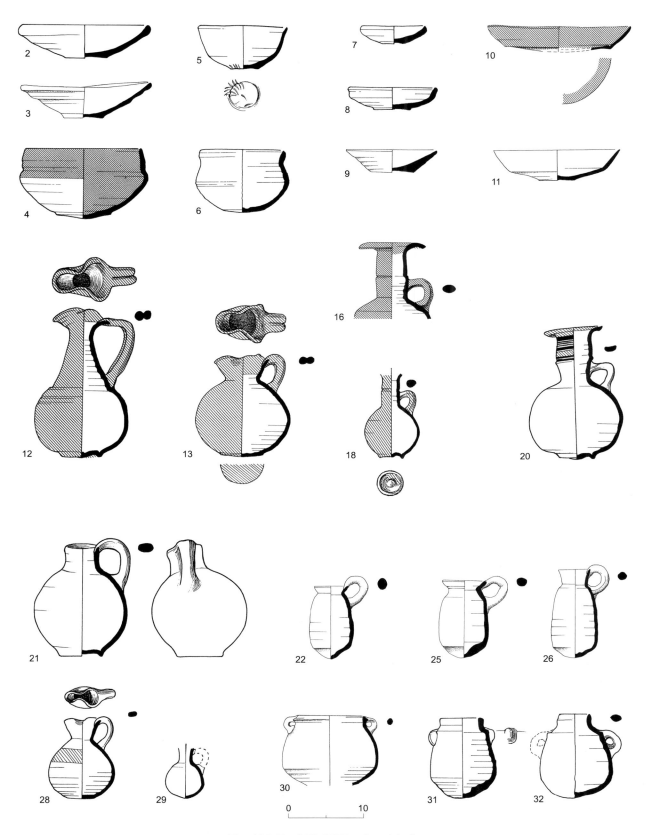

Fig. 4.21. Tomb ZR XXIX, selected finds.

Catalogue of Finds, Tomb ZR XXIX (contd., Fig. 4.21)

No.	Object	Type	IAA No.	Description	Dimensions (cm)		References
32*	Miniature jar	MV3	70-8166	Coarse reddish-brown ware, white grits.	H 12.5	W 8.5	
33*	Jug	CP2	70-8551	Reddish-brown ware, red slip, burnished. Black-painted decoration.	H 19.0	W 12 .0	
34*	Jug	CP3	70-8152	Light buff ware. Black- and red-painted decoration.	H 20.5	W 13.5	
35*	Juglet	CP6	70-8163	Reddish-brown ware, red slip, burnished. Black-painted decoration.	H 9.5	W 5.5	
36	Juglet	CP6	70-8162	Light buff ware, light red slip, burnished. Black-painted decoration.	H 9.5	W 5.5	
37*	Rhyton	M1	70-8180	Reddish brown ware, well-levigated.	H 9.5	D 8.5	

Small Finds

No.	Object	Type	IAA No.	Description	Dimensions (cm)		References
38*	Earrings		48-585	Bronze. Crescent-shaped. 31 fragments.		W 1.0–1.5	
39*	4 earrings		48-556	Silver. Crescent-shaped.		W 1.2–1.5	
40*	6 earrings		48-557	Bronze. Some fragments.		W 1.1–2.0	
41*	2 earrings		48-553	Bronze. Crescent-shaped.	L 2.5, 2.2	W 1.9, 1.5	
42*	5 earrings		48-583	Bronze. Crescent-shaped.	L 1.6–2.2		
43*	3 earrings or nose rings		48-584	Bronze.	L 2.0–2.1	W 1.4	
44*	Earring		48-554	Silver. Ends overlapping.	D 1.0		
45*	Earring		48-582	Silver. Crescent-shaped.	L 1.7	W 0.6	
46*	Earring		48-552	Silver and carnelian. With a threaded carnelian bead. Ends overlapping.	D 1.0		
47*	Finger ring		48-549	Bronze. Flat section.	D 2.0		
48*	Finger ring		48-558	Bronze. Round section.	D 2.2		
49*	2 bracelets		48-543	Bronze. Round in section. Overlapping ends.	D 5.4, 4.1		
50*	2 bracelets		48-544	Bronze. With encircling ridges and overlapping ends.	D 5.6, 3.9		
51*	3 bracelets		48-545	Bronze.	D 4.8, 4.2, 3.9		
52*	Bracelet		48-546	Bronze. Fragment.	D 4.5		
53	Bracelet		48-547	Iron. Fragment.	D 4.0		
54	Armlet		48-559	Iron. Fragment.	D 8+		
55*	Armlet		48-560	Iron.	D 10.0		
56*	Knee fibula		48-548	Bronze with iron pin	W 3.0	H 1.8	Lamon and Shipton 1939: Pl. 79:4
57*	Bead amulet		48-574	Faience. In shape of cowrie shell.	L 1.2	W 0.9	
58	Beads		48-571	Glass. Fragments. The glass is of Assyro-Phoenician type and should be dated to the late 8th–7th centuries BCE.	H 1.0, 0.8, 0.7		Hamilton 1935: Pl. XXV:b
59	Group of beads		48-572	Faience beads, disk-shaped, barrel-shaped and lentoid. Glass beads, cylindrical, biconical and barrel-shaped. Carnelian beads, barrel-shaped. Silver bead, barrel-shaped.	D 0.3–1.0		
60*	Bead		48-570	Faience. Serrated disk-shaped.	D 0.9		
61*	Ornament		48-592	Bronze. Square. Probably setting for a bead.	L 1.2	W 0.7	

Catalogue of Finds, Tomb ZR XXIX (contd., Fig. 4.21)

No.	Object Type	IAA No.	Description	Dimensions (cm)			References
62*	Pendant	48-550	Silver. Crescent-shaped with attached tube for threading. Similar pendants are known from Tell el-Far'ah (South) as well as from sites in the western Mediterranean such as Tharros, dated to the 7th–6th centuries BCE.	W 2.4			Petrie 1932: Pl. III: 29; Barnett and Mendelson 1987: Pl. 105: 16/22
63*	Pendant	48-555	Silver. Two attached cylinders.	L 0.8			
64*	Pendant	48-586	Bronze. Crescent-shaped with attached loop. Remains of chain inside loop.	L 2.4			
65*	Pendant	48-573	Carnelian. Lotus-bud-shaped.	L 2.2			
66*	Isis amulet	48-539	Greenish faience. Isis seated on throne, nursing her son Horus crowned, with Hathor horns flanking solar disk.	L 2.5	W 0.8	D 0.9	Petrie 1914: Pl. XXVI: 148h
67*	Bes amulet	48-540	Bluish faience.	L 2.7	W 1.4	D 0.6	Tufnell 1953: Pl. 34:14
68*	Thoth amulet	48-542	Bluish faience. Sitting baboon.	L 1.5	W 0.7	D 0.8	Petrie 1914: Pl. XXXVII: 206a
69*	Pateke amulet	48-563	Greenish faience, top of head—black glaze. With back pillar.	L 2.1	W 1.0	D 0.7	Petrie 1914: Pl. XXXI:178k; 176c
70*	Pateke amulet	48-541	Greenish faience. With scarab on head. Winged figure with Hathor horns (Isis?) on his back. Unclear hieroglyphs on base tablet.	L 1.4	W 0.8	D 0.6	Moscati 1988: 380
71*	Udjat amulet	48-567	Whitish faience, green glaze. Two fragments of a quadruple Udjat.	L 1.7	W 0.9		Petrie 1914: Pl. XXIV:104b
72*	Udjat amulet	48-565	Greenish faience. Openwork quadruple Udjat.	L 1.2	W 1.4		Petrie 1914: Pl. XXIV:140g
73*	Udjat amulet	48-564	Greenish faience. Openwork. Pierced lengthwise at center, almond shaped in section. Same decoration on both sides.	L 1.2	W 1.0		Pritchard 1988: Fig. 18: 34; Petrie 1914: Pl. XXIV: 139f, g
74*	Isis(?) amulet	48-578	Greenish faience. Upper part. Broken.	L 3+	W 0.8		
75	Demon amulet	48-569	Faience. Horned.	L 2.0	W 1.2	D 2.0	
76*	Demon amulet	48-537	Whitish faience. With high forehead, short horns, slanting eyes, broad nose and three parallel grooves indicating mouth.	L 2.1	W 1.6		Culican 1976a: 23:1
77*	Demon amulet	48-536	Bone? (blackened by fire) or black wood. With slanting eyes, broad nose, three parallel grooves indicating mouth; horns broken.	L 1.6	W 1.0	D 0.8	
78*	Scarab	48-579	Composite material. Light blue.	13.2 × 9.7 × 5.9 (mm)			See App. 2:40; Keel 1997:34: No. 40
79*	Scarab	48-581	Composite material. Light blue.	15.8 × 11.3 × 8.3 (mm)			See App. 2:41; Keel 1997:34: No. 41
80*	Female mask	44.255	Terracotta. Orange-buff, moldmade. Almost complete except for the right edge.	L 15.2	W 10.09	D 7.0	See Chap. 7: No. 20
81*	Bathing woman	44.57	Terracotta. Handmade, orange-buff ware with white and black grits.	L 10.5	W 6.5	H 7.5	See Chap. 7: No. 10
82*	Double-pipe player	44.56	Terracotta. Brownish-buff ware, red bands on the garment and black paint on the hair.	H 20.0	D 8.5		See Chap. 7: No. 4; Braun 1999: Pl. IV/2-2

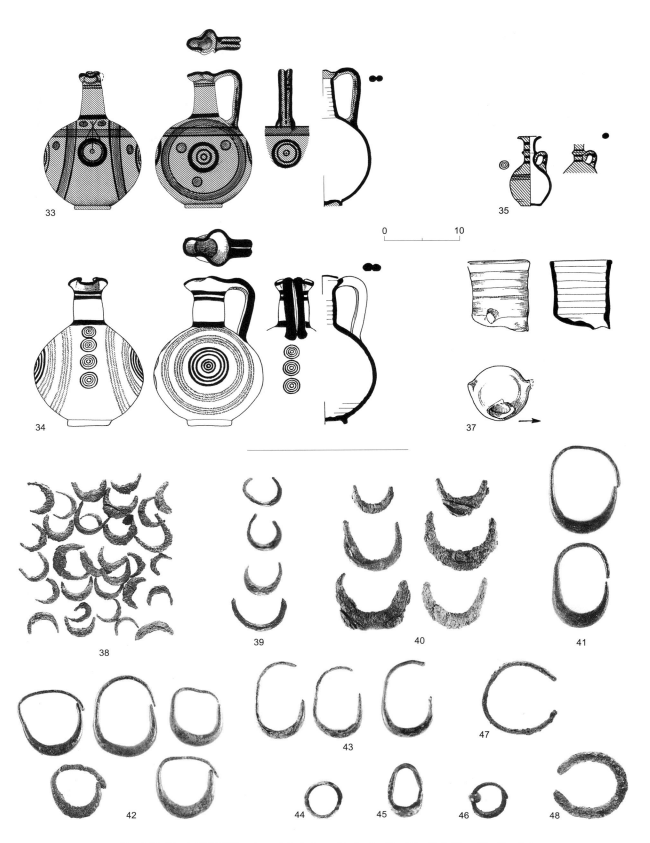

Fig. 4.21. Tomb ZR XXIX, selected finds (contd.). Scale: No. 38—3:4; Nos. 39–48—1:1.

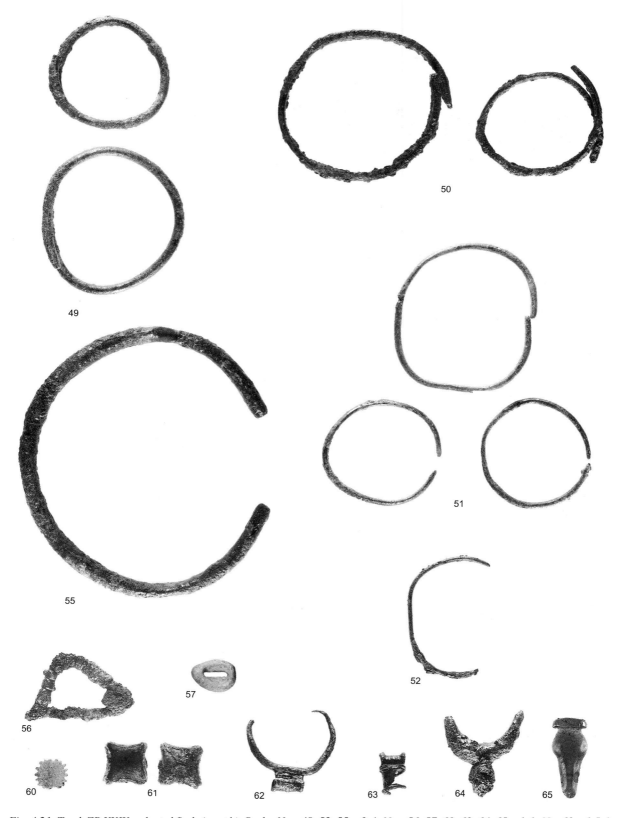

Fig. 4.21. Tomb ZR XXIX, selected finds (contd.). Scale: Nos. 49–52, 55—3:4; Nos. 56, 57, 60–62, 64, 65—1:1; No. 63—1.5:1.

Fig. 4.21. Tomb ZR XXIX, selected finds (contd.). Scale: Nos. 66–74, 76–79—1.5:1; Nos. 80–82—1:3.

Tomb ZR XXX (Type 1; Plans 4.1a, 4.12; Fig. 4.22)
The tomb is of the type common to this cemetery, consisting of a shaft with a stairway and a single burial chamber. The large shaft (1.38 × 1.75 m; unusual depth 2.75 m) is rectangular in shape. The stairway is broader than in other tombs (0.50 m), facilitating the descent.

The entrance to the burial chamber was blocked by masonry just outside the door frame. The chamber is not a direct continuation of the shaft, but veers a few degrees off center. It is roughly square (2.88 × 3.00 m; height 1.0 m) with a rock-hewn roof. The floor has an L-shaped outline with benches on three sides. The angular outline of the trench is most probably the result of the tomb's extreme proximity to Tomb ZR XXXII.

To the left of the trench lay the skeletal remains of one individual and to the right a heap of bones represented the remains of another individual.

According to the excavator, Tomb ZR XXXII (Plans 4.1a, 4.12) stood in the way of the builders of Tomb ZR XXX; consequently they had to cut their chamber so that the shaft was not on the same axis as the chamber. The tomb was looted and empty, except for a few finds buried in the debris of the shaft.

Chronology: This tomb, belonging to a common Phoenician type frequent in this cemetery, is lacking in datable objects, apart from the four scarabs, dated between the 10th and 7th centuries BCE (see Appendix 2:42–45; Keel 1997:36: Nos. 42–45).

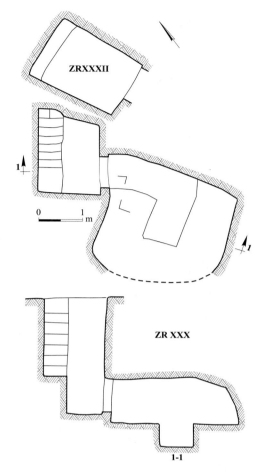

Plan 4.12. Tombs ZR XXX and ZR XXXII, plan and section.

Catalogue of Finds, Tomb ZR XXX
(For pottery types see Chapter 5. * = illustrated in Fig. 4.22)

No.	Object	Type	IAA No.	Description	Dimensions (cm)	References
Pottery						
1	Jug	JG6 I	69-7579	Orange-buff ware. Black- and red-painted decoration.	H 19.5+ W 12.5	
Small Finds						
2*	4 bracelets		48-599	Bronze. Two with overlapping ends, one with ends meeting.	D 4.3–5.0	
3*	Scarab		48-595	Steatite. White.	16.0 × 10.7 × 7.0 (mm)	See App. 2.42; Keel 1997:36: No. 42
4*	Scarab		48-596	Steatite(?) Remains of light-green glaze.	15.7 × 11.0 × 7.0 (mm)	See App. 2.43; Keel 1997:36: No. 43
5*	Scarab		48-597	Soft composite material. Yellowish, faint remains of bluish glaze.	12.0 × 9.3 × 6.6 (mm)	See App. 2.44; Keel 1997:36: No. 44
6*	Scarab		48-598	Clay(?) White glaze.	14.5 × 11.1 × 6.5 (mm)	See App. 2.45; Keel 1997:36: No. 45

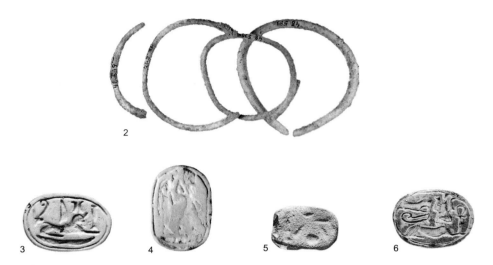

Fig. 4.22. Tomb ZR XXX, selected finds. Scale: No. 2—2:3; Nos. 3–6—1.5:1.

Tomb ZR XXXI (Type 1; Plan 4.1a; Fig. 4.23)
Tomb with rectangular shaft leading to rectangular burial chamber. Burials lay on the floor, grouped around a large central trench. Only the sketch in the plan of the cemetery is available.

Chronology: To judge by the description of this tomb, it belongs to Type 1, commonly found in this cemetery. It held only a few pottery bowls, such as Type B5 V dated to the 8th–7th centuries BCE, insufficient for a clear dating of the tomb. Of the three scarabs found, two are dated to the late 8th–6th centuries BCE (see Appendix

2:46, 47; Keel 1997:36: Nos. 46, 47); one is attributed to the second half of the XVth Dynasty, 16th century BCE (see Appendix 2:48; Keel 1997:38: No. 48) and is probably an heirloom.

Tomb ZR XXXII (Plans 4.1a and see 4.12)
The sketches in the plan of the cemetery and in Plan 4.12 are too minimal to provide any details. No further information is recorded.

The tomb may have been earlier than Tomb ZR XXX and may therefore have been damaged when the latter was built.

Catalogue of Finds, Tomb ZR XXXI
(For pottery types see Chapter 5. * = illustrated in Fig. 4.23)

No.	Object	Type	IAA No.	Description	Dimensions (cm)		References
Pottery							
1	Bowl	B4 VI	70-8565	Reddish-brown ware.	H 5.0	D 11.0	
2	Bowl	B4 VI	70-8566	Reddish-brown ware.	H 5.5	D 11.5	
3	Bowl	B5 V	70-8564	Yellow-buff ware. Red paint on rim.	H 4.5	D 12.5	
Small Finds							
4	2 earrings		48-607	Bronze. Crescent-shaped and ring-shaped. Fragments.			
5*	Finger ring		48-602	Bronze. Flat in section, ends meeting.	D 1.9		
6	Olive pits		48-608	Charred.	L 1.2		
7*	Scarab		48-600	Steatite. White.	14.4 × 11.2 × 6.9 (mm)		See App. 2:46; Keel 1997: 36: No. 46
8*	Scarab		48-601	Steatite. Gray.	13.4 × 9.6 × 6.9 (mm)		See App. 2:47; Keel 1997: 36: No. 47
9*	Scarab		48-605	Steatite. Gray, surface appearance white.	19.5 × 14.0 × 8.5 (mm)		See App. 2:48; Keel 1997: 38: No. 48

Fig. 4.23. Tomb ZR XXXI, selected finds. Scale: No. 5—1:1; Nos. 7–9—1.5:1.

Tomb ZR XXXIII (Fig. 4.24)
No description or plan available.

Chronology: The tomb contained a number of small finds, among them a scarab dated to the XXVIth Dynasty (664–525 BCE; see Appendix 2:49; Keel 1997:38: No. 49).

Catalogue of Finds, Tomb ZR XXXIII
(* = illustrated in Fig. 4.24)

Fig. 4.24. Tomb ZR XXXIII, selected finds. Scale: No. 1—1:1; No. 2—1.5:1; No. 3—1:2.

No.	Object	IAA No.	Description	Dimensions (cm)	References
Small Finds					
1*	Finger ring	48-611	Silver. Ends meeting.	D 2.2	
2*	Scarab	48-610	Steatite. White.	11.6 × 7.8 × 5.0 (mm)	See App. 2:49; Keel 1997:38: No. 49
3*	Necklace	48-609	23 beads, silver, faience, carnelian.	L 17.0	

Tomb ZR XXXIV (Type 1; Plans 4.1a, 4.13; Fig. 4.25)
The tomb is of the type common to this cemetery, consisting of a shaft with a stairway and a single burial chamber. The blocking slab was found in position, supported by a large block wedged against it. The roughly square shaft (1.62 × 1.75 m; depth 2.50 m) has seven rock-cut steps in the northwestern wall. An opening (0.25 m long) is hewn into the southeastern wall of the shaft.

The burial chamber is of irregular size and shape (roughly square, *c.* 3.60 × 3.60 m) with walls hewn in a clumsy, careless way. A large trench (1.50 × 1.90 m;

depth 0.38 m) in the center of the chamber has a small rectangular recess in the far right-hand corner.

The left chamber wall showed vertical cuts and traces of masons' marks indicating that the hewing of a niche was planned but not implemented, due perhaps to the poor quality of the rock.

Chronology: No pottery vessels were recovered from this tomb. The only reported finds are four scarabs, all dated to the XXVIth Dynasty (664–525 BCE; see Appendix 2:50–53; Keel 1997:38: Nos. 50–53).

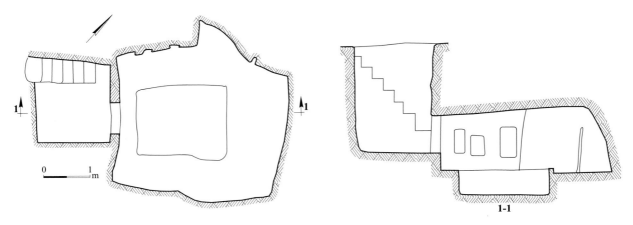

Plan 4.13. Tomb ZR XXXIV, plan and section.

Catalogue of Finds, Tomb ZR XXXIV
(* = illustrated in Fig. 4.25)

No.	Object	IAA No.	Description	Dimensions (cm)	References
Small Finds					
1*	Scarab	48-612	Soft composite material. White.	13.7 × 9.5 × 6.8 (mm)	See App. 2:50; Keel 1997:38: No. 50
2*	Scarab	48-613	Steatite. Gray, surface appearance white.	12.3 × 8.2 × 5.5 (mm)	See App. 2:51; Keel 1997:38: No. 51
3*	Scarab	48-614	Steatite. Surface appearance white.	15.1 × 11 × 7.7 (mm)	See App. 2:52; Keel 1997:38: No. 52
4*	Scarab	48-615	Steatite. Surface appearance white.	14.2 × 10.4 × 7.2 (mm)	See Keel App. 2:53; 1997:38: No. 53

1   2   3   4

Fig. 4.25. Tomb ZR XXXIV, selected finds. Scale—1.5:1.

Tomb ZR XXXV (Type 1.1; Plans 4.1a, 4.14; Fig. 4.26)
This tomb is of the type common to this cemetery, consisting of a shaft with a stairway and a single burial chamber. The roughly square shaft (1.50 × 1.75 m; depth 2.75 m) has nine steps leading down to the chamber. A blocking slab was held in position by several oblong dressed blocks wedged against it. An opening (length 0.25 m) leads into the roughly rectangular burial chamber (2.30 × 2.75 m; height 1.25 m) with a shallow (*c.* 0.15 m) trough in the center. The walls of the chamber slope slightly upward to a rock-hewn ceiling.

An unfinished niche in the left chamber wall was used as a burial place. Grooves on the right wall of the chamber indicate an attempt to cut a second niche.

Chronology: The tomb was looted. It contained no pottery vessels, and only a few non-diagnostic small finds.

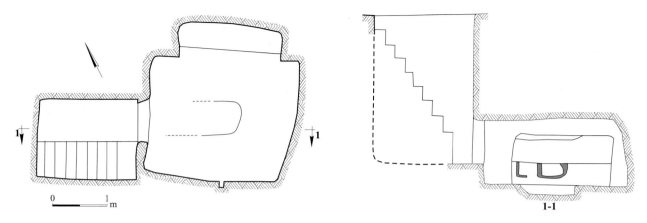

Plan 4.14. Tomb ZR XXXV, plan and section.

Catalogue of Finds, Tomb ZR XXXV
(* = illustrated in Fig. 4.26)

No.	Object	IAA No.	Description	Dimensions (cm)		Weight (gm)

Small Finds

No.	Object	IAA No.	Description	Dimensions (cm)		Weight (gm)
1*	Earring	48-618	Bronze. Crescent-shaped. Broken.		W 1.2	
2*	Earring	48-619	Bronze. Crescent-shaped.	L 1.8	W 1.2	
3*	Earring	48-620a	Bronze. Crescent-shaped.	L 1.5	W 1.0	
4*	Earring	48-620c	Silver. Crescent-shaped.	L 2.3	W 1.2	
5	Earring	48-620b	Bronze. Crescent-shaped. Fragment.			
6*	Crescent	48-617	Bronze. Remains of swivel mount. Fragment.		W 2.4	
7*	Bracelet	48-616	Bronze. Round in section, overlapping ends.	D 4.0		
8*	Weight	48-621	Hematite and bronze. Truncated pyramid, triangular in section, perforated at top with ring handle.	H 2.7		45.7156

Fig. 4.26. Tomb ZR XXXV, selected finds. Scale: Nos. 1–4, 6, 8—1:1; No. 7—3:4.

Tomb ZR XXXVI (Type 1; Plans 4.1a, 4.15; Fig. 4.27)
The tomb has a single burial chamber approached by a square shaft without steps (width 1.20 m; depth 1.67 m). The entrance (width 0.75 m) to the burial chamber was at 1.06 m below the surface and was found open. The chamber is roughly square in plan (2.50 × 2.80 m; height 1.85 m). The sloping walls form a dome-shaped ceiling. The burial chamber was full of earth, broken bones and potsherds. On the right side of the chamber, c. 1 m from the entrance, a black ashy area was discerned but the

examination did not reveal any remains of bones or objects.

Though disturbed, the tomb was unusually rich in finds. Apart from a large number of pottery vessels, it contained numerous small finds: scarabs, faience amulets, beads, and silver and bronze jewelry, as well as a figurine of a potter or phallus holder.

Chronology: The pottery vessels date from the 10th century BCE and continue down to the 8th–7th centuries BCE. Among the early types are pilgrim flasks (Type PF1). The bulk of pottery vessels clearly belongs to the 9th–8th centuries BCE, including characteristic 'Akhziv' types, such as the red-burnished mushroom-rim jugs (JG5 I, II), as well as 'Samaria' bowls (B8). The large number of scarabs recovered from the tomb also testifies to a long and continuous period of use (see Appendix 2:54–66; Keel 1997:40: Nos. 54–59; 42: Nos. 60–65; 44: No. 66).

This tomb provides a model of the continuous use of tombs in the er-Ras cemetery from the 10th–7th century BCE, its main period of use having been in the 9th–8th centuries BCE.

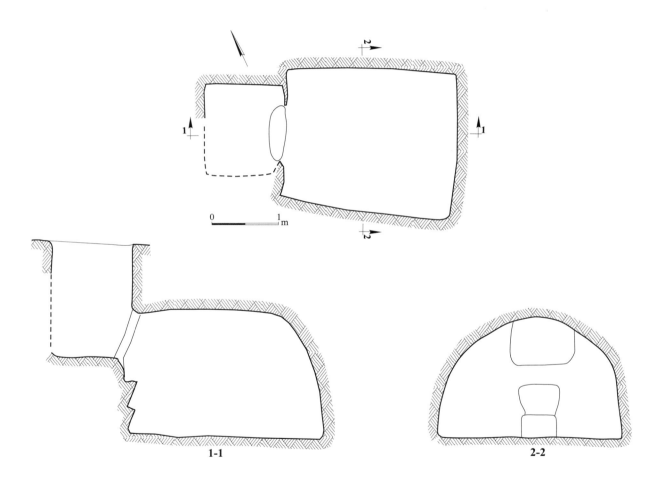

Plan 4.15. Tomb ZR XXXVI, plan and sections.

Catalogue of Finds, Tomb ZR XXXVI

(For pottery types see Chapter 5. Fr = fragment; * = illustrated in Fig. 4.27)

No.	Object	Type	IAA No.	Description	Dimensions (cm)		References
Pottery							
1*	Bowl	B1 I	69-7571	Coarse reddish-brown ware, white grits.	H 5.0	D 17.0	
2	Bowl	B1 I	69-7572	Reddish-brown ware, white grits.	H 5.0	D 17.0	
3*	Bowl	B2 I	69-7540	Coarse reddish-brown ware.	H 4.5	D 23.0	
4*	Bowl	B3 I	69-7573	Coarse yellowish-cream ware.	H 3.5	D 17.5	
5*	Bowl	B4 V	69-7574	Fine reddish-brown ware.	H 8.0	D 12.5	
6*	Bowl	B8 I	69-7539	Fine pinkish-yellow ware. Thick red slip inside and outside. Concentric red bands on bottom.	H 3.0	D 21.0	
7	Bowl	B8 IV	69-7545	Light buff ware, thick red slip. Concentric red bands on bottom.	H 4.0	D 18.5	
8*	Bowl	B8 IV	44.258	Fine pinkish-buff ware, red slip.	H 5.0	D 19.0	
9*	Bowl	B8 VI	69-7544	Pinkish-brown ware, thick red slip.	H 3.5		
10*	Bowl	B9 I	69-7543	Coarse reddish-brown ware. Black- and red-painted decoration.	H 4.0	D 20.0	
11	Storage jar	SJ 2	70-8533	Orange-buff ware.	H 51.0	W 26	
12	Jug	JG2 I	69-7500	Orange-buff ware, red slip, burnished.	H 20.5	W 10.0	
13	Jug	JG2 I	69-7501	Orange-buff ware, red slip, burnished.	H 20.0	W 10.0	
14*	Jug	JG2 I	69-7502	Buff ware, red slip, burnished.	H 22.0	W 11.0	
15*	Jug	JG2 I	69-7504	Orange-buff ware, red slip, burnished.	H 17.5	W 10.0	
16*	Jug	JG2 II	69-7505	Orange ware, red slip, burnished.	H 23.0	W 10.5	
17*	Jug	JG2 IV	69-7507	Reddish-brown coarse ware.	H 20.0	W 10.5	
18*	Jug	JG3 I	69-7506	Coarse reddish-brown ware, white grits.	H 21.5	W 11.5	
19*	Jug	JG3 III	69-7510	Coarse orange ware, white grits.	H 20.0	W 13.0	
20	Jug	JG3 III	69-7509	Coarse orange ware. Red and black bands.	H 25.0	W 16.0	
21	Jug	JG3 III	69-7508	Coarse reddish-brown ware.	H 20.0	W 11.5	
22	Jug	JG5 I	69-7517	Orange ware, dark red slip, burnished.	H 15.5	W 8.0	
23	Jug	JG5 I	69-7537	Orange-buff ware, dark red slip, burnished.	H 16+	W 8.5	
24	Jug	JG5 II	69-7513	Buff ware, red slip, burnished.	H 19.5	W 9.0	
25*	Jug	JG5 I	69-7518	Light buff ware, red slip, burnished.	H 21.5	W 11	
26	Jug	JG5 II	69-7538	Orange-light buff ware, red slip, burnished.	H 17.0	W 9.0	
27	Jug	JG5 II	69-7512	Light orange-buff ware, red slip, burnished.	H 17.0	W 8.5	
28*	Jug	JG5 II	69-7514	Orange ware, red slip, burnished.	H 21.0	W 11.0	
29*	Jug	JG5 IV	69-7534	Light buff ware, red bands.	H 17.5+	W 9.5	
30	Jug	JG5 IV	69-7532	Light buff thin ware. Black and red bands on upper part of neck.	H 21+	W 10.0	
31*	Jug	JG5 IV	69-7528	Reddish-brown ware.	H 18.5	W 10.5	
32	Jug	JG5 IV	69-7536	Reddish-buff ware.	H 17.5	W 7.0	
33	Jug	JG5 IV	69-7581	Brownish-buff ware.	H 9.5+	W 9.0	
34	Jug	JG5 IV	69-7580	Brownish-buff ware.	H 15+	W 12.0	
35*	Jug	JG5 V	69-7550	Pinkish coarse ware, black grits.	H 19.0	W 11.5	
36*	Jug	Misc.	69-7546	Reddish coarse ware, black grits.	H 16.0	W 10.0	
37	Jug	JG5 V	69-7522	Orange coarse ware, black grits.	H 16.5	W 8.0	
38	Jug	JG6 I	69-7531	Fine light buff ware. Red and black bands on neck.	H 21.0	W 15.0	
39	Jug	JG6 I	69-7525	Fine reddish-buff ware. Red and black bands on neck.	H 20.0	W 12.5	

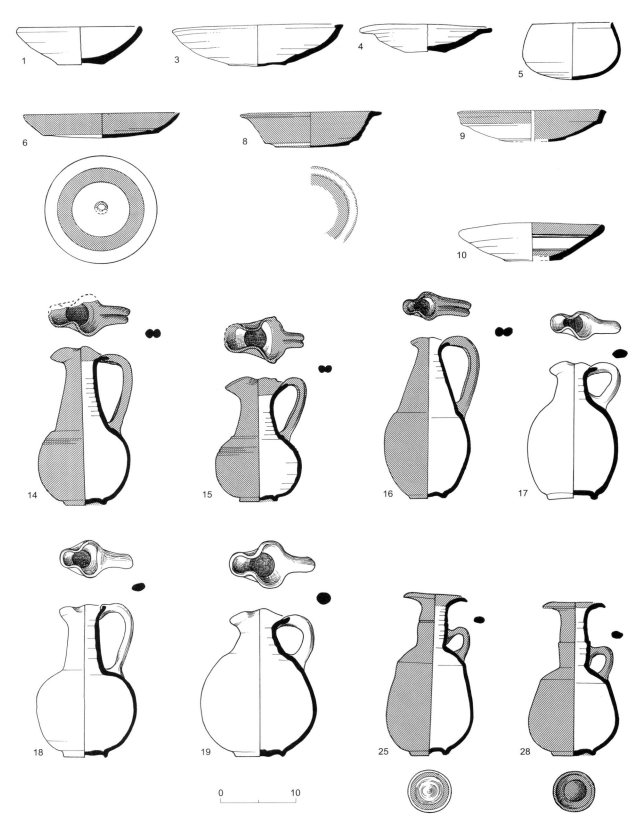

Fig. 4.27. Tomb ZR XXXVI, selected finds.

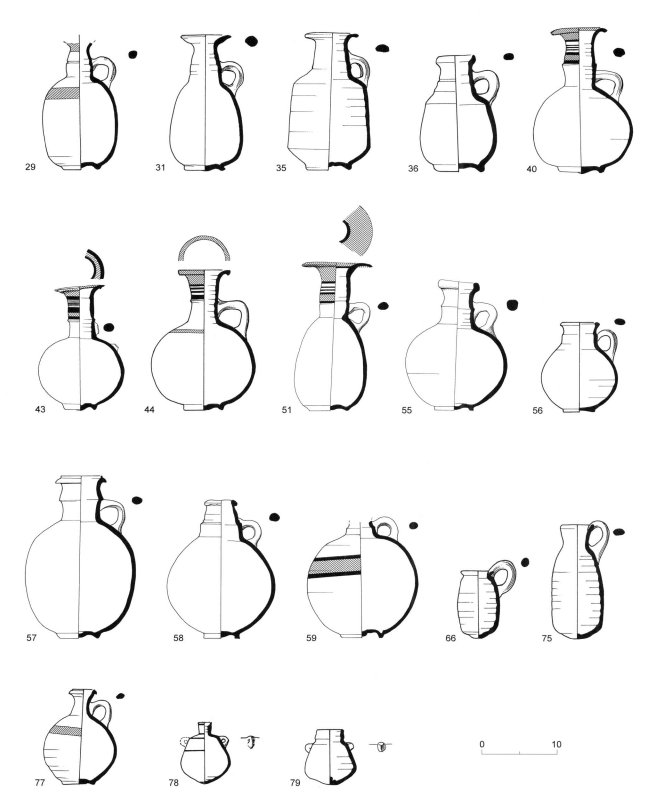

Fig. 4.27. Tomb ZR XXXVI, selected finds (contd.).

Catalogue of Finds, Tomb ZR XXXVI (contd., Fig. 4.27)

No.	Object	Type	IAA No.	Description	Dimensions (cm)		References
40*	Jug	JG6 I	69-7520	Reddish-buff ware. Red and black bands on neck.	H 20.0	W 13.0	
41	Jug	JG6 I	69-7527	Fine light buff ware. Black and red bands on neck.	H 18.5	W 10.5	
42	Jug	JG6 I	69-7519	Brownish-buff ware.	H 19.5	W 13.0	
43*	Jug	JG6 I	69-7521	Fine pinkish-light buff ware. Black and red bands on neck.	H 17.0	W 10.0	
44*	Jug	JG6 I	69-7524	Fine light buff ware. Black and red bands on neck.	H 20.5	W 12.5	
45	Jug	JG6 I	69-7529	Fine light buff ware. Black and red bands on neck.	H 18.0	W 11.5	
46	Jug	JG6 I	69-7526	Buff ware. Black and red bands on neck.	H 20.0	W 13.0	
47	Jug	JG6 I	69-7523	Reddish-brown ware. Black and red bands on neck.	H 16.0	W 9.5	
48	Jug	JG6 I	69-7533	Brownish-buff ware.	H 21+	W 10	
49	Jug	JG6 I	69-7578	Reddish-buff ware.	H 15+	W 10.5	
50	Jug	JG6 I	69-7551	Reddish-brown ware.	H 11+	W 10.0	
51*	Jug	Misc.	69-7511	Reddish-buff ware, red slip. Black and red bands on neck.	H 20.5	W 9.0	
52	Jug	JG6 III	69-7515	Fine reddish-buff ware. Red and black bands on neck.	H 23.5	W 11.0	
53	Jug	JG6 III	69-7535	Light buff ware. Red and black bands on neck.	H 16+	W 8.5	
54	Jug	JG6 V	69-7530	Coarse reddish-brown ware, white grits.	H 20.0	W 14.0	
55*	Jug	JG7 III	69-7547	Coarse reddish-brown ware, white and black grits.	H 18.5	W 12.0	
56*	Jug	Misc.	69-7549	Coarse brownish-buff ware.	H 12.5	W 9.5	
57*	Jug	JG7 III	69-7542	Coarse reddish-brown ware, white grits.	H 19.5	W 15.5	
58*	Jug	JG7 IV	69-7541	Reddish-brown ware, white grits.	H 18.0	W 15.0	
59*	Jug	JG7 V	70-8437	Orange-buff ware. Red and black bands on body.	H 16+	W 14.0	
60	Pilgrim flask	PF1	69-7566	Coarse reddish-brown ware. Black concentric circles on body.	H 9.0	W 6.0	
61	Pilgrim flask	PF1	69-7564	Coarse pinkish-buff ware. Black concentric circles on body.	H 8.5+		
62	Pilgrim flask	PF1	69-7577	Coarse reddish-brown ware. Black concentric circles on body.	H 6.8+	W 6.5	
63	Dipper juglet	DJ1	69-7516	Light buff ware, matt imprint on base.	H 11.5	W 6.0	
64	Dipper juglet	DJ1	69-7553	Light buff ware.	H 11.0	W 5.0	
65	Dipper juglet	DJ1	69-7554	Reddish-brown ware.	H 11.5	W 6.0	
66*	Dipper juglet	DJ1	69-7559	Light buff ware.	H 10.5	W 5.0	
67	Dipper juglet	DJ1	69-7557	Brownish-buff ware.	H 9.5	W 5.0	
68	Dipper juglet	DJ1	69-7558	Reddish-brown ware.	H 11.0	W 5.5	
69	Dipper juglet	DJ1	69-7555	Reddish-brown ware.	H 9.0	W 5.0	
70	Dipper juglet	DJ1	69-7560	Reddish-brown ware, white grits.	H 9.5	W 5.0	
71	Dipper juglet	DJ1	69-7582	Reddish-brown ware.	H 9.0	W 4.5	

Catalogue of Finds, Tomb ZR XXXVI (contd., Fig. 4.27)

No.	Object	Type	IAA No.	Description	Dimensions (cm)			References
72	Dipper juglet	DJ1	69-7562	Gray ware.	H 8.5+	W 6.0		
73	Dipper juglet	DJ1	69-7567	Reddish-brown ware.	H 9.5+	W 6.0		
74	Dipper juglet	DJ1	69-7583	Pinkish-buff ware.	H 10.5+	W 6.0		
75*	Dipper juglet	DJ2	69-7556	Reddish-brown ware, white grits.	H 16.0	W 7.0		
76	Dipper juglet	DJ2	69-7561	Reddish-brown ware.	H 14.0	W 6.5		
77*	Dipper juglet	J3	69-7548	Grayish-buff ware. Red-painted decoration.	H 13.0	W 9.5		
78*	Amphoris-kos	J6	69-7569	Light orange-buff ware. Thin dark brown bands.	H 8.0	W 6.5		
79*	Miniature jar	MV1	69-7576	Coarse reddish-brown ware.	H 7.5	W 6.5		
80*	Jug	CP4	69-7552	Light buff ware, thick white slip. Red and black matt decoration.	H 21+	W 15.0		
81*	Juglet	CP6	69-7563	Fine red ware, orange-red slip, highly burnished. Black-painted decoration.	H 8.5	W 4.0		
82	Juglet	CP6	69-7575	Fine red ware, reddish-orange slip, burnished. Black-painted decoration.	H 8.5	W 4.5		
83	Juglet	CP6	69-7568	Fine red ware, reddish-orange slip, burnished. Black-painted decoration.	H 9+	W 6.0		
84*	Juglet	CP12	69-7590	Fine orange-buff ware. Black-painted decoration.	Fr			

Small Finds

No.	Object	Type	IAA No.	Description	Dimensions (cm)			References
85*	Earring or nose ring		48-653	Gold. Crescent-shaped.	L 1.1	W 0.8		
86*	Earring		48-654	Silver and gold. Elliptical crescent-shaped. With loop (broken) at the bottom and an attached gold ring.	L 2.4+	W 1.5+		Pritchard 1988: Fig. 35:2
87*	Earring		48-655	Silver. Crescent-shaped. With small ring loop. Attachment soldered to bottom. Traces of another ring loop of an attached pendant.	L 1.6	W 1.1		Barnett and Mendelson 1987: Pl. 78: 3/13
88*	Earring		48-658	Silver. Elliptical.	L 2.7	W 1.7		
89*	Earring or nose ring		48-659	Silver.	L 0.8	W 0.9		
90*	2 earrings		48-689	Bronze.	L 1.5, 1.7	W 1.2		
91*	35 earrings		48-688	Bronze. Partly broken.	L 1.0–1.5	W 1.0–1.5		
92*	Finger ring		48-656	Silver.	D 2.3			
93*	7 finger rings		48-707	Bronze. 2 complete and 5 broken finger rings.	D 2.0–2.2			
94*	11 bracelets		48-684 48-685	Bronze. Some broken.	D 4.0–6.0			
95*	Fibula pin		48-686	Bronze. Broken.	W 3.3			
96	2 fibula pins		48-687	Bronze.	L 5.2+, 3+			
97	Bead		48-662	Silver. Cylindrical.	L 0.6	W 0.4		
98	Part of a handle(?)		48-703	Bone.	L 0.9	D 0.9		
99*	Bead		48-704	Glass.	L 0.7–0.8	D 1.0–1.1		
100*	Bead		48-639	Grayish faience. Rectangular. Pierced lengthwise.	W 0.7	L 1.3	H 0.3	

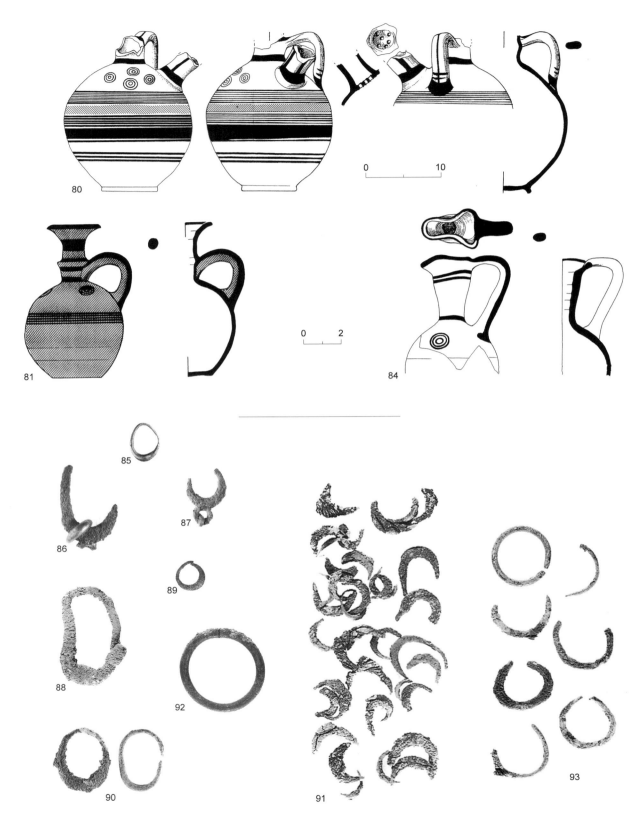

Fig. 4.27. Tomb ZR XXXVI, selected finds (contd.). Scale: Nos. 85–92—1:1; No. 93—3:4.

Fig. 4.27. Tomb ZR XXXVI, selected finds (contd.). Scale: No. 94—1:2; Nos. 95, 99, 100, 108–110, 112—1:1; Nos. 103–107, 111—1.5:1; No. 101—1:2.

Catalogue of Finds, Tomb ZR XXXVI (contd., Fig. 4.27)

No.	Object Type	IAA No.	Description	Dimensions (cm)	References
101*	Necklace of various beads	48-651	Carnelian. Barrel-shaped. Carnelian. Biconical. Carnelian. Melon-shaped. Amethyst. Long barrel-shaped. Black stone. Barrel-shaped. Dark blue glass. 2 irregular barrel-shaped beads. Light bluish faience. Fluted barrel-shaped. Silver. Broken. Light carnelian. Ovoid bead or pendant.	L 0.7–1.9 W 0.3–0.8 L 0.8–1.1 W 0.6–0.9 L 0.6–1.0 W 0.9 L 1.1–1.3 W 0.6–0.8 L 0.5 W 0.7 L 0.6–0.7 W 0.9 L 0.7 W 0.7	
102	Pendant	48-676	Serpentine. Leaf-shaped.	L 1.3 W 1.1	
103*	Udjat amulet	48-673	Whitish faience. Pierced lengthwise for suspension, carved on both sides.	L 1.1 W 0.8	Lamon and Shipton 1939: Pl. 75; Pritchard 1988: Fig. 18:32
104*	2 Udjat amulets	48-672	Greenish faience. Pierced lengthwise. Made in the same mold.	L 0.8 W 0.7, 0.3	
105*	Udjat amulet	48-649	Greenish faience. Pierced lengthwise for suspension, design on one side.	L 1.7 W 2.0, 0.5	
106*	Udjat amulet	48-648	Greenish faience. Pierced lengthwise for suspension, design on one side. The eye usually looks to the right; here it looks to the left.	L 1.3 W 1.9 D 3.0	
107*	Udjat amulet	48-644	Faience, black glaze on pupil. Pierced lengthwise, design on one side.	L 1.8 W 2.3 D 0.8	
108*	Bes amulet	48-647	Greenish faience. Four feathers in crown.	L 4.7 W 1.5, 0.9	Clerc et al. 1976: Pl. IX: Kit.:2952
109*	Bes amulet	48-650	Greenish faience. Crouching, bifrontal. Pierced at top for suspension.	L 3.9 W 2.9 D 1.5	
110*	Pateke amulet	48-646	Greenish faience. Pierced for suspension through the neck.	L 2.7 W 1.5	Johns 1933: Pls. 28:732, 33:885; Lamon and Shipton 1939: Pl. 74:30; Clerc et al. 1976: Pl. X: Kit.:772
111*	Pateke amulet	48-675	Greenish faience. Incised snake on bottom.	L 1.0 W 0.7, 0.5	
112*	Pateke amulet	48-641	Greenish faience. Right arm and leg broken, scarab on head, falcon on side.	L 2.8 W 1.5	
113*	Sekhmet amulet	48-642	Greenish faience. Seated on throne, holding enlongated object (sistrum?). Right arm missing.	L 5.9 W 3.2	
114*	Bastet amulet	48-670	Greenish faience. Sitting on hind legs. Pierced through the upper back for suspension, ear broken.	L 1.9 W 1.5	Petrie 1914:39: 227b
115*	Demon amulet	44.259	Bluish faience. Small ears, horns, slanted eyes, broad nose, wrinkled forehead. Perforated lengthwise.	L 4.0 W 2.8	Gjerstad 1948: Fig. 38:30; Culican 1976a: 22–23
116*	Bull's head amulet	44.262	Bluish faience. With ears and horns. The neck is pierced horizontally and vertically.	L 1.4 W 1.9	
117*	Ornament	48-623	Bone. Miniature-jar-shaped.	L 2.2 W 1.3	
118*	Pomegranate	48-671	Bone. With four leaves, remains of stick on which it was mounted.	L 1.4 W 1.1	
119*	Loomweight(?)	48-696	Clay(?).	L 1.5 D 3.5	
120*	Loomweight	48-697	Bone.	L 1.0 D 2.0	
121	Weight	48-681	Brown hematite with brown spots. Dome-shaped.	L 0.7 D 1.4 Wt 2.8 gm	

Fig. 4.27. Tomb ZR XXXVI, selected finds (contd.). Scale: Nos. 113, 115, 117, 119, 120, 123–129—1:1; Nos. 114, 116, 118—1.5:1.

Catalogue of Finds, Tomb ZR XXXVI (contd., Fig. 4.27)

No.	Object Type	IAA No.	Description	Dimensions (cm)			References
122	Weight	48-679	Bronze. Dome-shaped.	L 0.6	D 0.7	Wt 0.84 gm	
123*	Weight	48-665	Hematite. Pyramid-shaped, flattened on one side.	L 1.8	D 1.0	Wt 3.32 gm	
124*	Weight	48-666	Hematite. Grain-shaped, flattened on one side.	L 1.8	W 0.8	Wt 2.52 gm	
125*	Weight	48-622	Bronze. Grain-shaped with handle, traces of fabric attached.	L 3.4	W 1.3	Wt 23 gm	
126*	Weight	48-680a	Bronze. Grain-shaped. Flattened on one side, pierced at top for suspension.	L 1.1	W 0.8	Wt 4.3132 gm	Lamon and Shipton 1939: Pl. 88:20, 21
127*	Weight, pierced	48-680b	Bronze. Tortoise-shaped.	L 2.0	W 0.8	Wt 0.9900 gm	Reifenberg 1950:55, Fig. 4
128*	Hair ornament	48-692	Silver. Spiral. Solid.	D 1.6			Johns 1933:54, Pl. XVII: 408, 409
129*	2 hair ornaments	48-657	Silver. Spiral wire.	D 1.6, 2.1			Johns 1933:52, Fig. 5
130*	Spearhead	48-705	Iron. Wood remnants in socket.	L 45.0+			
131	Sickle blade	48-706	Iron.	L 20.5	W 4.0		
132*	Spindle whorl	48-698	Bone. Lentoid. Perforation square on one side.	L 0.8	D 2.3		
133*	Spindle whorl	48-699	Bone. Lentoid. Perforation square on one side.	L 0.6	D 2.2		
134*	Spindle whorl	48-700	Bone. Dome-shaped.	L 0.5	D 1.5		
135*	Spindle whorl	48-701	Bone. Dome-shaped.	L 0.5	D 0.9		
136*	Spindle whorl	48-702	Bone. Dome-shaped.	L 0.7	D 0.7		
137*	Crouching lion	44.261	Amber. Knob on box(?) Resembles a seal in the shape of a recumbent lion.	L 3.0	W 4.8		Coldstream 1982: Pl. 25:C
138*	Scarab	48-624	Steatite. Surface appearance white with ocher patches.	$16.2 \times 11.5 \times 7.3$ (mm)			See App. 2:54; Keel 1997:40: No. 54
139*	Rectangular plaque	48-625	Steatite. Gray. Remains of yellow coating.	$13.7 \times 9.9 \times 4.5$ (mm)			See App. 2:55; Keel 1997:40: No. 55
140*	Scaraboid	48-627	Steatite. Gray, remains of bluish glaze in depressions.	$15.2 \times 10.5 \times 5.9$ (mm)			See App. 2:56; Keel 1997:40: No. 56
141*	Scarab	48-628	Steatite.	$14.8 \times 9.8 \times 5.8$ (mm)			See App. 2:57; Keel 1997:40: No. 57
142*	Scarab	48-630	Limestone. Black.	$14.4 \times 9.4 \times 7.6$ (mm)			See App. 2:58; Keel 1997:40: No. 58
143*	Scarab	48-631	Steatite.	$16.4 \times 12.2 \times 6.9$ (mm)			See App. 2:59; Keel 1997:40: No. 59
144*	Scaraboid	48-632	Hard composite material. Bluish glaze.	$13.6 \times 9.8 \times 5.5$ (mm)			See App. 2:60; Keel 1997:42: No. 60
145*	Scarab	48-633	Steatite. White.	$15.7 \times 12.0 \times 8.1$ (mm)			See App. 2:61; Keel 1997: 42: No. 61
146*	Scarab	48-634	Steatite. Blue-gray.	$12.1 \times 8.7 \times 5.1$ (mm)			See App. 2:62; Keel 1997: 42: No. 62
147*	Scarab	48-635	Steatite. Remains of light-green glaze.	$13.0 \times 10.0 \times 7.0$ (mm)			See App. 2:63; Keel 1997:42: No. 63
148*	Scarab	48-636	Soft composite material. Light blue.	$14.4 \times 10.2 \times 7.0$ (mm)			See App. 2:64; Keel 1997:42: No. 64
149*	Scarab	48-637	?	$11.2 \times 6.9 \times 5.0$ (mm)			See App. 2:65; Keel 1997:42: No. 65
150*	Scarab	48-638	Bone(?) Steatite(?) Sunken parts ocher-colored.	$14.1 \times 11.4 \times 7.6$ (mm)			See App. 2:66; Keel 1997:44: No. 66
151*	Figure of potter or phallus holder	44.58	Terracotta. Pinkish-brown clay with white grits. Handmade.	H 12.0	W 5.0	L 8.9	See Chap. 7: No. 12

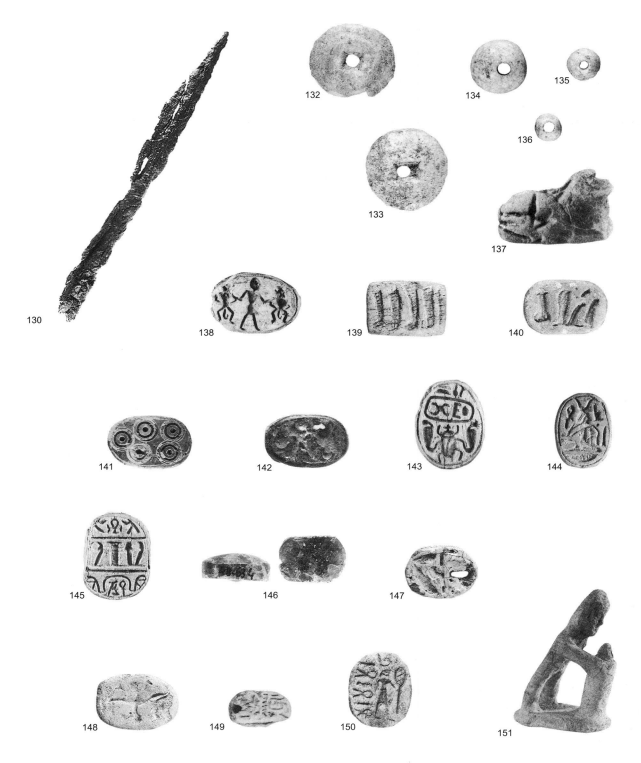

*Fig. 4.27. Tomb ZR XXXVI, selected finds (contd.). Scale: No. 130—1:5; Nos. 132–137—1:1;
Nos. 138–150—1.5:1; No. 151—1:3.*

Tomb ZR XXXVII (Type 1: Plans 4.1a, 4.16)
This tomb is of the common type in this cemetery, consisting of a shaft with a stairway and a single rock-cut
burial chamber. The shaft is roughly rectangular (1.30 ×
1.50 m; depth 2.10 m) with seven steps. The opening
(length 0.25 m) to the chamber was found blocked with a
slab. The roughly square chamber (2.70 × 2.75 m) has a
rectangular trench (0.75 × 1.30 m; depth 0.60 m) in the
middle. The chamber walls slope slightly upward to a
flat, rock-cut ceiling (cracked). A hole in the chamber
ceiling leading to surface level was probably used for
pouring liquid offerings.

The tomb contained no burials and yielded no objects,
with the exception of a few unspecified pottery sherds.

Chronology: This tomb cannot be dated. The only jug
reported, Type JG7 IV, is dated to the 9th–8th centuries
BCE.

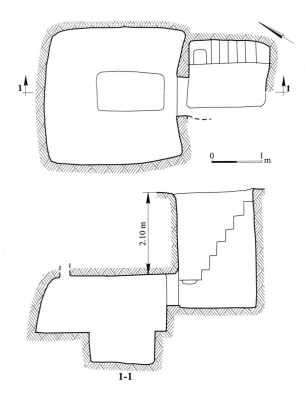

Catalogue of Finds, Tomb ZR XXXVII
(For pottery types see Chapter 5. Not illustrated)

No.	Object	Type	IAA No.	Description	Dimensions (cm)	
Pottery						
1	Jug	JG7 IV	70-8568	Orange-buff ware.	H 19.5	W 12.5

Plan 4.16. Tomb ZR XXXVII, plan and section.

Tomb ZR XXXVIII (Type 1; Plans 4.1, 4.17)
This tomb is of the type common to this cemetery, consisting of a shaft with stairway and a single burial chamber. The rectangular shaft (1.50 × 2.00 m; depth 2.50 m)
has nine steps on the eastern wall. The opening (length
0.23 m) was blocked with a high slab, divided into three
parts by parallel grooves cut into its surface and wedged
into position with an irregular stone. The burial chamber
is roughly square (*c.* 3.00 × 3.00 m; height 1.15 m); a
rectangular rock-cut trench (0.75 × 2.00 m; depth 0.62 m)
in the center has a step at one end. The trench was not
completed, as one side was not hewn. The chamber walls
slope slightly upward toward a flat rock-hewn ceiling.

The skeletal remains of four individuals, three adults
and a child, lay around the trench.

Chronology: No finds from this tomb were reported. Its
dating is therefore not possible.

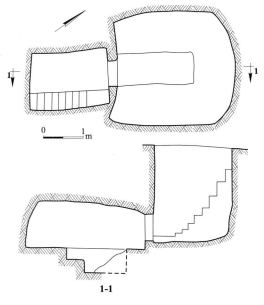

Plan 4.17. Tomb ZR XXXVIII, plan and section.

Tomb ZR XXXIX (Plan 4.1a; Fig. 4.28)

This tomb (see sketch in plan of cemetery) is the only masonry tomb in this cemetery, built entirely above surface level. It consists of a rectangular structure of two courses. The tomb was originally covered with very large slabs, only one of which was recovered. Although the tomb was found disturbed, it yielded a varied assemblage of pottery vessels and some small finds including earrings, fibulae, bracelets, etc.

Chronology: The earliest use of the tomb must have been in the 10th century BCE, as indicated by the presence of jug Type JG1 II. Other vessels from this tomb belonging to the 10th–9th centuries BCE, such as Type PF2, also attest to its early use. Three scarabs dated between the XXth and XXIInd Dynasties (1186–713 BCE) were recorded (see Appendix 2:67–69; Keel 1997:44: Nos. 67–69).

Catalogue of Finds, Tomb ZR XXXIX
(For pottery types see Chapter 5. * = illustrated in Fig. 4.28)

No.	Object	Type	IAA No.	Description	Dimensions (cm)			References
Pottery								
1*	Bowl	B2 II	70-8342	Reddish-brown ware, white grits.	H 5.0	D 16.0		
2*	Bowl	B4 I	70-8343	Reddish-brown ware, white grits.	H 7.0	D 14.0		
3*	Jug	JG1 II	70-8349	Orange-buff ware, thick red slip, burnished.	H 15+	W 10		
4*	Jug	JG3 II	70-8344	Orange-brown ware, buff wash all over.	H 22	W 15		
5	Pilgrim flask	PF2	70-8354	Orange-buff ware, white grits.	H 7.5	W 5.5		
6	Dipper juglet	DJ1	70-8351	Reddish-brown ware, white grits.	H 8.5	W 5.5		
7*	Juglet	J4	70-8345	Coarse gray ware, black slip, burnished.	H 9.5	W 6.0		
8*	Lamp	L3	70-8357	Coarse reddish-brown ware, white grits.	H 4.5	D 15.3		
9	Juglet	CP6	70-8353	Fine ware, badly encrusted. Black-painted decoration.	H 8.5	W 5.0		
Small Finds								
10*	Earring or nose ring		48-716	Bronze. Corroded.	L 1.1			
11	Bracelet		48-712	Bronze. Three-stranded, middle strand twisted. Fragment.	L 4.3			
12*	Fibula		48-720	Bronze. Fragment.	L 3.7			
13*	Bow fibula		48-721	Bronze. Flat in section, pin missing.	L 7.2			
14*	Bow fibula		48-722	Bronze. Profiled, with molded encircling rings on bow. Pin missing.	W 7.0			
15*	Eye bead		48-713	Glass(?) (Steatite[?] with glass inlay). Oblate triangular stratified.	H 2.0	D 2.8		Reich and Brandl 1985; Pritchard 1988: Fig. 21:51; Spaer 2001:79–81, 89, Fig. 38
16*	Weight		48-717	Hematite. Cylindrical.	L 1.4	D 1.2	Wt. 5.56 gm	
17	Hooked blade		48-708	Iron. With two nails inserted at one end. Broken.	L 19.0+			Pritchard 1988: Fig. 27:3, 4
18*	Bowl		70-8356	Bronze. Hemispherical, with squared-off rim.	H 7.5	D 13.0		Karageorghis 1983: Fig. CLXXX:73
19*	Spindle whorl		48-710	Bone. Truncated.	L 0.9	D 1.3		
20*	Spindle whorl		48-711	Bone. Truncated. Lower part missing	L 0.4	D 1.1		
21*	Scarab		48-714	Steatite. Surface appearance white.	15.7 × 11.8 × 7.7 (mm)			See App. 2:67; Keel 1997:44: No. 67
22*	Scarab		48-715	Bone? Yellowish.	14.3 × 10.7 × 6.4 (mm)			See App. 2:68; Keel 1997:44: No. 68
23*	Scarab		48-719	Steatite. White.	15.3 × 12.9 × 7.5 (mm)			See App. 2:69; Keel 1997:44: No. 69

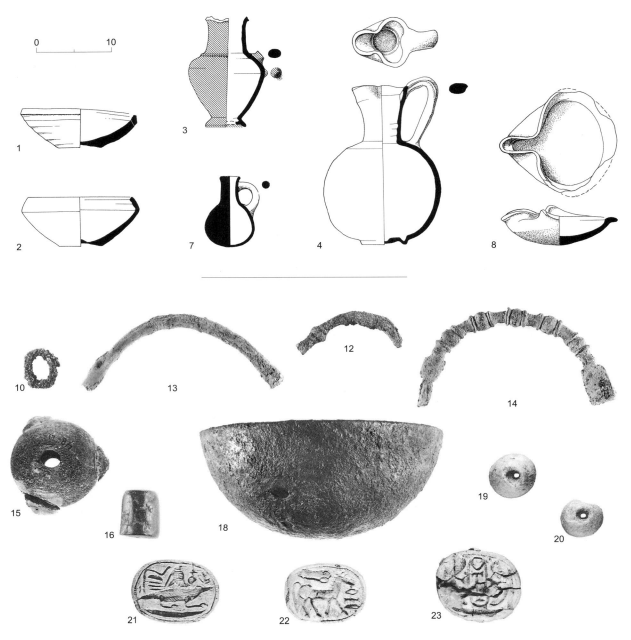

Fig. 4.28. Tomb ZR XXXIX, selected finds. Scale: Nos. 10, 15, 16, 19, 20—1:1; Nos. 12–14—3:4;
No. 18—1:2; Nos. 21–23—1.5:1.

Tomb ZR XL (Plan 4.1a)
Only the sketch in the plan of the cemetery is available.
No further information was recorded.

Tomb ZR XLI (Type 1; Plan 4.1a; Fig. 4.29)
Tomb consisting of deep square shaft with stairway,
leading to rectangular burial chamber. Only the plan in
the sketch of the cemetery is available. It contained fragments of decayed wood, evidently representing the remains of a coffin. Among the small finds were glass
eyeliner inlays, as well as some jewelry.

Chronology: The tomb was found looted, and only a few
objects, some of them unique to the Akhziv repertoire,
were left intact. Storage jar Type SJ2, as well as some
other diagnostic finds, dates to the Persian period.

Catalogue of Finds, Tomb ZR XLI

(For pottery types see Chapter 5. * = illustrated in Fig. 4.29)

No.	Object	Type	IAA No.	Description	Dimensions (cm)		References
Pottery							
1*	Storage jar	SJ2	70-8535	Orange-buff ware.	H 53.0	W 25.0	
Small Finds							
2*	6 earrings		44.234	Silver. Crescent-shaped. Partly broken.	L 2.5	W 1.6	
3*	Bracelet		44.241	Bronze. Broken, badly corroded.	L 7.0		
4*	2 beads		44.235	Carnelian. Oblate globular.	D 0.6		
5*	Kohl tube and stick		44.229	Bone and bronze. Tube decorated with molded double rings. Broken.	L 17+		Petrie 1927: Pl. XXII
6*	2 eyeliner inlays		44.232	Blue glass. One broken, elements forming a left and a right eyeliner for a mummy case.	L 7.0		Goldstein 1979: 171, No. 454
7	Eyeliner and eyebrow inlays		44.233	Blue glass. Fragments. (See No. 6.)			

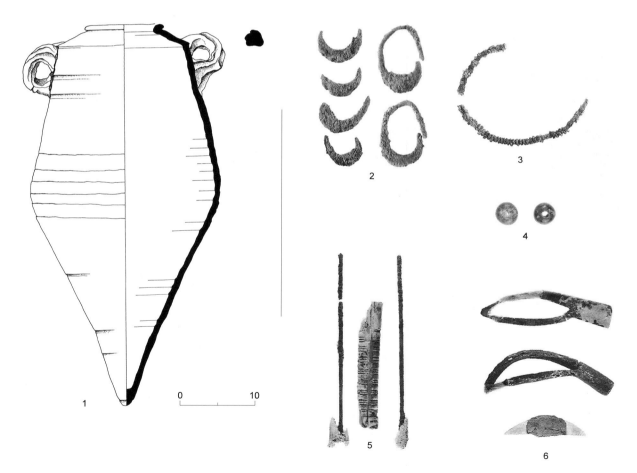

Fig. 4.29. Tomb ZR XLI, selected finds. Scale: No. 2—3:4; Nos. 3, 6—1:2; No. 4—1:1; No. 5—1:3.

Tomb ZR XLII (Type 1; Plan 4.1a; Fig. 4.30)
Tomb with a rectangular shaft and stairway leading to single burial chamber. The chamber has a central trench and benches all around. Only the plan in the sketch of the cemetery is available. A few pottery fragments were recovered.

Chronology: The few finds found in this tomb do not allow accurate dating, although the two storage jars date to the 6th–5th centuries BCE.

Catalogue of Finds, Tomb ZR XLII

(For pottery types see Chapter 5. * = illustrated in Fig. 4.30)

No.	Object	Type	IAA No.	Description	Dimensions (cm)	
Pottery						
1	Storage jar	SJ2	70-8525	Reddish-buff ware.	H 48+	W 26.0
2	Storage jar	SJ2	70-8526	Orange-buff ware.	H 54.0	W 25.0
Small Finds						
3*	Earring		44.245	Silver. Crescent-shaped. Broken.	W 1.6	
4*	Nails		44.246	Iron. Fragments.	L 1.8–3.8	

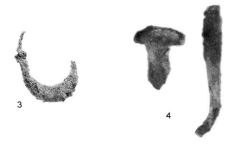

Fig. 4.30. Tomb ZR XLII, selected finds. Scale—1:1.

Tomb ZR XLIII (Type 1)
Tomb of rectangular shaft with stairway leading to single burial chamber. The chamber has a central trench and benches all around. No plan available. A few pottery fragments were recovered.

Catalogue of Finds, Tomb ZR XLIII

(For pottery types see Chapter 5. Not illustrated)

No.	Object	Type	Description	Dimensions (cm)	
Pottery					
1	Jug	JG5 IV	Pinkish-buff ware.	H 11.5+	W 6.5
2	Dipper juglet	DJ1	Reddish-brown ware.	H 9.0	W 5.0

Chronology: The two pottery vessels found date to the 8th–7th centuries BCE. However, they cannot be used to determine the period of use of this tomb.

Tomb ZR XLV
No description or plan available.

Catalogue of Finds, Tomb ZR XLV

(For pottery types see Chapter 5. Not illustrated)

No.	Object	Type	IAA No.	Description	Dimensions (cm)	
Pottery						
1	Storage jar	SJ1	70-8530	Reddish-brown ware.	H 42.0	W 21.0

Chronology: The single storage jar recovered, Type SJ1, is dated to the 8th–7th centuries BCE.

Tomb ZR XLVI (Fig. 4.31)
No description or plan available.

Chronology: The small number of objects found suggests that the tomb had been looted. However, it is worth noting that of the few urns found during this excavation, two were uncovered in this tomb. One urn (Type K1) contained a skull and bone fragments. This is an unusual phenomenon, given that in other Phoenician cemeteries urns were usually found in burial fields. The few pottery vessels date to the 7th–5th centuries BCE.

Catalogue of Finds, Tomb ZR XLVI

(For pottery types see Chapter 5. * = illustrated in Fig. 4.31)

No.	Object	Type	IAA No.	Description	Dimensions (cm)	
Pottery						
1*	Krater (urn)	K1	70-8480	Orange-buff ware with white grits. Found with skeletal remains.	H 28.0	W 25.0
2*	Krater (urn)	K2	70-8481	Light buff ware. Black- and red-painted decoration.	H 35.0	W 26.0
3	Storage jar	SJ2	70-8608	Orange-buff ware.	H 54.0	W 27.0
Small Finds						
4*	Earring		48-733b	Silver. Crescent-shaped.	L 1.8	
5*	9 earrings		48-733a	Bronze. Crescent-shaped. Fragments.	W 2.0–3.5	
6*	Finger ring		48-733c	Bronze. Broken.	D 2.2	
7*	Bracelet		48-728	Bronze. Overlapping ends.	D 7.0	
8*	Bracelet		48-729	Bronze. Overlapping ends.	D 7.0	
9*	Bracelet		48-731	Bronze. Gap between ends.	D 6.5	

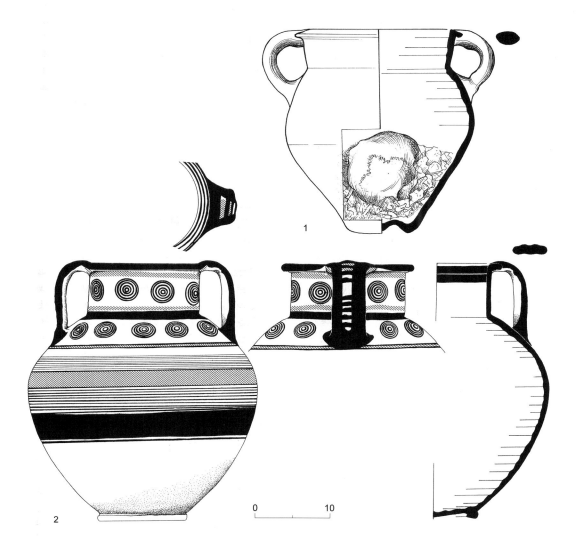

Fig. 4.31. Tomb ZR XLVI, selected finds.

Catalogue of Finds, Tomb ZR XLVI (contd., Fig. 4.31)

No.	Object	Type	IAA No.	Description	Dimensions (cm)
10*	Bracelet		48-732	Bronze. Gap between ends.	D 6.0
11*	Bracelet		48-733	Bronze. Ends meeting.	D 4.5
12*	Armlet		48-727	Bronze. Ends meeting.	D 10.5
13*	2 beads		48-734	Glass(?) Cylindrical.	L 0.5
14*	2 beads		48-735	Greenish faience. Oblate globular.	D 0.5, 0.6
15	Lump		48-737	Yellow ocher.	

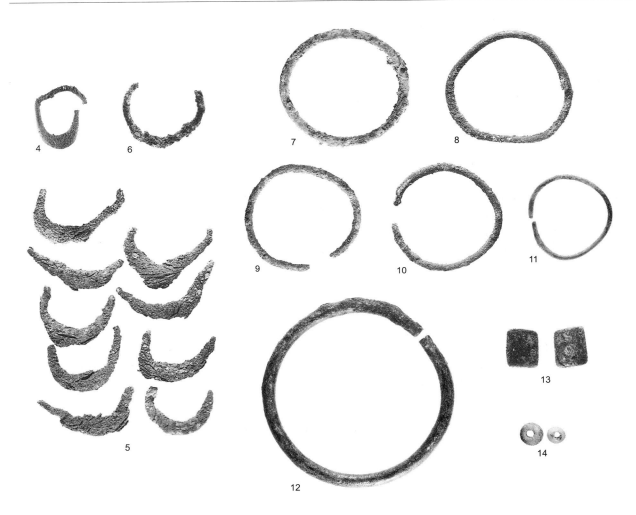

Fig. 4.31. Tomb ZR XLVI, selected finds (contd.). Scale: Nos. 4, 6, 14—1:1; No. 5—3:4; Nos. 7–12—1:2; No. 13—2:1.

Tomb ZR LIII (Fig. 4.32)
Shaft leading to burial chamber with tent-shaped ceiling. The chamber was found full of earth mixed with some small finds. No plan available. Of particular interest are glass eyeliner inlays.

Chronology: The few datable finds among the material recovered from this tomb are of the 6th–5th centuries BCE.

Catalogue of Finds, Tomb ZR LIII
(For pottery types see Chapter 5. * = illustrated in Fig. 4.32)

No.	Object	Type	IAA No.	Description	Dimensions (cm)		References
Pottery							
1	Storage jar	SJ2	70-8527	Reddish-buff ware.	H 53.0	W 26.0	
Small Finds							
2*	Finger ring		48-757	Bronze. Round in section, overlapping ends.	D 2.2		
3	Fibula pin		48-725	Bronze.	L 5.0		
4	Nail		48-756	Iron. Fragments.	L 4.5–7.5		
5	Nail		48-758	Bronze. Pointed, square in section. Fragment.	L 4.0		
6	Kohl stick		48-755	Bronze. Broken.	L 16.5+		
7*	2 eyeliner inlays		48-752	Blue glass. Broken elements forming a left eyeliner for a mummy case.	L 6.0–7.0		Goldstein 1979: 171, No. 454
8*	2 eyebrows		48-753	Blue glass. One fragmentary, elements forming eyes for a mummy case.	L 6.3–9.0		

Fig. 4.32. Tomb ZR LIII, selected finds. Scale: No. 2—1:1; Nos. 7, 8—1:2.

Tomb ZR LIV (Fig. 4.33)
Shaft with a stairway leading to a single burial chamber. Entrance blocked with a slab. No plan available.

Chronology: No pottery reported from this tomb, only a number of small finds which do not allow any definitive dating of this tomb.

Catalogue of Finds, Tomb ZR LIV
(* = illustrated in Fig. 4.33)

No.	Object	IAA No.	Description	Dimensions (cm)
Small Finds				
1*	Finger ring	48-762	Bronze. Square. Round in section.	D 2.0
2*	3 finger rings	48-761	Bronze. One with overlapping ends, rectangular in section. Two others, ends meeting, round in section.	D 1.6–2.0
3*	3 bracelets	48-760	Bronze. One with overlapping ends, rectangular in section. Two others round in section, ends not meeting.	D 4.2–6.0
4	Bracelet	48-765	Bronze. Oval in section. Fragment.	
5*	Eye bead	48-763	Greenish glass. Stratified, eye missing.	D 1.0
6*	Bead	48-764	Greenish glass. Globular.	D 1.0
7*	Hook	48-766	Bronze. Broken (key?).	L 4.5

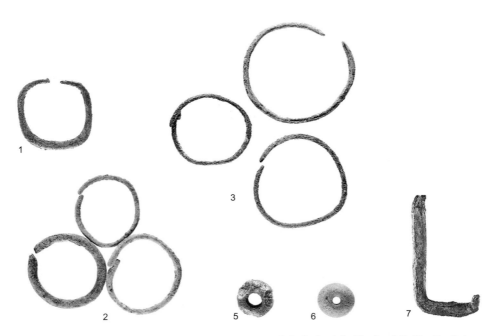

Fig. 4.33. Tomb ZR LIV, selected finds. Scale: Nos. 1, 2, 5, 6—1:1; No. 3—1:2; No. 7—3:4.

Tomb ZR LV (Fig. 4.34)

Shaft with stairway leading to single burial chamber. The entrance was partly closed with a rough, irregular boulder. No plan available. The tomb was re-used in Roman times.

Chronology: The tomb was found almost empty, with only a few non-diagnostic small finds, which do not allow an exact dating.

Catalogue of Finds, Tomb ZR LV
(* = illustrated in Fig. 4.34)

No.	Object	IAA No.	Description	Dimensions (cm)
Small Finds				
1*	Bell	48-767	Bronze. Dome-shaped, tongue missing.	D 1.9
2*	Center piece	48-768	Silver. Composed of a ring between two tubular ribbed and collared stringing attachments.	L 2.3

Fig. 4.34. Tomb ZR LV, selected finds. Scale—1:1.

CHAPTER 5

POTTERY TYPOLOGY

The typology of the Akhziv tomb pottery assemblage was organized according to the shape and profile of the vessels rather than by families. The only exception is the Cypriot and Cypro-Phoenician pottery. The Akhziv tombs have yielded mainly jugs, juglets and bowls, as well as jars—a clearly funerary repertoire. Concomitently, domestic vessels, such as cooking pots and oil lamps, are notably absent.

The bulk of the vessels from the Akhziv tombs belongs to the 9th–8th centuries BCE, although a considerable number of vessels are of the 7th century BCE.

The Akhziv pottery has some distinctive forms, dominant among which is the red-slipped jug. The jug's pedestal base is characteristic of some of the earlier examples, dated to the 10th century BCE. They were replaced in the 9th–8th centuries BCE by the 'Akhziv base', a kind of depressed or reversed omphalos (see, e.g., Fig. 5.7:5) which is one of the main features of this pottery. In the late 8th–7th centuries BCE, these bases were superseded by ring bases.

Another typical feature of the Akhziv pottery is the handle, which can be of two main types: a handle drawn from rim to shoulder, usually in the form of a double strap, and a handle drawn from a ridge on the neck to the shoulder. In degenerate shapes a simple handle is drawn from rim to shoulder.

The degenerate shapes, for which no exact parallels were found, presented a difficulty. They differ from the other pottery in their coarse clay, lack of slip and careless manufacture. Their close affinity to popular Phoenician types strongly suggests that they were made especially to be placed in tombs. However, one should not exclude the possibility that the vessels were made by an inexperienced potter, in an effort to imitate the flawless Phoeni-cian ware. As to their date, there is no doubt that they are either contemporary with or a little later than the 'original' shapes.

The Cypriot and Cypro-Phoenician vessels belong to types known from Cyprus—the 'White-Painted' family, the 'Black-on-Red' family and the plain wares. No classical bichrome pottery was found. Its absence suggests that the use of the cemeteries probably did not begin until the 10th century BCE.

The vessels of reduced size form an interesting group, which was difficult to date due to the absence of comparative material. The parallels given are usually with reference to full-scale vessels.

It is noteworthy that no torpedo jars, characteristic of the 8th century BCE, were recorded at Akhziv, a phenomenon that occurs also at Tell Keisan.

There was some difficulty in deciding which sites provide the closest parallels to the Akhziv pottery. The variety of types is so wide-ranging that no single site in the Phoenician homeland can be said to offer comprehensive comparative material.

TYPE B — BOWLS (Figs. 5.1–5.3)

Type B1
Bowls with rounded wall, simple rounded or slightly squared-off rim, flat or disk base.

Type B1 I. Simple rounded rim. Coarse, reddish-brown ware with grits.

Similar bowls are known from Samaria Period III, late 9th century BCE (Crowfoot, Crowfoot and Kenyon 1957: Fig. 4:3) and Kition (Karageorghis et al. 1981: Pl. 26:17).

Tombs: Z IE:1–4; Z IW:1–3; Z X:1; Z XI:1, 2; Z XIV:1; Z XVIII:1; Z XX:1–5; ZR XVII:1, 2; ZR XXIX:1, 2; ZR XXXVI:1, 2.

Type B1 II. Bowl characterized by an outer ribbed wall with a ridge about halfway down. Gritty reddish-brown ware.

This type of bowl occurs in Tyre, Stratum I, 7th century BCE (Bikai 1978b: Pl. I:7).
Tomb: ZR XXIX:3.

Type B2
Bowls with rounded wall, various rims, flat or disk base.

Type B2 I. Flat inverted rim, flat base. Coarse reddish-brown ware.
Tomb: ZR XXXVI:3.

Type B2 II. Flat squared-off inverted rim, flat base. Characterized by its thick and heavy reddish-brown ware, rich in white grits.
Tomb: ZR XXXIX:1.

Type B2 III. Flat rim, slanting slightly inward, disk base. Coarse reddish-brown ware with white grits.
Tombs: Z IE:5, 6; Z IW:4; Z VI:1; Z X:2; Z XI:3; ZR VIII:1.

Type B2 IV. Thickened down-turned cut rim, flat base. Coarse reddish-brown ware.
Similar bowls are known from Sarepta, Substratum C2, 8th–7th centuries BCE (Anderson 1988: Pl. 35:6) and Ḥazor Area A, Stratum VI, 8th century BCE (Yadin et al. 1961: Pl. CLXXXII:7).
Tombs: Z IE:7, 8; Z IW:5; Z XXI:1.

Type B3
Shallow bowls with straight wall, inner carination at base of flattened rim and flat base.

Type B3 I. Wide, slightly everted rim. Coarse yellowish-cream ware.
This type of bowl occurs frequently at Tyre, Stratum III, 8th century BCE (Bikai 1978b: Pl. VIIIA; 27, 31, 45) and is known at Khalde, Level III, 8th century BCE (Saidah 1966:61:8), where it probably served as a cover for urns (Saidah 1966: Pl. II: Tomb III; Pl. III: Tomb 121).

It also occurs at Tell Keisan, Stratum 5, late 8th–7th centuries BCE (Briend and Humbert 1980:167: Type b).
Tombs: Z IE:9–12; Z VI:2–4; ZR XXXVI:4.

Type B3 II. Wide everted rim which appears as a direct continuation of the body wall. No exterior signs of the carination. Fine buff ware, well-levigated. The interior has a smoother finish than the exterior.
Bowls of this type have been found at Tell Keisan, Stratum V, late 8th–7th centuries BCE (Briend and Humbert 1980: Pl. 38: 7g), Tyre, Stratum I, *c.* 700 BCE (Bikai 1978b: Pl. I:8–10), Sarepta, Stratum B, 6th–5th centuries BCE (Anderson 1988: Pl. 38:21) and al-Mina, Stratum V, 7th century BCE (Taylor 1952:80, Fig. 6:39).
This type of bowl appears in the latter part of the 8th century BCE and continues well into the 7th and even the 6th century BCE.
Tombs: Z I Vestibule:1; ZR VIII:2; ZR XXVI:1

Type B3 III. Everted horizontal rim and 'step' or articulation point on exterior wall below rim. Reddish-yellow ware.
A parallel for this bowl comes from Tyre, Strata III–II, 8th century BCE (Bikai 1978b: Pl. IX:15).
Tombs: Z III:1; Z X:3; Z XVII:1.

Type B3 IV. Wide, slightly concave rim. Slight depression on outer wall below rim. Coarse reddish-brown ware.
Similar bowls are known from Tell Keisan, Stratum V, late 8th and 7th centuries BCE (Briend and Humbert 1980: Pl. 38:5), as well as from Kition (Bikai 1987b: Pl. XX:532).
Tomb: Z X:4.

Type B4
Rounded bowls, some carinated.

Type B4 I. Rounded wall ending in an inverted rim tapering to a rounded rim. String-cut base. Heavy reddish-brown ware, rich in white grits.
Tomb: ZR XXXIX:2.

Type B4 II. Carination above middle of vessel wall, rising vertically to a sharp rim. Disk-base, slightly concave. Reddish-brown ware. Red slip on interior going over rim and upper part of vessel. Wheel-burnished on the outside.

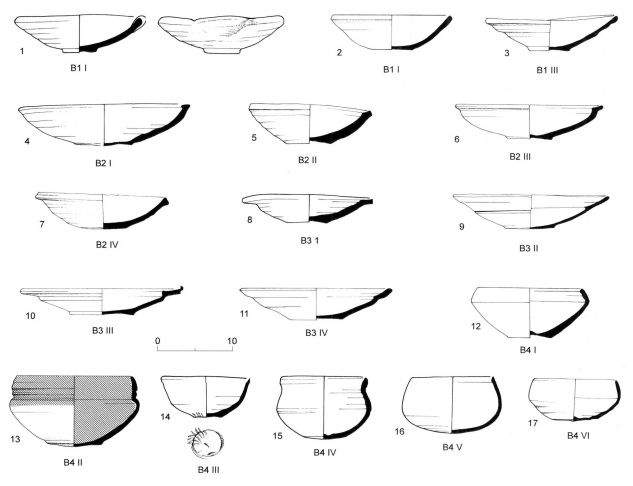

Fig. 5.1.

A bowl of similar shape comes from Tyre, Stratum III–II, 8th century BCE (Bikai 1978b: Pl. X:19). *Tomb:* ZR XXIX:4.

Type B4 III. Small deep bowl. Rounded wall, vertical rim and flat string-cut base. Relatively coarse grayish-brown ware, white grits.

A similar bowl is known from Ḥazor, Area B, Stratum II, 4th century BCE (Yadin et al. 1958: Pl. LXXIX:28). *Tomb:* ZR XXIX:5.

Type B4 IV. Bulging body. The wall above bulge is concave and ends in a flaring rim with an externally thickened lip. Flat string-cut base. Light buff-pinkish ware. *Tomb:* ZR XXIX:6.

Type B4 V. Hemispherical bowl. Thin walls, vertical or incurved rim and rounded base.

Such bowls are known from Tyre, Stratum III, 8th century BCE (Bikai 1978b: Pl. X:20). *Tombs:* Z XI:4; ZR XVII:3; ZR XXXVI:5.

Type B4 VI. Hemispherical bowl. Slight carination at two-thirds of its height, ending vertically in a simple rim. Coarse reddish-brown to orange ware. *Tombs:* Z I Vestibule:2; ZR XXXI:1, 2.

Type B5
Small bowls.

Type B5 I. Rounded wall, flat rim slanting slightly inwards, string-cut flat base. Gritty reddish-brown ware, gray core. *Tomb:* Z XX:6.

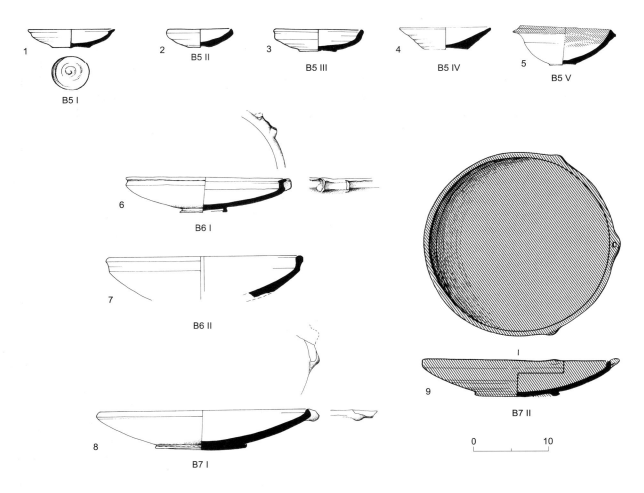

Fig. 5.2.

Type B5 II. Shallow bowl. Thick flaring walls, ending in a cut-off rim. Flat string-cut base. Coarse reddish-brown ware, white and black grits.

A similar bowl was found at Ḥazor, Area B, Stratum IX, 9th century BCE (Yadin et al. 1961: Pl. CCVIII:6). *Tombs:* Z XX:7; ZR XXIX:7.

Type B5 III. Carinated bowl. Wall above carination is slightly flaring, ending in a rounded rim. Flat string-cut disk base. Reddish brown coarse ware, white and black grits.

A similar bowl was found at Ḥazor, Area B, Stratum VA, 8th century BCE (Yadin et al. 1961: Pl. CCXXV:5). *Tomb:* ZR XXIX:8.

Type B5 IV. Shallow bowl. Sloping walls ending in a thin rounded rim. A variant of this type has an internal cutoff rim. Flat thickened base. Coarse reddish-brown ware, white grits. A variant has a thick white slip.
Tombs: Z IW:6; Z XVIII:2, 3; Z XXIX:9.

Type B5 V. Wide pendent rim with sharp ridge at base of rim. Flat string-cut base. Orange-buff ware. Red slip on rim.

Bowls similar in shape, mainly of the rim, come from Tell Keisan, Stratum 5, late 8th–7th centuries BCE (Briend and Humbert 1980: Pl. 40:6, 6a). Identical bowls were discovered in the Tophet at Carthage dated to the second half of the 8th century BCE (Gehrig and Niemeyer 1990: Nos. 159, 168).
Tombs: ZR VI:1; ZR XII:1; ZR XXXI:3.

Type B6
Carinated shallow bowls.

Type B6 I. Carinated at about two-thirds of the bowl height. Flaring rim ending in a slightly inverted flat lip. Occasionally, there is a bar handle below the rim. Ring base, sometimes step above base. Reddish-buff ware.
Tombs: Z XI:5; ZR IX:1.

Type B6 II. The vertical wall above the carination is relatively short, ending in a thickened rounded rim. Reddish-brown ware, grits.
Similar bowls are known from Ḥazor, Area A, Stratum VIII, 9th century BCE (Yadin et al. 1960: Pl. LIII: 8–11), as well as from Tell Abu Hawam, Stratum III, 10th–9th centuries BCE (Hamilton 1935:21:72).
Tomb: Z XI:6, 7.

Type B7
Large shallow bowls.

Type B7 I. Wall ending in inturned rim. Knob on rim. Disk base. Pinkish-buff ware, grits.
A bowl with a similar rim (base missing) was found at Sarepta Stratum C2, 9th century BCE (Anderson 1988: Pl. 35:20).
Tomb: Z XVI:1.

Type B7 II. Rounded wall, inverted rim, ring base. Pierced lug handle and two small knobs on outside of rim. Grayish-buff ware with thick red slip, wheel-burnished on the outside and irregularly hand-burnished inside.
Tombs: Z VI:5; Z XX:8.

Type B8
'Samaria bowls'.

Type B8 I. Mostly thin-walled, red-slipped and burnished. Vertical or slightly convex wall, ending in a sharp rim. Flat or slightly rounded base with groove on interior defining the juncture with the base. Light buff ware, well-levigated, well-fired and highly wheel-burnished all over. The common decoration is an over-all thick red slip on the interior and alternating bands of red and yellow slip on the base. In some cases, the bowls are red-slipped inside and outside with most of the base left plain.

Such bowls are known from Tyre, Strata III–II, 8th century BCE (Bikai 1978a:52–54; 1978b: Pl. XI:12–14), Samaria, Period IV, 8th century BCE (Crowfoot, Crowfoot and Kenyon 1957: Fig 18:7) and Tel Mikhal, Stratum XII, 8th century BCE (Herzog, Rapp and Negbi 1989:83, Fig. 7:4:1). The most famous of these are the band-decorated bowls found at Samaria. Other examples were found at Sarepta, Stratum C1, 8th century BCE (Anderson 1988: Pl. 38:3, 4), Khalde, Level III, 8th century BCE (Saidah 1966:61:10) and Kition (Karageorghis et al. 1981: Pl. 24:1–14). The wide distribution of these bowls in the Phoenician sphere suggests their Phoenician origin.
Tombs: Z XI:8; Z XVII:2; Z XVIII:4; ZR XVII:4; ZR XXIX:10; ZR XXXVI:6.

Type B8 II. Shallow bowl. Slightly convex, exceptionally thin walls. Straight sharp rim and flat ring base. Light buff ware, no traces of slip are visible; well-levigated, well-fired and wheel-burnished.
A similar bowl, though red-slipped, comes from Ḥazor, Area B, Stratum IX, early 9th century BCE (Yadin et al. 1961: Pl. CCVIII:26). This type of bowl without a red slip is fairly uncommon (Bikai 1978b:26–27).
A variant of this bowl is characterized by a thicker and gritty ware, a carinated wall, and a flat disk base. It is of reddish-brown ware and lacks any slip or burnish. A similar bowl is known from Lachish, Stratum III–II, 7th–early 6th centuries BCE (Tufnell 1953: Pl. 98:571).
Tombs: Z XX:9; ZR XXIX:11.

Type B8 III. Small bowl. Straight or slightly rounded wall ending in a thin rounded rim. Disk base, slightly carinated. Fine ware, though less thin than Type B8 I. Brownish-buff ware, well-levigated; red-slipped on interior, going over rim to just below carination. A wide red band encircles the base. Well-burnished all over.
A similar bowl is known from Tell Abu Hawam, Stratum III, 9th century BCE (Hamilton 1935: Pl. XIII:68).
Tomb: ZR XXVI:2.

Type B8 IV. Deep bowl. Rounded wall, ending in a flat, slightly pendent rim. Stepped disk base, carinated close to the base. Fine buff ware covered with a thick red slip. In some cases only the interior is red-slipped, while in other examples, most of the bowl is covered with a red slip, except for the area below the carination and the center of the base. Wheel-burnished all over.

This type of bowl is known mainly from Phoenician sites. It appears at al-Mina, Stratum VIII, late 9th–8th centuries BCE without a slip (Taylor 1959: Fig. 6:10, 13), at Qraye (Chapman 1972: Fig. 28:302) and at Sarepta, Substratum C1, 8th century BCE (Anderson 1988: Pl. 38:1). It is also known from Tell Keisan, Stratum 5, late 8th–mid 7th centuries BCE (Briend and Humbert 1980: Pl. 40:3). This bowl should be dated to the late 9th–8th centuries BCE.
Tombs: Z IE:13; Z IW:7; ZR XXXVI:7, 8.

Type B8 V. Shallow bowl. Slightly convex wall, carinated at two-thirds of its height. Pendent rim tapering to a sharp edge. Flat base. Orange-buff ware covered with a red slip inside and on rim, burnished all over.

Close parallels to this bowl are found at Sarepta, Substratum C2, late 9th–8th centuries BCE (Anderson 1988: Pl. 35:9), at Tell Keisan, Stratum 5, late 8th–mid 7th centuries BCE (Briend and Humbert 1980: Pl. 40:2, 2a) and at Kition (Bikai 1987b: Pl. XX:545).
Tomb: ZR XVII:5.

Type B8 VI. Shallow bowl. Disk base carinated at two-thirds of its height. Vertical, thick wall above carination ends in flattened rim. Orange-buff ware, red slip inside and over the rim, burnished all over.
Tomb: ZR XXXVI:9.

Type B9
Bichrome decorated bowls with rounded walls, simple or thickened rims, flat or ring bases.

Type B9 I. Straight-sided wall, rounded rim and flat base. Reddish-brown ware. The interior is decorated with a red band on the rim and near the base and groups of black lines bordering the red bands.

Similar bowls are known from Tyre, Stratum III, 8th century BCE (Bikai 1978b: Pl. X:13) and Sarepta, Stratum D1, 10th–9th centuries BCE (Anderson 1988: Pl. 33:14).
Tomb: ZR XXXVI:10.

Type B9 II. Wall tapering to rim thickened on outside. Ring base. Yellow-buff ware. Concentric black- and red-painted bands on interior. In some cases, groups of black strokes on rim.

This type of bichrome bowl is known from various sites: Tell Keisan, Stratum VII, first half of the 9th cen-

tury BCE (Briend and Humbert 1980: Pl. 53:4, 5); Tell Abu Hawam, Stratum IV, 12th century BCE (Hamilton 1935:29:153); Tell Qasile, Stratum XI, late 11th century BCE (A. Mazar 1985a: Fig. 18:9); Ḥazor, Area B, Stratum IX, late 10th–early 9th centuries BCE (Yadin et al. 1961: Pl. CCVIII:29); and Kh. Silm (Chapman 1972: Fig. 25: 135, 138).
Tomb: Z XI:9, 10.

Type B9 III. Slightly convex wall ending in rounded rim. Flat base. Brownish-gray ware rich in white grits. Wide red bands between single black lines on interior. Red band on exterior of rim.

Parallels come from Tell Keisan, Stratum 7, 9th century BCE (Briend and Humbert 1980: Pl. 53:1) and from Joya (Chapman 1972: Fig. 25:258).
Tomb: Z IW:8.

Type B10
'Black-on-Red' bowls.

Type B10 I. Rounded wall tapering to a straight rim. Ring base. Horizontal handle below rim; there was probably another handle, now broken, on the opposite side. Orange-buff ware covered with thick red slip and black concentric circles on the inside.

The appearance of horizontal handles on the common round-sided Iron Age bowl suggests an Aegean influence (A. Mazar 1985a:36).

Similar bowls are known from Tell Qasile, Stratum XI, late 11th century BCE (A. Mazar 1985a: Fig. 18:11), Megiddo, Stratum VA, 10th century BCE (Loud 1948: Pl. 90:1) and from Ḥ. Rosh Zayit (Gal 1989: No. 5). A further parallel is known from Palaepaphos-Skales, Type BOR II (IV; Karageorghis 1983: Pl. CLXII:141).
Tomb: Z IE:14.

Type B11
Bowls with spiral decoration.

Type B11 I. Slightly convex, ribbed wall, inverted rim, two horizontal handles on rim, disk base. Reddish-brown ware. Black spiral inside, bordered by black concentric lines.

This round-sided bowl is characteristic of the Iron Age (see Type B1). Its horizontal handles and spiral decoration suggest an Aegean–Philistine influence.

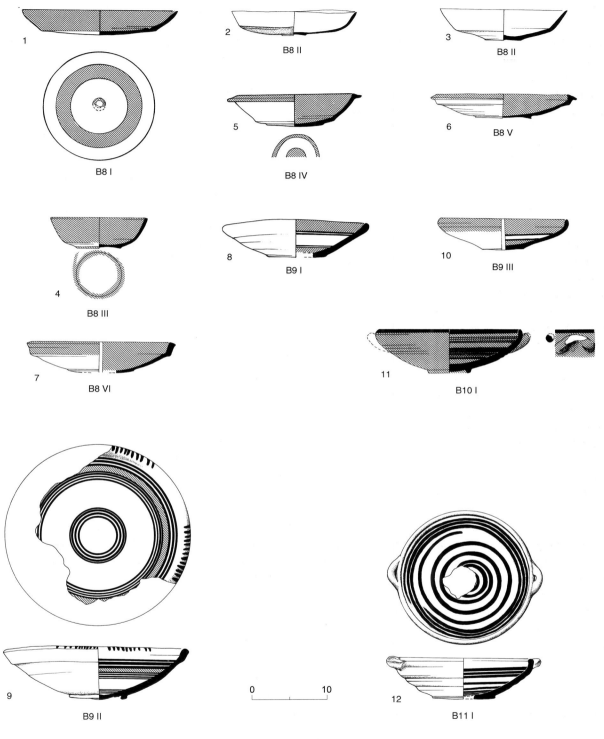

Fig. 5.3.

A bowl of similar shape and decoration was found at Tell el-Farʿah (South), Tomb 542 (Petrie 1930: Pl. XXV: 542). A bowl similar in shape and spiral decoration, though with a red slip, comes from Tell Qasile, Stratum X1, late 11th century BCE (A. Mazar 1985a:38). *Tomb:* Z IE:15.

Type K — Kraters (Fig. 5.4)

Type K1 — Urns

Jar-shaped urn with depressed ring base, piriform body, short wide neck with rim thickened, flattened and slightly sloping outward. Handles drawn from rim to shoulder. Orange-buff ware, white grits. No traces of slip have survived.

This type of urn is recorded at er-Ruqeish (Culican 1973:73:R7), Kh. Silm (Chapman 1972: Fig. 19:81) and Tell Keisan, Stratum 4, mid 7th–early 6th centuries BCE (Briend and Humbert 1980: Pl. 28:9).
Tombs: Z III:3; ZR XVII:7; ZR XLVI:1.

Type K2

Bichrome krater. Piriform body, ring base. Wide cylindrical neck, flat out-turned rim. Two strap handles drawn from rim to shoulder. Light buff ware with black and red decoration: concentric black circles around neck and shoulder; black and red bands and concentric rings encircle rim, neck and body; transversal black and red strokes on outer part of handles; black lines and bands on flat part of rim and inside upper neck.

This amphora of Bichrome III ware is known from Cyprus (Gjerstad 1948: Fig. XXIV:2) and has a close parallel at Tell 'Ira in the Negev, dated to the early 6th century BCE (Biran 1985:27). Further examples are known from Rashidiyeh, early 6th century BCE (Culican 1982:69:b).
Tomb: ZR XLVI:2.

Type SJ — Storage Jars (Figs. 5.5, 5.6)

Type SJ1

Storage jar. Long, straight body, vertical sides, pointed base. High flat wide carinated shoulder, angled up and inward, ending in short squared-off rim. A variant of this type appears with a broad, squat body. Two small loop handles, sometimes carelessly made, are drawn from carinated shoulder to body. Reddish-brown to orange-buff ware.

Parallels to this type of jar are known from Tyre, Stratum II, 8th century BCE (Bikai 1978b: Pls. III:2, IV:2), Tell Keisan, Stratum 4, 7th century BCE (Briend and Humbert 1980: Pl. 25: 2, 3), Ashdod, Stratum VIIb, 7th century BCE (M. Dothan and Porath 1982: Fig. 22:2) and Tel Batash, Stratum II, 7th century BCE (Kelm and Mazar 1985: Fig. 18:1). This type of jar clearly belongs

to the late Iron Age repertoire and should be dated to the 7th–early 6th centuries BCE.
Tombs: Z III:4; ZR VI:2, 3; ZR VIII:3; ZR X:1; ZR XI:1; ZR XVII:8; ZR XXIV:1; ZR XLV:1.

Type SJ2

Storage jar. Broad flat shoulder, sharply carinated, straight and short thickened rim. Elongated body, concave below carinated shoulder, widening toward the center of the body or slightly below it and tapering sharply toward an elongated pointed base. A variant of this type has a short pointed base. A pair of carelessly made loop handles is drawn from carination to body. Brittle, reddish-brown to orange-buff ware.

The jars date from the Persian period and occur mainly in the 5th century BCE, though there are earlier examples in the 6th BCE century from Tell Keisan, Strata 5–4 (Briend and Humbert 1980: Pls. 25:5, 47:2). The numerous examples from the Persian period come from sites such as Shikmona (Elgavish 1968: Pl. LI:106), 'Atlit (Johns 1933: Fig. 16:K, M) and Tel Mikhal, first half of the 5th century BCE (Herzog, Rapp and Negbi 1989: Fig. 9.1:23).
Tombs: ZR VI:4; ZR VIII:4; ZR X:2, 3; ZR XII:2; ZR XIII:1; ZR XXXVI:11; ZR XLI:1; ZR XLII:1, 2; ZR XLVI:3; ZR LIII:1.

Type SJ3

Storage jar, sharply carinated shoulder. Long waisted body narrowing below shoulder and gradually widening in its lower part. The rim is fashioned by folding the clay outward, forming a collar-like band. Two carelessly made loop handles are drawn from shoulder to body. Greenish-buff, coarse and porous ware, rich in large black grits.

Examples of this shape of jar were found at Tyre, Stratum II, mid-8th century BCE (Bikai 1978b: Pl. II:3), as well as at Tel Keisan, Stratum IV, mid 7th–early 6th century BCE (Briend and Humbert 1980:Pl. 25:4). The Akhziv examples seem to be later, judging by the quality of ware and color and their careless workmanship. They should be dated to the 6th–5th centuries BCE.
Tombs: Z IE:16, 17; Z IW:9; Z XXI:2.

Type SJ4

Storage jar. Elongated body, wide sloping shoulder, carinated, sharply contoured under carination. Thickened rim folded over and flattened. The body is waisted, widening at the center and tapering gradually to a pointed base.

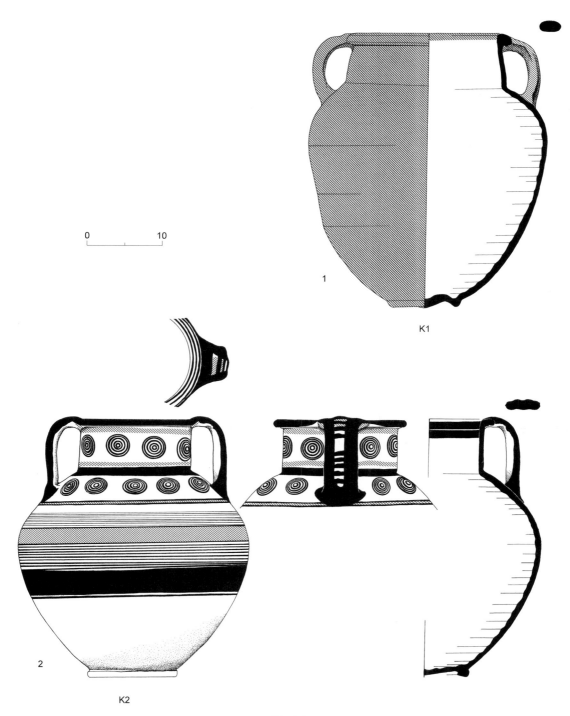

Fig. 5.4.

Two handles drawn from carination to body. Reddish-brown ware, white grits, well-levigated.

The careful workmanship of these jars and the quality of their ware point to an Iron Age date in the 7th century BCE. Similar storage jars are known from Tell Keisan,

Stratum 5, late 8th–7th centuries BCE (Briend and Humbert 1980: Pl. 47:2) and Tel Batash, Stratum II, 7th century BCE (Kelm and Mazar 1985: Fig. 18:7), although the rim is different.

Tomb: Z IE:18, 19.

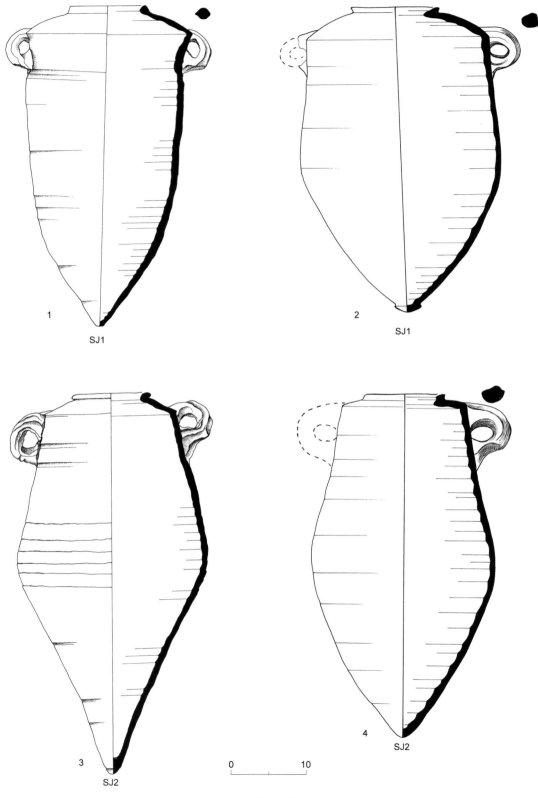

Fig. 5.5.

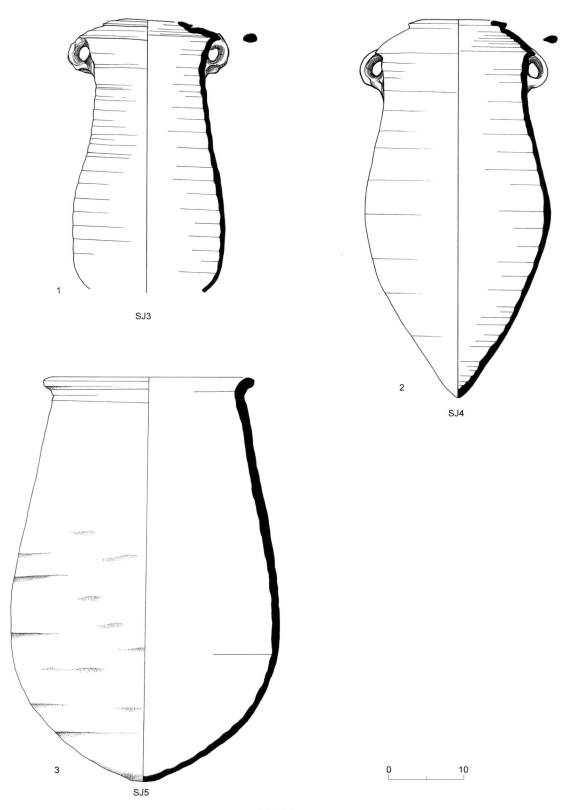

Fig. 5.6.

Type SJ 5

Holemouth jar. Long sack-shaped body, wall widening gradually, reaching its maximum width below center, narrowing toward a rounded base. No shoulder, thick everted rim. Coarse reddish-brown ware. This jar is the only example of its kind in the Akhziv repertoire.
Tomb: Z X:5.

TYPE HJ — HOLEMOUTH JARS (Fig. 5.7:1)

Type HJ1

Piriform body, deep depressed ring base. Curved wall ending in rounded thickened rim. Brownish-buff ware. Red paint covers the body except for a wide black band between pairs of black lines around the shoulder. Wheel-burnished all over.

This jar is unique in the Akhziv repertoire. Similar red-slipped jars were found at Amathus in Tomb 13 (Gjerstad 1948: Pl. XIX:1).
Tomb: Z III:6.

TYPE JG — JUGS (Figs. 5.7:2–9, 5.8–5.10)

Type JG1

Biconical-bodied jugs.

Type JG1 I. Biconical body, pedestal base. Elongated straight neck, trefoil mouth with two small knobs on rim at each side of the handle (Culican 1982:64). Handle drawn from rim to body slightly below neck. There are no incised lines and no ridge. Orange-buff ware, highly burnished dark red slip that goes over mouth. The jug is well-proportioned and the ware is metallic.

A close parallel comes from Ḥazor, Area A, Stratum IX–X, dated to the mid 10th–early 9th centuries BCE (Yadin et al. 1961: Pl. CLXXVII:15). Further examples are known from Kh. Silm (Chapman 1972: Fig. 27:148; Culican 1982: Fig. 8:a). This type of jug appears also in Cyprus, probably not before the early 8th century BCE (Gjerstad 1948: Fig. XLIII:11; Bikai 1987b: Pl. XIV: 363).

This type of trefoil-mouth jug seems to be a 10th century BCE precursor of the globular and piriform shapes that became widespread during the 9th–8th centuries BCE.
Tomb: Z XX:10.

Type JG1 II. Biconical body, pedestal base. Wide cylindrical neck with ridge at base. Single handle drawn from rim to shoulder. Knob below handle. Orange-buff ware with a thick red-burnished slip.

This jug is closely related to Type JG1 I, differing mainly in its wider neck. Its features are reminiscent of metal jugs. It has a close parallel at Ḥazor, Area A, Stratum IX–X, 10th century BCE (Yadin et al. 1961: Pl. CLXXVII:16).
Tombs: Z IW:10; ZR XXXIX:3.

Type JG1 III. Biconical body, pedestal base. Short, broad neck ending in trefoil mouth. Handle drawn from rim to shoulder with knob at base of handle and ridge at the base of neck. Gray ware, thick black-burnished slip.*

In character, this jug belongs to the Phoenician red-slip repertoire. A close parallel was found at Kh. Silm (Chapman 1972: Fig. 27:147) and a more remote comparison at Lachish (Tufnell 1953: Pl. 86:240). Another close parallel is known from Amathus, dated mid 9th– mid 8th centuries BCE (Bikai 1987a: Pl. IV:2). At Kition, it was suggested that black-burnished jugs with a similar body but a different neck were Phoenician (Karageorghis et al. 1981:27, Pl. XXVI:5).
Tombs: Z XX:11.

Type JG2

Trefoil-mouth jugs.

Type JG2 I. Globular or squat body, Akhziv base. Conical neck, ending in trefoil mouth. The width of the mouth varies considerably. Double-strand handle or flattened strap handle drawn from rim to base of neck. Ridge at base of neck and usually three incised lines around shoulder, probably imitations of decorations on metal vases. The ware is usually orange-buff, covered by a dark red slip extending over the mouth. The body is wheel-burnished, while the neck is vertically hand-burnished.

The vessel is outstanding in its good proportions and elegance. Its distinctive features suggest that it developed from metal prototypes.

Red-slip ware made up a good proportion of the pottery in the Phoenician homeland. This trefoil-mouth jug type is known from al-Mina, Strata VII–VI (Taylor 1952:83, Fig. 7:7), although fragments have been found already in Strata X–VIII, late 9th–8th centuries BCE.

---

*According to Ephraim Stern (pers. comm.), this was originally a red-slipped jug whose color changed as a result of blackening fire.

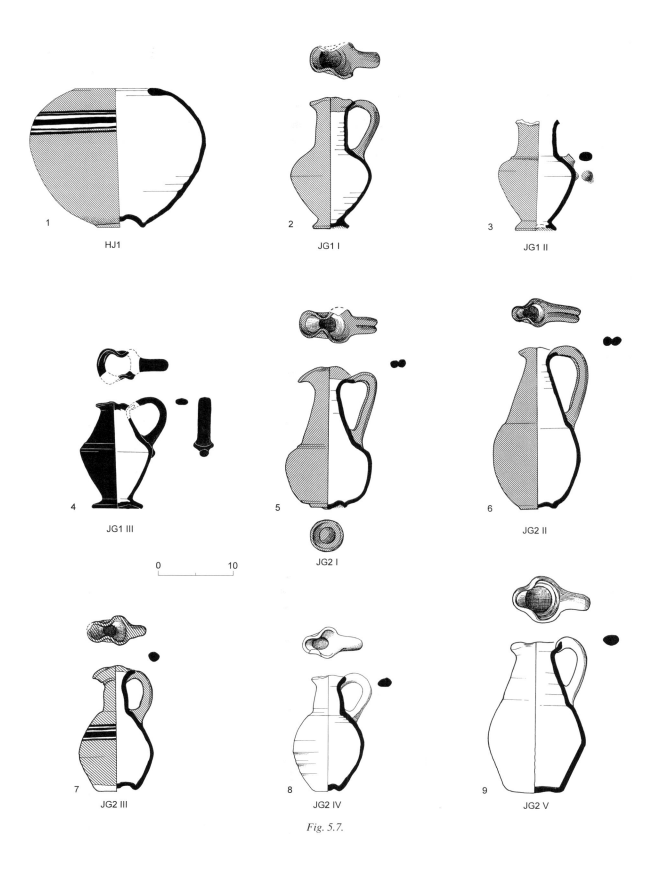

1 HJ1

2 JG1 I

3 JG1 II

4 JG1 III

5 JG2 I

6 JG2 II

0   10

7 JG2 III

8 JG2 IV

9 JG2 V

Fig. 5.7.

Further examples come from Khalde, Tomb III, late 9th–8th centuries BCE (Saidah 1966:61:9), Sarepta, Substratum C1, 8th–mid 7th century BCE (Anderson 1988: Pl. 37:1), Tyre, Stratum IV, mid 8th century BCE (Bikai 1978b:36) and Kh. Silm (Chapman 1972: Fig. 26:139). This type of jug, though with a wider base, makes an early appearance at Ḥazor, Area A, Stratum VII, 9th century BCE (Yadin et al. 1958: Pl. L:25). A late 9th–8th century BCE date seems appropriate for the Akhziv type.

Red-slipped jugs of this type occur frequently in Cyprus (Gjerstad 1948: Fig. XLIII:13; Bikai 1987b: Pl. XVI:391), as well as in the Punic world in the 7th–6th centuries BCE (Cintas 1950: Pl. LXXXI: 150, 151, 160, 193–195; Chapman 1972:167).
Tombs: Z IE:20–32; Z IW:11–16; Z III:7–9; Z V:1; Z XVIII:5, 6; Z XXI:3, 4; ZR IX:2, 3; ZR XI:2; ZR XIV:1–3; ZR XVII:9, 10; ZR XXIX:12; ZR XXXVI:12–15.

Type JG2 II. This jug is closely related to Type JG2 I. Piriform body, tapered neck and fairly wide Akhziv base. The trefoil mouth is relatively smaller than in Type JG2 I. A double rope handle extends from mouth to base of neck. Ridge where neck is joined to body and numerous incised lines around upper body. This type of jug has been influenced by manufacturing techniques for metal jugs (Amiran 1969:272). Orange-buff ware, red-slipped, burnished horizontally on body and vertically on neck and handle.

This jug type is probably later than Type JG2 I, beginning to appear in the latter part of the 8th century BCE. Parallels to this jug are known from Cyprus: a similar jug (upper part missing) comes from Salamis, Tomb 79, late 8th century BCE (Karageorghis 1974: Pl. CCXXVI:901); further parallels come from Amathus (Bikai 1987b: Pl. XVI: 373, 374).

Similar jugs are known particularly from Punic sites in the West, where they appear in metal, pottery and glass. They were found in graves in Spain at Almunecar (Prov. Granada), together with proto-Corinthian pottery dated to the early 7th century BCE (Catalan 1963: Pls. 4, 5). Further examples from Spain come from Toscanos, late 7th–6th centuries BCE (Lindemann et al. 1972:138, Fig. 6), and from Algarrobo (Prov. Malaga; Niemeyer et al. 1964:76, Fig. 2).
Tombs: Z IE:33–36; Z IW:17, 18; Z X:6–8; Z XXI:5, 6; ZR IV:1, 2; ZR XII:3, 4; ZR XXXVI:16.

Type JG2 III. Elongated ovoid body, Akhziv base. Tall narrow cylindrical neck ending in pinched mouth. Deep groove at base of rim. Single handle drawn from rim to shoulder. Coarse orange-yellow to brownish-yellow ware, covered with red slip, with the exception of the base. Shoulder decorated with black-painted bands, probably an attempt to imitate the traditional Black-on-Red decoration.
Tomb: ZR XI:3.

Type JG2 IV. Ovoid body, roughly made Akhziv base. Truncated neck ending in a pinched rim. Single handle drawn from rim to shoulder. Coarse reddish-brown ware rich in white grits. This type of jug shows a close resemblance to Type JG2 III in its general shape and ware. It differs mainly in the shape of its neck and in its lack of decoration.
Tombs: ZR V:1; ZR XXXVI:17.

Type JG2 V. Biconical body, Akhziv base. Truncated neck ending in funnel-shaped pinched rim. Single handle drawn from rim to shoulder. Coarse reddish-brown ware rich in white grits. The jug is an imitation of inferior quality of the classical Akhziv trefoil-mouth jugs (see Type JG2 II). Its degenerate form indicates a date not earlier than the late 8th–7th centuries BCE.
Tomb: ZR XI:4.

Type JG3
Jugs.

Type JG3 I. Globular body, ring base. Slightly truncated long neck, pinched mouth. Handle drawn from rim to shoulder. This type is closely related in shape to Type JG2 I, though inferior in quality and made of coarse reddish-brown ware; it should be dated to the late 8th–7th centuries BCE. A variant of this type has a red-burnished slip.
Tombs: Z X:9; Z XX:14; ZR XVII:11; ZR XXXVI:18.

Type JG3 II. Globular body, Akhziv base. Tall flaring neck ending in pinched rim. Strap handle drawn from rim to shoulder. Orange-brown ware, buff wash all over. The jug is close in its shape and coarse ware to Type JG3 I, but with a different neck. It is another variant of the traditional Akhziv pinched-mouth jug.
Tombs: Z XX:12; ZR XXXIX:4.

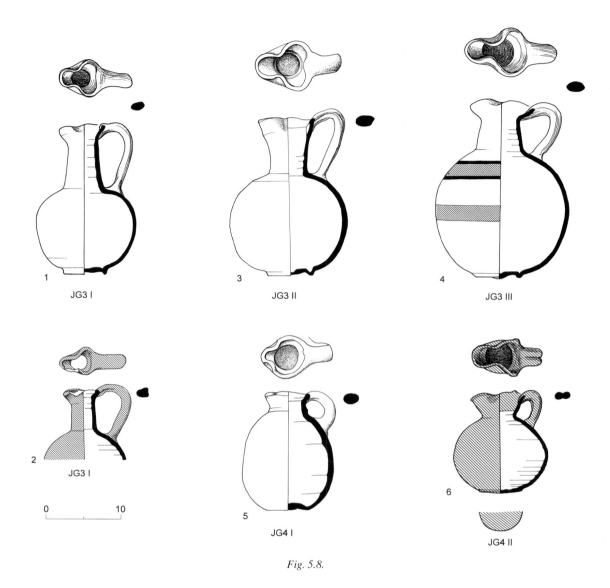

Fig. 5.8.

Type JG3 III. Globular or ovoid body, Akhziv base. Short truncated neck, ending in pinched rim. Single handle drawn from rim to shoulder. Coarse reddish-buff ware. Some specimens have a bichrome decoration of reddish bands, between black lines.

A smaller variant of this type is of well-levigated ware, red-slipped and burnished.
Tombs: Z III:10; ZR IX:4, 5; ZR XXXVI:19–21.

Type JG4
Type JG4 I. Piriform body. String-cut base. Short, wide flaring neck, with ridge at base, ending in a pinched rim.

Handle drawn from rim to shoulder. Coarse pinkish-brown ware, white grits.
Tomb: ZR XIV:4.

Type JG4 II. Globular body, flat disk base. Short flaring neck, pinched mouth. Two small knobs on rim at each side of handle. Double handle drawn from rim to shoulder. The fine orange-buff ware is well-levigated. Dark red slip extending over the mouth, wheel-burnished all over.

The jug is outstanding in its good proportions. Its shape, including the two knobs on the rim, suggests a metallic prototype. An example in silver is known from

Cyprus (Gjerstad 1948:160:5). The jug belongs to the classic red-slipped jugs of the 9th–8th centuries BCE. Several identical jugs of this type were found at Akhziv. *Tombs:* Z IE:37; ZR IX:6, 7; ZR XXIX:13, 14.

Type JG5
Jugs with mushroom or related rims.

Type JG5 1. This type of jug is notable for its classic Phoenician mushroom rim. Ovoid body, Akhziv base. The shoulder is carinated with incised lines immediately below it. Elongated neck divided into two parts by pronounced ridge or two grooves. Lower part roughly cylindrical, while upper part narrows toward the top, tapering to strongly everted mushroom rim. Small handle drawn from near base of neck to shoulder. Orange-buff, well-levigated ware, covered with a thick dark red burnished slip, which extends over the whole surface including base and rim.

The general shape of these jugs is strongly reminiscent of the decanter, one of the most popular shapes of the period, found mainly in the southern and central parts of Israel. The Akhziv jugs are, on the whole, of a better finish than the decanter, but the affinity is striking.

The red-slipped jug with a mushroom rim is very common at Akhziv. It is otherwise known on the mainland, for instance, from Ḥazor, Area B, Stratum VA, 8th century BCE (Yadin et al. 1960: Pl. 88:5).

At Tyre it was common in Strata III–II, second half of the 8th century BCE (Bikai 1978b: Pls. V: 19, 20; VI:5). Such jugs are also known from Khalde, Tomb I (Saidah 1966:58:2) and Qraye (Chapman 1972: Fig. 27:300), as well as al-Mina, Levels VII–VI, 8th century BCE (Taylor 1952:84).

Similar jugs occur at various sites in Cyprus such as Kition (Karageorghis et al. 1981: Pl. XXII:4), Salamis (Karageorghis 1974: Pl. CCXXVI:79) and Amathus (Bikai 1987b: Pl. XIII: 274, 285). They are commonly found on Punic sites in the west dated to the 7th century BCE: Carthage (Cintas 1950: Types 65, 66); Algarrobo (Niemeyer et al. 1964: Fig. 2:a); and Almunecar (Catalan 1963: Fig. 11:3; 12:3).
Tombs: Z IE:38–46; Z IW:19; Z III:11, 12; Z X:10–12, 14, 15; Z XVIII:7; Z XXI:7, 8; ZR XI:5; ZR XVII:12; ZR XXIX:15, 17; ZR XXXVI:22, 23, 25.

Type JG5 II. This type is closely related to Type JG5 I in having a mushroom rim and a similar neck, handle and base. The main difference lies in the body, which is squat–globular, reminiscent of the classic decanter body. Orange-buff ware, dark red burnished slip. This vessel represents the typical features of the classical red-slip jugs dated to the 9th–8th centuries BCE.
Tombs: Z III:13, 14; Z X:17; ZR IX:8; ZR XXIX:16; ZR XXXVI:24, 26–28.

Type JG5 III. Small jug. Globular body, Akhziv base. Long cylindrical neck with groove in the middle. Loop handle drawn from lower part of neck to shoulder. Rim missing. Orange-buff ware with thick dark red burnished slip. The shape of the vessel suggests a strongly everted rim.

Similar small jugs are known from Tell Abu Hawam, probably Stratum III, 9th century BCE (Hamilton 1935: Pl. XIII:67) and Megiddo, Stratum III, 8th century BCE (Lamon and Shipton 1939: Pl. 1:40). This type of jug occurs in Cyprus in Tomb 367/51–2 in Amathus, dated to the 8th century BCE (Bikai 1987b: Pl. XIII:295).
Tombs: Z IE:47; Z X:18; ZR XXIX:18.

Type JG5 IV. This group is definitely related to Type JG5 on account of the mushroom rim and the shape of the neck. The main difference lies in the shape of the body, which is piriform and lacks a defined shoulder. The ware is plain, buff in color and rarely covered with a slip. The lack of slip and burnishing is compensated in some cases by painted red bands on the upper half of the neck or shoulder. A small variant of this type, differing mainly in its flat base, is also known from the Akhziv burials.

Similar jugs are known from Tell Keisan, Stratum V, late 8th–7th centuries BCE (Briend and Humbert 1980: Pl. 44:3) and from Tyre, Stratum I, c. 700 BCE (Bikai 1978b: Pl. I:3). In Cyprus they occur at sites such as Kition (Karageorghis et al. 1981: Pl. XXII:4). This Phoenician jug is a common type at Akhziv and should be dated to the last third of the 8th century BCE.
Tombs: Z IE:48, 60; Z X:19; ZR XI:6; ZR XIV:5–7; ZR XVII:14; ZR XXXVI:29–34; ZR XLIII:1.

Type JG5 V. Elongated body, carinated above base and at shoulder, ring base. Truncated neck, with ridge at base, ending in narrow mushroom rim. Coarse reddish-brown ware. This jug is a degenerate variant of the classic mushroom-rim. The body is reminiscent of the decanter.
Tombs: ZR XII:5; ZR XXXVI:35, 37.

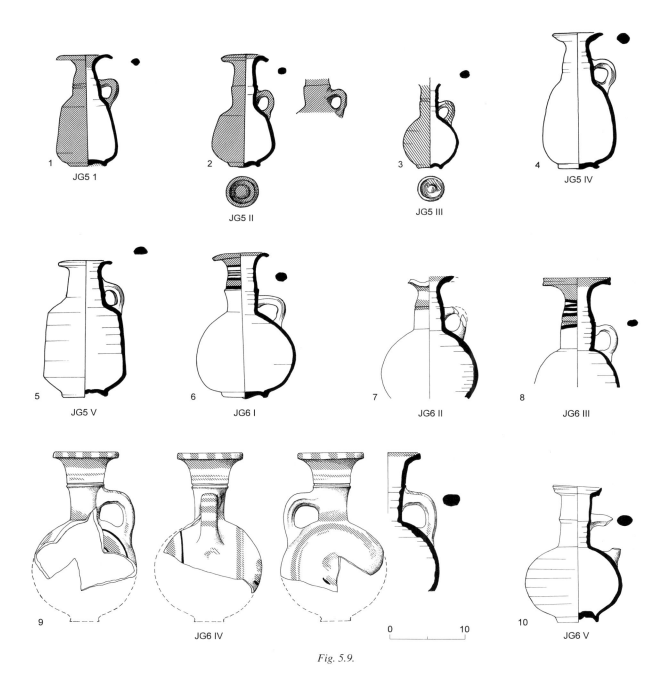

1 JG5 1
JG5 II
JG5 III
4 JG5 IV
5 JG5 V
6 JG6 I
7 JG6 II
8 JG6 III
9 JG6 IV
10 JG6 V

0 10

Fig. 5.9.

Type JG6

Jugs with broad rims and usually decorated.

Type JG6 I. This type of jug is characterized by its mushroom-shaped or broadly flaring rim and bichrome decoration on neck. Globular body, Akhziv base. Ridge on neck and small loop handle drawn from ridge, or just below it, to shoulder. In some specimens, the handle is thick and coarse. The rims are basically of two types: a squared-off rim or a wider tapering mushroom rim. Most of these jugs are of pinkish-yellow ware. They are decorated in the bichrome style with dark reddish-purple and black bands on the neck and rim above the ridge, and lack a red slip. Some are burnished all over.

This type of jug is very common on the Phoenician coast, where it can be traced as early as the late 10th–early 9th centuries BCE. Similar in shape and decoration is a jug found at Ḥazor, Stratum Xb, mid 10th century

BCE (Yadin et al. 1961: Pl. CCCLV:13). These jugs are also known from Megiddo, Stratum IV, 9th century BCE (Loud 1948: Pl. 91:4). Further parallels come from Sarepta, Stratum E (Anderson 1988: Pl. 31:15); Kh. Silm (Chapman 1972: Fig. 6:33, 40, 41, 178); al-Mina, Stratum VIII, late 9th–8th centuries BCE (Taylor 1959: Fig. 2:9–11, 13) and Tyre, Stratum IV, mid-8th century BCE or earlier (Bikai 1978b: Pl. 14:5).

This type is infrequent in Cyprus. However examples are known from Kition (Bikai 1981: Pl. 23:2–4). In Cyprus, it appears also in silver (Myres 1914:466:4586). Such jugs were also found at Carthage and at almost every other Punic site. Their presence at sites beyond the Phoenician sphere reflects extensive trade (Chapman 1972:154).

Tombs: Z IE:50–54; Z IW:21; Z I Vestibule:3; Z IV:1–3; Z VI:6; Z X:20; Z XX:15–21; ZR II:1; ZR IX:10, 11; ZR XVII:15, 16; ZR XXIX:19, 20; ZR XXX:1; ZR XXXVI:38–50.

Type JG6 II. To a certain degree, this group is related to Type JG6 I in its globular body, the shape of its neck, the loop handle drawn from neck to shoulder and the painted decoration. The main difference lies in the style of decoration which consists of red bands only on the upper neck and rim. The buff ware is well-levigated and burnished.

Tombs: Z III:15, 16, ZR IX:9.

Type JG6 III. Elongated ovoid body, long truncated neck tapering to strongly everted mushroom rim, occasionally squared-off. Loop handle drawn from neck to shoulder. Upper part of neck and rim decorated with black and red bands. Reddish-brown to orange-buff ware, sometimes burnished. This type of jug is a later imitation of the JG6 I jugs, but differs in the shape of the body and the careless attention to decoration.

Similar jugs were found in burials at 'Atlit (Johns 1938:143: Fig. 7:1). They are known from Tyre, Stratum III, second half of the 8th century BCE (Bikai 1978b: Pl. V:14), as well as from Cyprus (Bikai 1987b: Pl. XII: 271).

Tombs: Z IE:56–59; Z IW:22; Z XVIII:8; ZR XIV:8, 9; ZR XXVI:4; ZR XXXVI:52, 53.

Type JG6 IV. Globular body, long flaring ridged neck, ending in an everted squared-off rim. Single handle drawn from below ridge to shoulder. Orange-buff ware. Red concentric circles on body, confined by traces of a black line. Red horizontal strokes on handle, red bands around base of neck and upward from ridge.

Similar jugs with bichrome decoration are known from Megiddo dated to the Iron I (Guy and Engberg 1938: Pl. 66:20). Further examples are known from Tyre, Strata VIII–IX, 9th century BCE (Bikai 1978b: Pl. XXI:9, 10), Kh. Silm and Qasmieh (Chapman 1972: Figs. 5:57, 32:313), as well as from sites in Cyprus such as Episkopi and Pentakomo (Bikai 1987b: Pl. IX:168–169). This Phoenician jug should be dated to the 9th–8th centuries BCE in view of its parallels and the context in which it was found.

Tomb: Z IW:23.

Type JG6 V. Globular body, degenerate Akhziv base. Tall ridged neck, funnel-shaped rim. Handle drawn from ridge to shoulder.

This type of jug is closely related in shape to Type JG6 I, but is made of heavy, coarse, grayish-brown ware and lacks decoration. The careless execution of this vessel suggests a date not before the late 8th–7th centuries BCE. An identical jug was found in Prausnitz's excavations at Akhziv (Prausnitz 1972:152:4, 155).

Tombs: Z IE:61, 62; Z XI:11, 12; Z XVIII:9; ZR XXXVI: 54.

Type JG7
Jugs related to Type JG6.

Type JG7 I. This type of jug is closely related to Type JG6 I on account of its globular body, Akhziv base, long ridged neck and bichrome decoration. Unlike Type JG6 I, it ends in a straight to slightly everted rim. Buff ware, decorated on neck above ridge, on rim and on body with red bands between black lines.

A similar neck is known from Tyre, Strata III–II (Bikai 1978b: Pl. VI:6). Reminiscent in shape is a jug from Megiddo, Stratum V (Lamon and Shipton 1939: Pl. 7:172) and a jug from a tomb on Mt. Carmel (Guy 1924: Pl. III:27). This jug should be dated to the late 9th century BCE.

Tombs: Z IW:24; ZR XVII:3; ZR XXIX:21.

Type JG7 II. Globular body, Akhziv base. Cylindrical ridged neck, widening above ridge. Loop handle drawn from neck, below ridge, to shoulder. Wide red band on upper part of neck. Pinkish-buff ware with gray core. A similar jug was found in Shikmona, dated to the Persian period (Elgavish 1968: Pl. XXXIII:16).

Tomb: ZR XXVI:5.

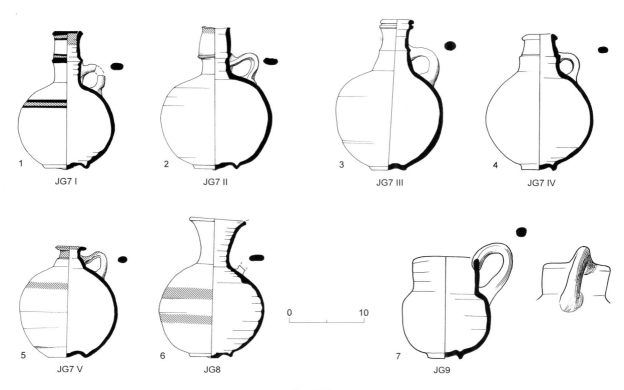

Fig. 5.10.

Type JG7 III. Jugs with ridged neck. This jug is closely related to Type JG7 IV, whose globular body is here slightly piriform. It has an Akhziv base and belongs to the 'neck ridge' family. Handle drawn from ridge to shoulder. Concave neck, taller than Type JG7 IV, ending in thickened rim with deep groove in the middle. Reddish-brown, coarse, heavy and gritty ware.
Tombs: Z IE:63; Z XX:22, ZR XXXV:55, 57.

Type JG7 IV. Globular body, Akhziv base. Wide and ridged neck, narrowing toward an everted rim. Reddish-brown to light buff coarse ware, rich in white grits. This type of plain, ridged-neck jug appears at Ḥazor, Area A, Stratum VIII, 9th century BCE (Yadin et al. 1960: Pl. LVIII:20). It is also known from Tyre, Stratum III, second half of the 8th century BCE (Bikai 1978b: Pl. V:5), as well as from Joya (Chapman 1972: Fig. 7:176).
Tombs: Z IE:64; Z IW:25; ZR IX:12, 13; ZR XXXVI:58; ZR XXXVII:1.

Type JG7 V. Globular body, Akhziv base. Short swollen neck, sometimes ridged, tapering to an everted flattened rim. Small loop handle drawn from mid-neck to shoulder.

Brownish-buff ware. The decoration varies between a red band on body and rim, to bichrome decoration on body and red paint on rim, occasionally burnished.

This Phoenician jug has close parallels at Ḥazor, Area A, Stratum VI, 8th century BCE (Yadin et al. 1958: Pl. LII:23), as well as at Tyre, Stratum III, second half of the 8th century BCE (Bikai 1978b: Pl. V:1–4). Similar jugs occur in Cyprus at Ayia Irini (Bikai 1987b: Pl. X:330).
Tombs: ZR IV:3; ZR VI:5, 7; ZR XXXVI:59.

Type JG8
Globular body, Akhziv base. Long flaring neck ending in everted rounded rim. Handle drawn from rim to shoulder. Brownish-buff ware, well-levigated and burnished all over. Wide red bands on body. This type of jug shows strong connections to Type JG6 I in its globular body, base and ware, differing mainly in its flaring neck, rim and handle.

A jug from Megiddo, Stratum V (Lamon and Shipton 1939: Pl. 7:173) is similar in shape, although its decoration is different.
Tomb: Z IW:26.

Type JG9

Squat body, Akhziv base. High straight and wide neck ending in rounded rim. High loop handle drawn from rim to shoulder. Light reddish-brown ware, rich in white grits.

A jug from Samaria (Crowfoot, Crowfoot and Kenyon 1957: Fig. 5:3) is reminiscent in shape. A closer parallel comes from Tyre, Stratum III, second half of the 8th century BCE (Bikai 1978b: Pl. VI:7).
Tomb: ZR IX:14.

Jugs — Miscellaneous

Included here are jugs which are variants or very similar to the above sub-types, but did not quite fit into any of those categories.

TYPE PF — PILGRIM FLASKS (Fig. 5.11:1–3)

Type PF1

Lentoid body, occasionally with protruding center. In some cases one side of body is flat and the other rounded. Long and flaring neck ends in simple rim. Two handles are drawn from mid-neck to shoulder. Coarse reddish-brown to grayish ware. The flasks are decorated with black concentric circles on both sides of the body, but some are time-worn so that the decoration has disappeared.

This type of flask is of typical Phoenician style. Several such flasks are known from Khalde (Saidah 1966: Nos. 50, 51, 54) and Kh. Silm (Chapman 1972: Fig. 13:63, 73). They appear in a tomb at Tell el-Far'ah (South) (Petrie 1930: Pl. XLI:221) and at Tell Abu Hawam, Stratum III (Hamilton 1935:19:54, 55). Large numbers were found in Cyprus, e.g. in Palaepaphos-Skales Tombs 49 and 76, dated to the 10th century BCE (Karageorghis 1983: Figs. LXXX:189, 191; CXL:2). These flasks were found in large numbers in the Akhziv tombs and they are probably not later than the 10th century BCE.
Tombs: Z IE:65–70; IW:27–33; Z VI:7; Z X:21–23; Z XI:13–20; Z XX:23–34; ZR IV:4; ZR XVI:1; ZR XXXVI:60–62.

Type PF2

Miniature pilgrim flask. Globular body, rounded base, long neck and flaring rim. Two outsize irregular handles are drawn from mid-neck to body. Coarse brownish-gray ware, well-fired.

These carelessly made small flasks were probably produced specially as funerary offerings. They are fairly common at Akhziv.

A close parallel comes from Tell Abu Hawam, Stratum III, dated 10th–9th centuries BCE (Hamilton 1935:19:56).
Tombs: Z XX:35–40; ZR XXXIX:5.

Type PF3

Asymmetrical body, one side lentoid, the other convex. Shoulder tapering to short wide cylindrical neck ending in straight rim. A groove runs along both sides bridged by four lug handles, each pierced twice. Gray ware, thick black-burnished slip.

This unique vessel is a reduced version of large pilgrim flasks with similar features known from Megiddo, Stratum IV (Lamon and Shipton 1939: Pl. 36:2; Loud 1948: Pl. 91:9) and Joya (Chapman 1972: Fig. 17:195). No parallels were found to this small flask, which must have contained some precious liquid.
Tomb: Z XX:41.

TYPE DJ — DIPPER JUGLETS (Fig. 5.11:4–7)

Type DJ1

Sack-shaped body, carelessly formed. Irregular rounded base often protruding in center. Wide short everted rim rising from sharp angle on the body. High loop handle drawn from rim to shoulder. Rather coarse clay, usually light buff to reddish-brown.

This juglet appears frequently in tombs. It is common at Tyre, Stratum III, 8th century BCE (Bikai 1978b: Pl. XXI:1–16). Examples were found at many other sites such as Tell Keisan, Levels V–IV, 8th–7th centuries BCE (Briend and Humbert 1980: Pls. 28:11, 43:8–8a), Ḥazor, Area B, Stratum VB, 8th century BCE (Yadin et al. 1961: Pl. CCXXIV:7) and Megiddo, Strata III–I, 8th–7th centuries BCE (Lamon and Shipton 1939: Pl. 1:13).
Tombs: Z IE:71, 72; Z IW:34–37; Z III:17; Z X:24, 25; Z XVIII:10–13; ZR V:2–4; ZR VI:6; ZR IX:15–17; ZR XI:7–12; ZR XII:6–9; ZR XIV:10, 11; ZR XVII:17, 18; ZR XXVIII:1–3; ZR XXIX:22–25; ZR XXXVI:63–74; ZR XXXIX:6; ZR XLIII:2.

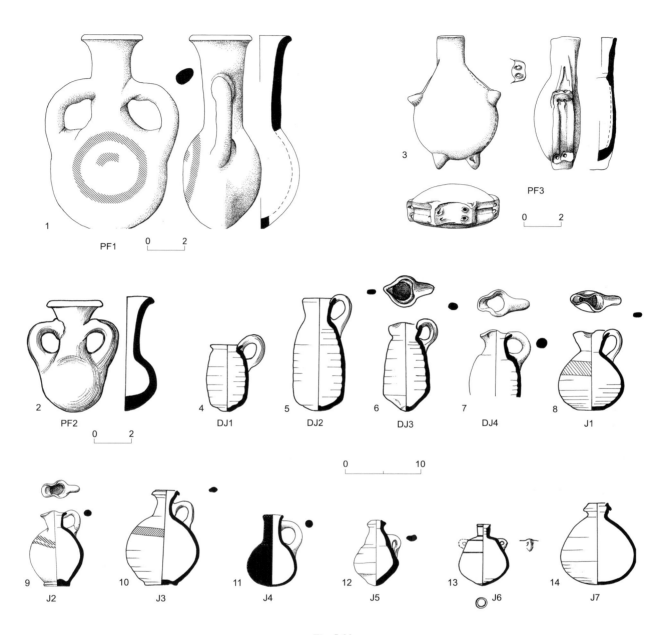

Fig. 5.11.

Type DJ2

Cylindrical body, rounded base. Flaring neck ending in a simple rim. Loop handle drawn from rim to shoulder. The gritty coarse ware is reddish-brown.

This dipper juglet is a very common form in the Iron Age and is frequently found in burials. It appears at Khalde, Level III, 8th century BCE (Saidah 1966:71:34), Tyre, Stratum III, 8th century BCE (Bikai 1978b: Pl. XII:18–20) and Kh. Silm (Chapman 1972: Fig. 23:86).

Further examples come from Ḥazor, Area A, Stratum VI, 8th century BCE (Yadin et al. 1960: Pl. LXX:2, 3).

Tombs: Z IE:73–82; Z IW:38–41; Z III:18–21; Z IV:4, 5; Z X:26, 27; Z XVIII:14; Z XX:42–46; Z XXI:9, 10; ZR IX:18; ZR XXIX:26, 27; ZR XXXVI:75, 76.

Type DJ3

Cylindrical body, irregular pointed base. Flaring neck tapering to a pinched rim. Loop handle drawn from rim to

shoulder. Coarse greenish-light buff ware. This type of juglet is closely related to Type DJ1, differing mainly in its pinched rim.
Tomb: ZR IX:19.

Type DJ4

Cylindrical body, concave flaring neck ending in a pinched rim. Handle drawn from rim to shoulder. Pinkish-buff ware with white grits.

Similar juglets are known from Ḥazor, Area A, Stratum VI, 8th century BCE (Yadin et al. 1960: Pl. LXX:8), Tell Abu Hawam, Stratum III, 10th–9th centuries BCE (Hamilton 1935:20:57) and other sites.
Tomb: Z XI:21.

TYPE J — JUGLETS (Fig. 5.11:8–14)

Type J1

Juglet. Piriform body, flat base. Short flaring neck and pinched mouth. Loop handle drawn from rim to shoulder. Light buff ware, well-levigated, wide red band on shoulder.
Tomb: ZR XXIX:28.

Type J2

Juglet. Piriform body, flat base. Short cylindrical neck ending in pinched rim. Handle drawn from rim to shoulder. Orange-buff ware. White wash. Red band on shoulder.

A close parallel is known from Shikmona, dated to the Persian period (Elgavish 1968: Pl. XXXII:2). A jug similar in shape from Salamis is dated to the 6th century BCE (Karageorghis 1970: Pl. LXX:4).
Tomb: ZR XII:10.

Type J3

Juglet. Globular body, flat base. Concave neck ending in everted rim. Loop handle drawn from mid-neck to shoulder. Reddish-brown ware. White wash. Red band on shoulder below handle.
Tomb: ZR XXXVI:77.

Type J4

Juglet. Globular body, slightly pointed or rounded base. Straight or slightly concave neck, simple rim. Handle drawn from below rim to shoulder. Grayish coarse ware, black burnished slip.

These juglets are found at numerous sites, both in the north and the south of Israel. They appear in the 10th century BCE at sites such as Tel Mevorakh (Stern 1978: Pl. 31:6, 7) and Megiddo (Guy and Engberg 1938: Pl. 62:14, 63:6). They continue throughout the Iron Age at Megiddo, Stratum III, 8th century BCE (Lamon and Shipton 1939: Pl. 2:44, 49, 50), Tell Beit Mirsim, Stratum A (Albright 1943: Pl. 18:8) and Be'er Sheva', Stratum II, 8th century BCE (Aharoni 1970: Pl. 69:16).
Tombs: ZR IX:20; ZR XXIX:29; ZR XXXIX:7.

Type J5

Juglet. Piriform body widening below center and narrowing toward rounded base. Bulging neck, tapering to narrow mouth, defined by a thick sloping rim. Handle drawn from mid-neck to shoulder. Thick coarse reddish-brown ware.

Juglets of this type, frequently called ampullae, are rare on mainland sites. They appear mainly in the western Mediterranean. A large number of such ampullae are reported from Mogador (Culican 1970:5). Further parallels are known from Utica (Culican 1970:5) and other sites, all dated to the 7th century BCE. These juglets are associated with oil or perfume and may have served as lamp-oil containers (Culican 1970:6).
Tomb: ZR XXIV:2.

Type J6

Amphoriskos. Sack-shaped body, convex base, bottom marked with small incised circle. Carinated shoulder, narrow neck, relatively thick in section, forming a narrow opening. Diagonally inverted rim. Small perforation on shoulder facilitated the pouring of liquids. Two pierced vertical lug handles drawn from carination on shoulder to body. Orange-buff ware, burnished. Thin black line decorates middle of body, shoulder and rim.
Tombs: ZR XXXVI:78.

Type J7

Bottle. Piriform body, rounded base. Short narrow neck ending in sharply everted rim. No handles. Light buff ware.

Identical bottles were found at sites on the inner Judean plain such as Tel Batash, dated to the 7th century BCE (Kelm and Mazar 1985:115:4). This type of bottle is influenced by the Assyrian tradition and shows great similarity to Assyrian bottles, examples of which are known from Megiddo, Strata II–I (Lamon and Shipton 1939: Pl. 9:4–7).
Tomb: ZR IX:21.

Type C — Cooking Pots (Fig. 5.12:1–4)

Type C1

Two handles and thick, straight ridged rim. Handles drawn from ridge to shoulder. Reddish-brown coarse ware rich in white grits.

Similar cooking pots are known from Ḥazor, Area B, Stratum Va, 8th century BCE (Yadin et al. 1960: Pl. XCIV:16), Tel Mikhal, Stratum XII, 8th century BCE (Herzog, Rapp and Negbi 1989: Fig. 7.4:5) and other sites.

Tomb: Z VI:8.

Type C2

Carinated shoulder ending in ridge at the base of the neck. Short thickened and rounded rim. Handles drawn from ridge to shoulder. Coarse reddish-brown ware with white grits.

A similar cooking pot is known from Ḥazor, Area A, Stratum VIII, 9th century (Yadin et al. 1960: Pl. LVII:26).

Tombs: ZR XIV:12; ZR XXVIII:5.

Type C3

Biconical wall inclined sharply inward, tapering to squared-off rim, thickened on exterior. Two handles drawn from rim to shoulder. Grayish coarse ware, white grits.

This type of cooking pot appears at Ḥazor, Area A, Stratum VI, 8th century BCE (Yadin et al. 1961: Pl. CLXXXIV:6) and Gezer, Stratum VIA, mid 8th century BCE (Gitin 1990: Pl. 22:5), as well as at Taanach, Period V, in the first half of the 7th century BCE (Rast 1978: Fig. 76:6).

Tombs: Z IE:83; Z IW:42.

Type C4

Miniature cooking pot. Carinated near base. Rounded base, center missing. Rim is thickened on exterior, forming an angle just below rim edge. Short neck, two small loop handles drawn from rim to shoulder. Fine reddish-buff ware, well-levigated.

A cooking pot similar in shape occurs at Tyre, Stratum III, 8th century BCE (Bikai 1978b: Pl. XII:24).

Tombs: Z XXI:11; ZR XXIX:30.

Type MV — Miniature Vessels (Fig. 5.12:5–10)

Type MV1

Miniature jar. Squat body, rounded base. Carinated shoulder, wide straight neck ending in squared-off or rounded rim. Two vertical lug handles below carinated shoulder. Reddish-brown ware, white grits.

This type of vessel shows affinities to the Iron Age pyxis, e.g. an example from Megiddo, Stratum III, 8th century BCE (Lamon and Shipton 1939: Pl. 9:35). However, some of its features suggest a closer affinity to the group of miniature jars.

Tomb: ZR XXXVI:79.

Type MV2

Miniature jar. Sack-shaped body, rounded base. Wall tapering to carinated shoulder, straight wide neck ending in thickened flat squared-off rim. Vertical knob handles project from the carination. Reddish-brown ware, white grits.

Tomb: ZR XXIX:31.

Type MV3

Miniature jar. Squat body, widening toward rounded base. Wide slanting shoulder forms a sharp angle with vessel wall. Straight neck tapers to slightly thickened rounded rim. Loop handles drawn from carinated shoulder to body. Reddish-brown ware, white grits.

This type of vessel is a reduced form of jars known from sites such as 'Atlit (Johns 1938: Fig. 7:2), where they were used as burial urns.

Tomb: ZR XXIX:32.

Type MV4

Miniature jar. Sack-shaped body, widening toward rounded base. Sharply carinated shoulder, short vertical square rim with flattened lip. Pierced lug handles drawn from carination to body. Coarse reddish-brown ware, white grits.

This vessel is a smaller form of sack-shaped storage jars known from sites such as Megiddo, Stratum I, Persian period (Lamon and Shipton 1939: Pl. 14:73) and Tel Mikhal, Stratum IX, Persian period (Herzog, Rapp and Negbi 1989: Fig. 9.3:7, 8).

Tomb: ZR XXVIII:4.

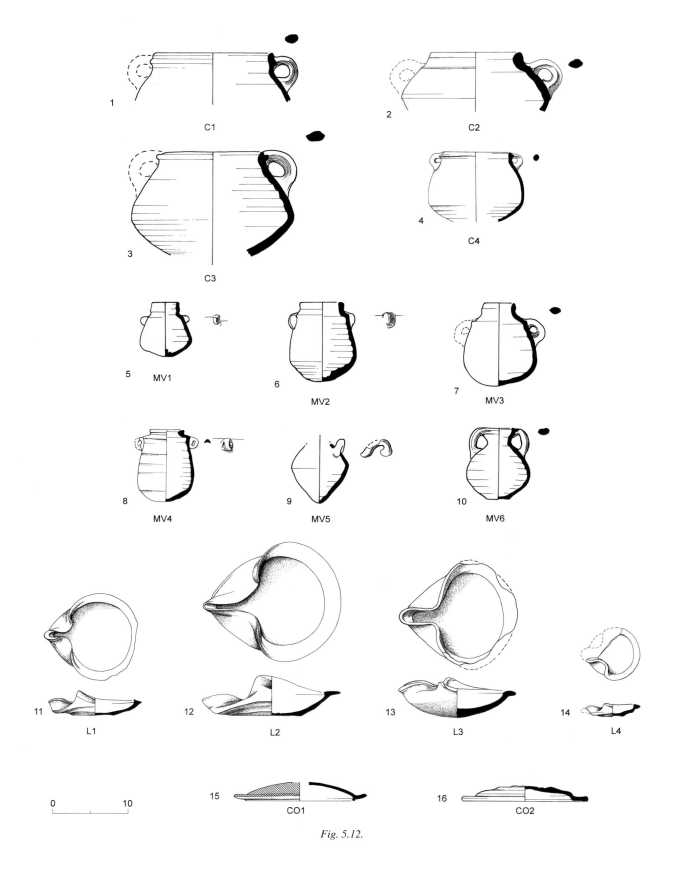

Fig. 5.12.

Type MV5

Miniature amphora. Conical body, tapering to pointed base. Carinated shoulder. Two carelessly attached basket handles rise from shoulder. Fairly thin yellowish-buff ware.

This type of vessel is a miniature form reminiscent of the basket-handled storage jar of the Persian period. It was locally produced and was used for funerary offerings.

Large amphorae of this kind were widespread in the maritime trade of the period and have been found along the Mediterranean coast. They appear at the end of the Iron Age at Meṣad Hashavyahu (Naveh 1962: Fig. 6:13), and are known from the 6th–5th centuries BCE at numerous sites such as Tell Keisan (Briend and Humbert 1980: Pl. 24:1, 4) and Tel Mikhal (Herzog, Rapp and Negbi 1989:116–118).
Tomb: ZR XII:11.

Type MV6

Miniature amphora. Globular body, flat base. Wide flaring neck, flat rim. Two handles drawn from rim to shoulder. Ribbed surface, greenish-buff ware.

This vessel is a small version of the amphorae of the Persian period.
Tomb: ZR XII:12.

Type L — Lamps (Fig. 5.12:11–14)

Type L1

Shallow saucer with broad horizontal flange ending in tapered lip and well-pinched mouth. Rounded shaved base. Pinkish-buff ware.

This characteristically Persian-period lamp is known from Tel Megadim (unpublished) and other sites.
Tomb: Z XIII:1.

Type L2

Deep saucer, broad horizontal flange ending in tapered rim, pinched long mouth, flat base.

This typically Persian-period lamp is known from the 6th century BCE and throughout the Persian period. It has parallels at Tel Mikhal, Stratum XI (Herzog, Rapp and Negbi 1989: Fig. 9.1:8) and Stratum VIII (Herzog, Rapp and Negbi 1989: Fig. 9.7:6, 7) and Dor (Stern 1994b:148), as well as Shikmona (Elgavish 1968: Pl. LI:108).
Tomb: Z XIII:2.

Type L3

Deep saucer, convex everted flange, rounded base, pinched mouth. Coarse heavy reddish-brown ware, white grits.

Similar lamps dating to the Persian period are known from Tel Michal, Stratum VII (Herzog, Rapp and Negbi 1989: Fig. 9.8:12).
Tombs: Z XVIII:15; ZR XXXIX:8.

Type L4

Small lamp. Shallow saucer, flattened disk base, stepped wall ending in flat everted flange. Brownish-buff ware.
Tomb: ZR XII:13.

Type CO — Covers (Fig. 5.12:15, 16)

Type CO1

Shallow domed dish-shaped cover, wide, flat everted rim. Pronounced ridge on interior. Pinkish-buff ware, red slip and burnish on exterior, plain on interior. Center missing.

Similar covers, mostly with knob handles, are known from Tyre, Strata III–II, 8th century BCE (Bikai 1978b: Pl. X:3, 5, 6) and Kition (Bikai 1981: Pl. XX:7–11). Examples of similar covers placed on urns are known from the Punic cemetery at Carthage (Stager and Wolff 1984:30–51). Several urn covers were found in burials in the southern cemetery at Akhziv excavated by Prausnitz (Prausnitz 1982:35).
Tomb: ZR XVII:19.

Type CO2

Cover(?). Shallow dish, wide horizontal thickened rim, squared-off rim, flat base. Coarse reddish-brown ware.

Close parallels defined as urn covers are known from Khalde, dated to the late 9th–8th centuries BCE (Saidah 1966:61:7). Further parallels come from Tyre, Stratum III, 8th century BCE (Bikai 1978b: Pl. IX:12).
Tombs: ZR XXIV:3.

Type CP — Cypriot and Cypro-Phoenician Vessels (Figs. 5.13–5.15)
Black-on-Red and Bichrome vessels.

Type CP1

Jug. Globular body, Akhziv base. Cylindrical ridged neck, slightly flaring toward thickened rim. Handle

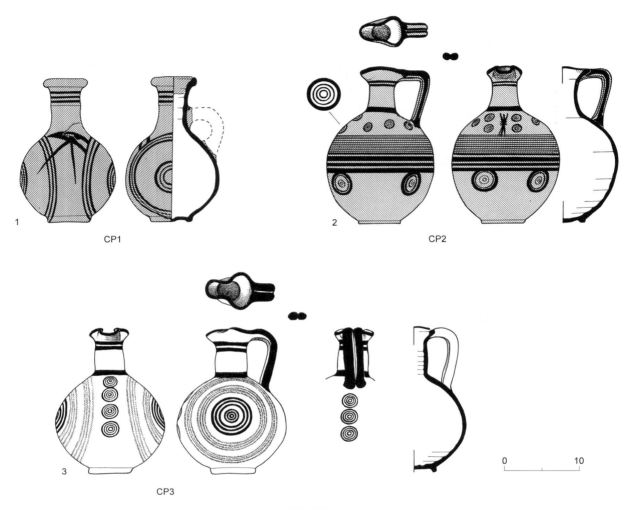

Fig. 5.13.

drawn from ridge, or just below it, to shoulder. Orange-buff ware. Dark red slip, hand-burnished. Black concentric circles on both sides of body and black lines on neck and handle. Black-painted star opposite handle.

This type of jug was influenced by the Cypriot Black-on-Red jugs and should be dated to the early 9th century BCE.

Tomb: Z XX:47, 48.

Type CP2

Jug. Piriform body, ring base. Narrow cylindrical neck, pinched mouth. Double handle drawn from rim to shoulder. Thin, light orange ware, covered with thick orange-red, wheel-burnished slip. These jugs are decorated with a band of horizontal black lines encircling the shoulder,

sometimes intersected by a group of vertical lines around each side of body, and a black star opposite the handle. In addition, groups of small black circles fill the empty spaces. Black lines on neck, rim and handle.

Several examples recorded in Cyprus were defined by Gjerstad as Black-on-Red II (IV) ware (Gjerstad 1948: Fig. XXXIX:2). A further example of Black-on-Red II (IV) ware is known from Palaepaphos-Skales, dated to the mid 8th–7th centuries BCE (Karageorghis 1983: Pl. CXXVIII:9). Additional examples are known from a number of sites: Amathus, Tomb 7, *c.* 900 BCE (Gjerstad et al. 1935: Pl. IX); Stylli, Tomb 17 (Gjerstad et al. 1935: Pl. XXXV:1) and others. This type should be dated to the mid 8th–7th centuries BCE.

Tombs: Z XX:49–51; ZR XXIX:33.

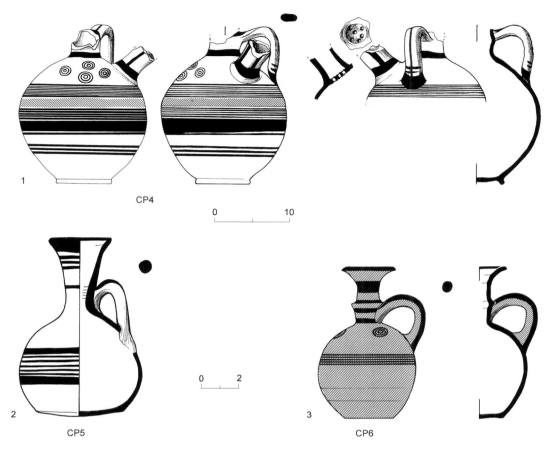

0   10

0   2

Fig. 5.14.

Type CP3

Jug. Globular body, ring base. Narrow cylindrical neck, pinched rim. Double handle drawn from rim to shoulder. Light buff ware. Painted with black and red vertically arranged concentric circles which encircle the body on either side. The empty spaces below handle and pinched rim contain a column of smaller black concentric circles. Black lines on neck, rim and handle.

Close parallels to this jug are Bichrome IV and Bichrome V jugs from Salamis dated to the 7th–6th centuries BCE (Karageorghis 1970: Pls. LXIV:103, 104; CIII:31). No exact parallels to the jug could be traced on the mainland. A petrographic analysis carried out by Yuval Goren showed that its clay is of foreign, probably Cypriot, origin.
Tomb: ZR XXIX:34.

Type CP4

Jug. Spherical body, ring-base. Tubular strainer spout on shoulder and handle at right angles to spout. Upper part of neck missing. Light buff ware, thick white burnished slip. Black and red horizontal bands on body below spout and handle. Painted bands also on spout, handle and base of neck. Black concentric circles on shoulder opposite handle. Only a single specimen of this type of jug was recorded.

The petrographic analysis carried out by Y. Goren indicates that this is probably an imported vessel, most likely from Cyprus. This bichrome jug has parallels in Cyprus, defined by Gjerstad as Bichrome III (Gjerstad 1948: Fig. XIII:7, 8).
Tomb: ZR XXXVI:80.

Type CP5

Juglet. Squat body, wide, flat, slightly rounded base. Long flaring neck with simple rim. Handle drawn from lower part of neck to shoulder. Fine yellowish-buff ware, well-levigated. The vessel is covered with a light buff slip, decorated with black horizontal lines on body, neck and handle. Black band on rim with red traces under it. Black paint going over inside of rim, burnished all over.

A similar juglet was found in Tomb 22a at Tell el-Far'ah (South), mid 10th–early 9th centuries BCE (Petrie 1930: Pl. XXXIX:82). A close parallel comes from Salamis, Tomb 50A, dated to the 11th century BCE (Karageorghis 1978:11, Pl. III:2).
Tombs: Z X:28; Z XX:52.

Type CP6

Globular body, flat base. Narrow neck with pronounced ridge and everted rim. Loop handle drawn from ridge to shoulder. These juglets are characterized by their fine ware, high degree of firing and highly polished red slip. Black horizontal lines on body and neck, groups of black concentric circles on shoulder and black bands on rim and handle. A variation of this type is the juglet with a piriform body.

The Black-on-Red juglets were widely distributed throughout Palestine and Cyprus over a long period of time. This particular type was common in Cyprus; it has been classified as BoR II (IV) and dated to the mid 8th–7th centuries BCE. Examples have been found at Palaepaphos-Skales (Karageorghis 1983: Pl. CXXVIII: 19, 37). Birmingham (1963:36), however, has proposed a much earlier date for its first appearance on the island—the late 11th–10th centuries BCE.

Black-on-Red juglets were found in Palestine, particularly in the north and on the coastal plain, but also in the south. Such juglets were uncovered at Ḥazor, Strata X–IX (Yadin et al. 1961: Pl. CLXXVII:14), Tel Mevorakh, Tomb 100 and Stratum VII (Stern 1978:55–57), as well as at Tel Mikhal, Stratum XIV (Herzog, Rapp and Negbi 1989:77). These examples are dated to the 10th century BCE, but as they consist only of the neck and rim, a clear distinction between BoR I (III) and BoR II (IV) is not possible. A similar juglet with the handle attached to the middle of the neck was found at Rosh Zayit; it is dated to the mid 10th–mid 9th centuries BCE (Gal 1992: Fig. 5:12). The Akhziv juglets belong to the BoR II (IV) ware and have their closest parallels in Cyprus (see above).
Tombs: Z IE:84; Z XI:22; Z XX:53–56; ZR XXIX:35, 36; ZR XXXVI:81–83; ZR XXXIX:9.

Type CP7

Juglet. Bichrome style, pinkish-buff ware, ovoid body,

flat base, narrow ridged neck, wide and thick everted rim, handle from ridge to shoulder. Body decorated with wide red band between two black lines. Groups of black concentric circles on body above and below band. Painted bands on neck above ridge and on rim, inside and outside.

Similar in shape and some of the decorative elements is a Cypro-Geometric III juglet from Salamis, Tomb 44, dated to the 8th century BCE (Karageorghis 1978:4–6; Pl. I:13).
Tomb: Z III:22.

Type CP8

Conical juglet. Flat base, wall narrowing gradually toward ridged flaring neck, ending in simple rim. Handle drawn from ridge to body. Red-orange ware, well-levigated and highly burnished. Black horizontal bands on body, neck and handle.

This type of miniature vessel occurs in the Phoenician homeland as well as in Cyprus, within the Black-on-Red family. It appears in the 10th century BCE at several sites: Rosh Zayit, mid 10th–mid 9th centuries BCE (Gal 1992: Fig. 5:11); Ta'anach, Period IIB, 10th century BCE (Rast 1978: Fig. 93:6); Megiddo, Stratum VA–IVB, second half of the 10th century BCE (Loud 1948: Pl. 88:18); and further south, in Tomb 120 at Lachish, second half of the 10th century BCE (Tufnell 1953: Pl. 88:330). It is a common type found at various sites in Cyprus and classified as BoR II (IV) ware, mid 8th–7th century BCE (Gjerstad 1948: Fig. XXXVIII:12).
Tomb: Z XX:57.

Type CP9

Barrel-shaped juglet. Nipple on both sides of body, narrow concave neck and simple rim. Handle drawn from lower neck to mid-body. Fine buff ware, well-levigated, matt slip. Concentric black lines around body; several narrow black circles and one red or black band at both ends of body. Neck painted with narrow horizontal black lines and/or a wide red band on the outside of the rim.

This type of juglet appears mainly in tomb groups. It occurs in an 11th century context at Tel Zeror (Ohata 1967: Pl. X:3; Gilboa 1989:212–214) and in southern Palestine between 950 and 850 BCE at Tell el-Far'ah (South) (Petrie 1930: Pl. XXXIX:86D) and Lachish (Tufnell 1953: Pl. 88:329). An interesting parallel comes from Azor, where in Tomb 79 barrel-shaped juglets were found together with Black-on-Red juglets (M. Dothan

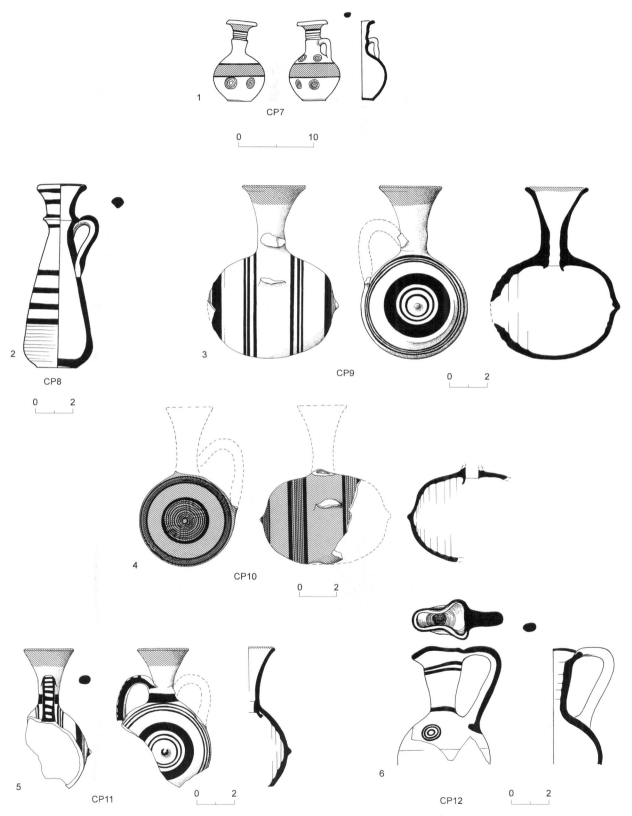

Fig. 5.15.

1961:173–174; Pl. 34:5). They occur frequently in the southern cemetery of Akhziv and are known also from Sarepta, Substratum D2, late 11th–mid 10th century BCE (Anderson 1988: Pl. 32:20) and Kh. Silm (Chapman 1972: Fig. 31:167). In Cyprus, they were classified as Bichrome III ware. Such juglets were found in Palaepaphos-Skales, mid 9th–8th centuries BCE (Karageorghis 1983:Pl. LXXVI:20). They were also discovered at Amathus, where they were recorded shortly before the appearance of the Black-on-Red ware (Birmingham 1963:38).

Tombs: Z IE:85, 86; Z IW:43, 44; Z X:29; Z XI:23–27; ZR XVII:20.

Type CP10

Barrel-shaped BoR juglet, identical in shape to Type CP9. Fine orange-buff ware, well-levigated. Body covered with dark red slip, decorated with groups of concentric black lines arranged vertically and burnished all over.

Black-on-Red barrel-shaped juglets are very rare in the Phoenician homeland. A single specimen of this type was found at Akhziv, recovered in a tomb which contained at least five barrel-shaped juglets of Type CP9. A similar juglet of Black-on-Red (III) ware is known from Cyprus (Karageorghis 1983: Pl. CLIII:12).

Tomb: Z XI:28.

Type CP11

Pilgrim flask. Lentoid body, knob in center of both sides of body. Cylindrical neck, flaring rim. Handles drawn from lower neck to mid-body. Fine ware, matt slip, black concentric circles on body. Black line at base of neck and black strokes on handles. Wide red band on outside of rim.

This type of Cypro-Geometric III flask is closely related to the barrel-shaped juglet (Type CP9) in ware, workmanship and style of decoration. It differs only in the shape of the body. A similar vase is known from Rizokarpaso, found in a tomb (Christou 1986: Pl. XXIV:3). Identical flasks are recorded at Oran in Algeria (Shefton 1982: Pl. 32:a, b). Based on the decoration and flaring rim it should be dated between the mid 9th and early 8th centuries BCE.

Tomb: Z XI:29.

Type CP12

Juglet. Piriform body, flaring neck and simple rim pinched to form a spout. Handle drawn from rim to shoulder, base missing. Orange-buff ware. Black concentric circles on shoulder, black lines on neck, rim and handle. The juglet is worn and it may have been red-slipped and burnished, as most of its parallels come from the Black-on-Red family.

A similar juglet was found at Joya (Chapman 1972: Fig. 31:266) in southern Lebanon and another example comes from Tabbat el-Hammam (Braidwood 1940: Fig. 4:5). They are widespread in Palestine at sites such as Rosh Zayit, mid 10th–mid 9th century BCE (Gal 1992: Fig. 5:9), Megiddo, Stratum VA–IVb, second half of the 10th century BCE (Loud 1948: Pl. 88:6) and a tomb in Lachish dated to the mid 9th century BCE (Tufnell 1953: Pl. 88:338).

Tomb: ZR XXXVI:84.

TYPE M — MISCELLANEOUS (Fig. 5.16)

Type M1

Cylindrical cup-like vessel. Rounded splayed mouth, rounded base with projection on each side. Reddish-brown ware, well-levigated.

This unique vessel may represent the head of a young animal, with the projections at the base standing for the ears and the splayed opening for a wide-open mouth. If this is the case, it may have served as a rhyton. Alternatively, it may have functioned as a funnel.

Tomb: ZR XXIX:37.

Type M2

Shallow bowl. Rounded base, wall tapering to simple rounded rim, interior handle. Pinkish-buff ware.

This vessel resembles spinning bowls known from various sites in Palestine, from as early as the 14th century BCE down to the 7th century BCE (T. Dothan 1963). The common Iron Age spinning bowls usually have two loop handles, though there are some examples with one, three or four handles. However, the shallowness of this bowl, its rounded base and single handle without grooves on its underside suggest a different use (lid?).

Tomb: ZR IX:22.

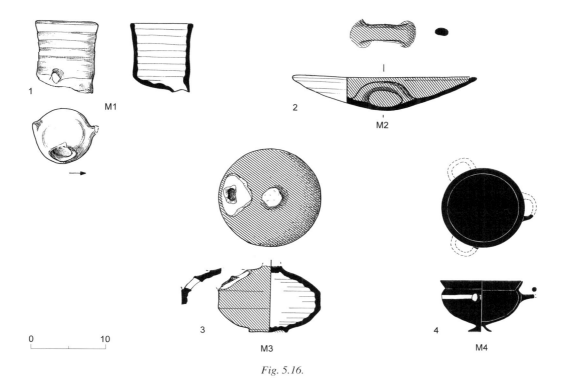

Fig. 5.16.

Type M3

Askos. Biconical body composed of two bowl-shaped parts attached by a wide straight band forming the shoulder of the jug. Originally, it had a long, angular spout on the shoulder ending in a trefoil mouth. Handle drawn from rim to shoulder, depressed ring base. Reddish-brown ware, white grits. Red-slipped and burnished.

This jug has elements in common with the *askos* of the Aegean sphere. Close parallels are known from Megiddo, Stratum V, 10th century BCE (Lamon and Shipton 1939: Pl. 5:117) and from tombs at Tell en-Nasbeh (Wampler 1947: Pl. 35:263). Both are red-slipped and burnished. This type of *askos* is dated to the 10th–9th centuries BCE. Further examples are known from tombs at Hama (Riis 1948:67). For a comprehensive discussion of this type of vessel, see M. Aharoni 1979.

Tombs: Z VI:9; ZR XVI:2.

Type M4

'Ionian' cup. Deep hemispherical bowl resting on flaring pedestal foot, flaring rim. Three horizontal handles have been reconstructed. Remains of only two asymmetrically placed handles have survived. However, similar cups appear with two handles as well. Exceptionally thin pale-orange ware, covered with brownish-black paint inside and outside, apart from narrow gap on shoulder.

'Ionian' cups were found at Meṣad Hashavyahu as part of a rich assemblage of East Greek pottery, dated to the last third of the 7th century BCE (Naveh 1962:97–98, Fig. 7; Fantalkin 2001:78, Fig. 28:IC2). Close parallels are known from Tharros, dated there to the mid 6th century BCE (Barnett and Mendelson 1987: Pls. 79:4/6, 96:12/2).

Tomb: ZR XVII:21.

CHAPTER 6

SMALL FINDS

Most of the Akhziv tombs contained various types of small finds. Like the tombs themselves and the pottery assemblage, these finds reflect the social background of the community interred in the ez-Zib (Buqbaq) and er-Ras cemeteries. The small finds from the Akhziv tombs are not, for the most part, made of the finest materials available at the time; this lends support to the assumption that the individuals buried in these cemeteries were probably commoners. However, the facts that the tombs were re-used in later periods and that most were looted, have influenced the number of precious objects that were recorded.

In Cyprus and throughout the Punic world, the material most commonly used in the jewelry industry was gold (Moscati 1988:370). Popular techniques included granulation, filigree and embossing. In contrast, the majority of the jewelry recovered at Akhziv is made of bronze and the above-mentioned techniques are seen infrequently. Although some objects made of precious materials, such as gold and silver, were recovered, they are rare.

Most of the jewelry from Akhziv is non-diagnostic chronologically, consisting of shapes and motifs that were popular over a long period of time. In addition, the custom of passing down jewelry from generation to generation also presents a problem in precise dating. In some instances, the number of pottery vessels found corresponds to the number of small finds in the tomb (ZR XXIX and ZR XXXVI). Sometimes, however, the ratio is inverted, e.g. Tomb Z I was rich in pottery and poor in small finds, and Tomb ZR IX yielded little pottery but many small finds. An important source of comparative material for jewelry is the excavation at Tharros, although many items have parallels at Sarepta and other sites.

The small finds fall into several major categories, including earrings, finger rings, bracelets and armlets, fibulae, beads, amulets and pendants, terracottas (Chapter 7, below), stelae (see Cross, Appendix 1, below) and scarabs (see Keel, Appendix 2, below). These have been catalogued and illustrated above according to tomb.

EARRINGS

A large number of earrings were uncovered in the tombs. Most are of the 'boat-shaped' type (known also as 'leech-shaped'), made of either circular or elliptical wire. This common type is known from the third millennium BCE (Maxwell-Hyslop 1971:4–5) through the Roman period. The boat-shaped earrings from the Iron Age are more elongated than those from earlier periods. In many cases, the thin wire of the loop has corroded, and only the 'boat' has survived. A special boat-shaped earring with a glass eye-bead threaded on it was found in Tomb ZR II:3.

Another type is the basket-shaped pendant earring, which occurs in most Phoenician settlements of the 7th–6th centuries BCE (Barnett and Mendelson 1987: Pl. 80:4/164). Two examples of this type were recovered at Akhziv (Tomb ZR XII:17 and possibly ZR IV:11). The basket-shaped pendant usually hangs from a loop attached to the bottom of the earring. Occasionally, a pyramid formed by granules is attached to the top of the basket.

FINGER RINGS

Bronze, iron, silver and gold rings, made of either wire or flattened coils, were found at Akhziv. The ends of the rings either meet, overlap or are soldered together. They are round, elliptical or flat in section.

Of particular interest are the swivel rings, of which two types were found. The first has tapered ends (Tomb ZR IX:41), while the second has enlarged pointed ends, formed to fit into a pierced scarab (Tomb ZR IX:42). In both cases, the ring is made of silver and the seal has not survived.

The tombs also yielded a few examples of square rings with rounded inner faces. This type is rare.

BRACELETS AND ARMLETS

The bracelets and armlets are of bronze, usually plain, open-ended (Tomb Z I Vestibule:4), round in section (Tomb ZR XIII:5) and tapering at the ends (Tomb Z XIX:1), which are sometimes flattened. A few of the bracelets are decorated with parallel incised lines at the ends.

FIBULAE

Only a few fibulae were recovered. A fragment of the spring and catch of what may belong to the earliest fibula type known in the East Mediterranean, asymmetrical with an elongated bow and forearm (Stronach 1959:183), was found in Tomb Z IE:92. Most of the fibulae known from Akhziv, however, have semicircular–arched bows or triangular bows ('knee' or 'elbow' fibulae). Though these types overlap in time, the more rounded forms disappear in the late 7th or early 6th century BCE, while the more angular types continue into the Hellenistic period (Stronach 1959:185).

The 8th century BCE saw an increase in the production of semicircular bow fibulae throughout the Near East. This led to the development of many new variations of this type, which existed alongside other forms for another two centuries (Stronach 1959:186). One fibula of this type (Tomb ZR XXXIX:14) has a semicircular bow with collared bead molding and bent catches at both ends. This type was common in the 7th century BCE.

Another fibula has an arched bow with a collared bead on each arm. The arched fibula type can be regarded as a link between the early rounded types and the later triangular types (Stronach 1959:190). Between 800 and 600 BCE, this type developed further, especially in Syria and Palestine, where it was already known.

The fibulae with a triangular bow ('knee' or 'elbow' fibulae) represent the most common type in the Near East. They spread from Egypt to Persia, spanning a long period of time between the 8th century BCE to the 1st century CE. Most examples are of bronze, though a few

from Syria and Palestine have an iron pin (Stronach 1959:193). One example (Tomb ZR XXIX:56) is made of bronze and has an iron pin.

BEADS

The beads found at Akhziv are made of various materials. The most common are carnelian or glass, but beads of faience, silver, agate and other semi-precious materials were also found.

The beads are of various shapes: oblate–globular, melon-shaped, globular, prism-shaped, lentoid, ring-shaped, barrel-shaped, ribbed, biconical, disk-shaped, cylindrical, lozenge-shaped, lotus-shaped, etc. The relatively large number of glass beads recovered is interesting, as glass vessels are rare in the period when the Akhziv tombs were in use. Of special interest are the numerous stratified glass eye-beads (Tombs ZR II:20, ZR X:12, 13), characteristic of the Persian period. The triangular stratified glass eye-bead (Tomb ZR XXXIX:15) of Assyrian type appears in the 8th century BCE and is represented at many sites in the East Mediterranean, except Egypt. Lotus flower-shaped beads of glass (Tomb ZR X:22) were current in the late Iron Age (Barnett and Mendelson 1987:112). Amphora-shaped glass beads (Tomb ZR VI:10) occur in the Persian period (Johns 1938:145).

AMULETS AND PENDANTS

The amulets found at Akhziv reflect a strong Egyptian influence, evident in the many Egyptian gods and divine symbols represented on them. Examples include 'the Eye of Horus' (Udjat), Isis, Shu, Pateke and Bes.

Despite this evidence of Egyptian influence on Phoenician culture, it is noteworthy that the Phoenicians frequently modified the Egyptian symbols according to their needs. Some of the amulets bear specifically Phoenician symbols, such as the 'sign of Tanit' on a conical seal from Akhziv (Tomb ZR II:34; see Appendix 2:11; Keel 1997:24: No. 11). The Phoenician amulets thus demonstrate a measure of iconographic and stylistic independence (Moscati 1988:399). Most of the Akhziv amulets are made of faience (glazed composition), green and blue in color. Parallels can be found at numerous Phoenician and Punic sites, echoing contacts between East and West.

Egyptian Gods

Bes. This dwarf-god with bow legs is usually shown wearing a feathered headdress. Bes was believed to ward off evil spirits and was the protector of women in childbirth (e.g. Tomb ZR XXIX:67).

Isis. Spouse of Osiris and mother of Horus, Isis is usually shown standing with a pillar, a rectangular shaft covering much of her back. She is wearing a sun-disk and the horns of Hathor; occasionally, however, she appears seated on a throne, sometimes holding the child Horus (Tomb ZR XXIX:66).

Khnum. The ram-headed god, Khnum is represented in Akhziv in a crouching position. He was seen as the creator of life and living things (Tomb ZR X:26).

Pateke. This dwarf-like figure was linked to the creator god Ptah, as dwarfs were considered to be skilled artisans. The appearance of Pateke on amulets was meant to ward off danger (e.g. Tomb ZR XIII:41, 42).

Sekhmet. The lioness goddess, wife of Ptah and mother of Nefertum, Sekhmet was believed to be a destroyer of the enemies of the sun. She also had the power to heal, and the 'Priests of Sekhmet' formed one of the oldest medical associations (Tomb ZR XXXVI:113).

Thoueris. This hippopotamus-headed goddess was an apotropaic deity associated with pregnancy and childbirth (Tomb ZR XIII:37).

Shu. Shu is depicted with bent knees and raised arms. He symbolizes the atmosphere and was considered to be responsible for holding the heavens over the earth, separating Geb, the Earth, from his wife Nut, the Sky (Tomb ZR X:25).

Other Amulets

Demons. Demon heads are a Phoenician phenomenon. Almost all these amulets are frightening and were certainly meant to ward off evil spirits. They are clearly related to the grotesque terracotta masks and are quite common in the Punic world (e.g. Tomb ZR XXIX: 76, 77).

Udjat. A popular funerary amulet, the 'Eye of Horus' had a regenerative character, but served also for apotropaic purposes. It is found in most Phoenician and Punic sites and appears in various forms—in openwork, in quadruple, etc. (e.g. Tomb ZR XXIX:72).

Animals

Apes. The ape was a manifestation of the god Thoth, moon god and the god of writing and wisdom. Most apes are depicted in a squatting position (e.g. Tomb ZR XXIX:68).

Sow. The sow, a popular Egyptian fertility symbol, appears with or without piglets. At Akhziv, the sow is shown grazing, without piglets (Tomb ZR XIII:46).

Lion. The lion was a symbol of strength, regarded as a guardian and protector (Tomb ZR X:24). Lion amulets are known from several Punic sites and usually come from the later tombs (Barnett and Mendelson 1987:114).

Hawk. A popular Egyptian amulet, representing a form of Horus (Tomb ZR XIII:40).

Bull. The bull was a symbol of power and fertility. The amulet found at Akhziv was in the form of a bull's head (Tomb ZR XXXVI:116).

Frog-Shaped Pendants. The frog was associated with the concepts of new life and fertility (Tomb ZR III:15).

CHAPTER 7

TERRACOTTAS

Ben-Dor's excavations at Akhziv (1941–1944) yielded an impressive group of anthropomorphic and zoomorphic figurines. Some are finely executed, others fairly crude, but they all provide an interesting glimpse into Phoenician culture, shedding light on such areas as religion, art, crafts and relations with foreign lands. The figurines were probably meant to accompany and please the dead in the afterlife, by reminding them of this world. Among the terracottas in this category are the baker, the bathing woman and the boat. Terracottas were also used to provide a link between the dead and their deities, as is the case with the masks and the model shrines.

The use of molds made it possible to mass produce the figurines. In some cases, the entire front of the figurine was moldmade; additional clay was added to form the back, which was then smoothed flat. In other cases, only the face was moldmade, while the body was made on the wheel. Another group of figurines was handmade according to a certain iconographic style (the bather, the baker, etc.).

The Akhziv assemblage of terracottas includes a prominent group of figures representing musicians. It is not clear, however, whether they depict musicians playing in sanctuaries or scenes from everyday life. Music was an integral part of daily life in the ancient world, accompanying festivals, feasts and victory celebrations. Yet it is also found in the context of mourning, as for instance, David's lament over the deaths of Saul and Jonathan (2 Samuel 1:17–27).

Despite the many references to music in the Bible, we have no descriptions of the instruments themselves. Archaeological finds, therefore, provide a means of filling in some of the gaps in our knowledge of music in ancient times.

HUMAN FIGURINES

1. Tambourine (Frame-Drum) Player (Fig. 7.1)
Tomb ZR XXVIII (Reg. No. 44.264).
Dimensions: H 20.6 cm; D 8 cm.
Reddish-buff ware, decorated with red and black paint.

This figurine is the most graceful and finely executed of the three frame-drum players at Akhziv (see Nos. 2 and 3, below). Her features are delicately outlined, and her posture is proud and erect. Her dress is covered with red paint and decorated on the sides with vertical black stripes. The frame-drum, thicker and more solid than the others, is painted red, as is her face. This is the only human figurine from Akhziv with an airhole beneath the left ear, as opposed to the usual location at the back of the head.

2. Tambourine (Frame-Drum) Player (Fig. 7.2)
Tomb ZR XIII (Reg. No. 44.54).
Dimensions: H 21.9 cm; D 8.2 cm.
Reddish-buff ware, with traces of black paint on the hair.

This tall, thin figurine, with her stooped posture, contrasts sharply with her graceful counterpart (No. 1). The crown of her head is strikingly high, and her hair hangs low over her forehead. The figurine has an airhole at the back of the head to allow gases to escape during firing.

3. Tambourine (Frame-Drum) Player (Fig. 7.3)
Tomb ZR XII (Reg. No. 70-8043).
Dimensions: H 19+ cm; D 6+ cm.
Brownish-buff ware, traces of black paint on the hair and red paint on the body and frame-drum.

This figurine was made with much less care than the others, probably by a less experienced artisan. While identical to the others in overall conception, it lacks their charm. Although the hairstyle resembles that of the other figurines, the locks are much thinner. Airhole at the back of the head.

As seen, these three figurines are similar in conception but strikingly different in execution. Each depicts a woman holding a disk-shaped object, a frame-drum pressed to her chest between her breasts. The body, which is bell-shaped, was formed on the potter's wheel. The head, inserted into the body, consists of a moldmade face with clay added to form the back of the head. Each of the figurines has an airhole which allowed the gases to escape during firing.

The figurines have an identical hairstyle, consisting of long, heavy locks reaching below the breasts and hair over the forehead. In the back, the line of the hair is emphasized with additional clay that extends below the shoulders. The arms and the drum were handmade and added separately. In each case, the instrument is held in the left hand, and struck with the right.

The frame-drum, a popular instrument used to accompany song and dance, may have been played mainly by women (Exodus 15:20). This could explain why it is not recorded as part of the Temple cult (Keel 1978:340).

The iconographic origin of this type of figurine is Mesopotamia (Karageorghis 1987:18), whence it passed to Syria, Palestine and Cyprus sometime in the 7th century BCE. Many such figurines have been discovered in tombs and shrines in these countries. Examples are known from Ḥorbat Qitmit (Beit-Arieh 1995:162–168), Sarepta (Pritchard 1988: Fig. 11:28, 29), Kharayeb (Chéhab 1953–1954: Pl. 1:4), Tyre (Bikai 1978b: Pl. LXXXI:2) and Shikmona (Elgavish 1993:1374). Further examples are in the Israel Museum collections (Ornan 1986:32–33), as well as in the Semitic Museum at Harvard (Meyers 1987). These terracottas were more common in Cyprus than on the eastern Mediterranean coast. Karageorghis carefully distinguishes between 'tambourine holders,' one of the most popular types at

1   2   3

Figs. 7.1–7.3. Frame-drum players.

Amathus (Karageorghis 1987:18) and 'tambourine play-ers.' Two of the latter type were found at Amathus; these are quite similar to the Akhziv examples (Kara-georghis 1987:17). Figurines of this type have also been found at Kition (Gehrig and Niemeyer 1990:147 No. 63).

4. Double-Pipe Player (Fig. 7.4)
Tomb ZR XXIX (Reg. No. 44.56).
Dimensions: H 20 cm; D 8.5 cm.
Brownish-buff ware, red bands on the garment and black paint on the hair.

The bell-shaped body, fashioned on the wheel, tapers at the top to join the neck and head. The dress is decorated with red stripes on the front. The face was moldmade and a flat piece of clay was added to form the back of the head, which has an airhole. Careful attention was given to the details of the face. The almond-shaped eyes are large and wide, extending almost to the temples. The ears are particularly large, and the nose is broad and bulbous. The mouth is marked by two parallel lines, which seem to be slightly upturned at the edges, lending the face a joyful, but controlled, expression. The short hairstyle is indi-cated by black paint, ending in a straight line at the back of the neck and emphasized by parallel grooves on the forehead. The head was inserted into the upper part of the body and secured with soft clay. The arms, modeled separately, hold a double-pipe, the mouthpiece of which is missing.

Pipes (aerophones) are mentioned in the Bible in conjunction with the ecstatic band of prophets described in 1 Samuel 10:5: "... a band of prophets coming down from the high place with a lute, and a timbrel and a pipe, and a lyre before them and they shall prophesy." They are also referred to in the context of banquets (Isaiah 5:12), pilgrimages to Jerusalem (Isaiah 30:29) and Solomon's procession from Gihon to Zion (1 Kings 1:40). While the Bible does not include the pipe among the list of instru-ments used in the Temple orchestra, it was clearly an integral part of daily life.

Pipes were known in Mesopotamia and Egypt as early as the third millennium BCE. In Egypt, double-pipes were made of cane and were long and thin. Along with the lyre and the frame-drum, the double-pipe is fre-quently depicted in scenes of votive processions of musi-cians marching toward an enthroned deity. Such themes are known from both Mesopotamian and Egyptian art.

Fig. 7.4. Double-pipe player.

This kind of musical ensemble also appears on several Phoenician metal bowls dated to the 9th–8th centuries BCE (Markoe 1985:246, 253, 316), as well as on ivory pyxides from Nimrud, dated to the 8th century BCE (Barnett 1957: Pls. XVI:XVII).

Terracottas of double-pipe players are known in Cy-prus from the Cypro-Archaic II period (Flouerentzos 1991: Pl. II:2–5; Myres 1914:340, No. 2043). A depic-tion of a double-pipe player also occurs on a cylinder seal from Tel Keisan, dated to the 9th–8th centuries BCE (Gorali 1977: No. 114). A Canaanite orchestra, including a musician playing the double-pipe, appears on a pottery stand from Ashdod from the 10th century BCE (M. Dothan 1970:310). Two limestone sculptures from Cy-prus, apparently of the Early Cypro-Classical I period, also show double-pipe players (Flouerentzos 1991: Pl. I). At Megiddo, a bronze cult stand was discovered bearing the figure of a woman playing the double-pipe, probably of the 9th century BCE (Schumacher 1908: Pl. 50). A double-pipe player figurine, dating to the late 7th century BCE, was also found at Tel Malḥata (Beit-Arieh 1995:315, Fig. 9.4), as well as at Ḥorbat Qitmit (Beit-Arieh 1995:166).

5. Woman Holding a Dove (Fig. 7.5)
Purchased during the excavation (Reg. No. 44.50).
Dimensions: H 18 cm; D 5 cm.
Brownish-buff ware, traces of red paint on body and black paint on hair.

The figure has a bell-shaped wheelmade body into which a mold-formed head was inserted. The face was shaped in a shallow mold and completed by adding a slab of clay to form the back. The face, on which faint traces of red paint can be seen, is meticulously modeled and bears a serene expression. The almond-shaped eyes, originally painted white, are framed by graceful eyebrows. The high cheekbones and nose are delicately shaped; the mouth is small and closed. The hair is indicated by vertical grooves rising above the forehead. The arms are crossed below the chest, holding a dove (or a duck?), against the breasts. The arms and the dove were separately fashioned and joined to the body. This type may represent a woman presenting an offering.

Figurines holding doves are known from Tel Keisan (Briend and Humbert 1980: Pl. 103:16, 17). Another similar figurine, though different in hairstyle, was found at Sarepta (Pritchard 1988: Fig. 11:24). Further parallels come from Cyprus (Cassimatis 1986: Pl. 37:1–3). A female holding a dove to her breast is known from Locri, dated to the early 5th century BCE (Higgins 1954: No. 1201).

6. Seated Pregnant Woman (Fig. 7.6)
Tomb ZR XXVIII (Reg. No. 44.263).
Dimensions: H 19 cm; D 5.4 cm.
Pinkish-buff clay, covered with white wash. Traces of red paint on face and ears, black paint on hair.

This beautifully preserved figurine is an embodiment of a woman patiently awaiting the birth of her child. The woman is depicted sitting on a chair, her feet resting on a stool. She wears a long robe, which clings softly to her full breasts and distended belly. The arms protrude from the sleeves so that only the forearms and hands are exposed. Both her hands rest on her knees. The hairdress is arranged in long locks flowing below the shoulders. Her face is softly modeled, the eyes framed with black paint, and her ears are fairly pronounced.

The figure was made in two parts, leaving the interior hollow and the base open. The front and sides were cast in a mold, the plain back was added by hand and smoothed over.

Many such figurines are known from sites in Syria, Israel and Cyprus, mostly dated to the 7th–6th centuries BCE. They were found at Kharayeb (Kaoukabani 1973: Pl. 7:4), Sarepta (Pritchard 1988:50–52, Fig. 12:34, 39) and Byblos (Dunand 1950: Pl. 168:9047). Numerous examples come from sites in Israel, such as Tel Ṣippor (Negbi 1966: Pl. 6:19, 20), Tell Abu Hawam (Hamilton

Fig. 7.5. Woman holding a dove.

Fig. 7.6. Seated pregnant woman.

1935:16: No. 25; 17, No. 26), Makhmish (Avigad 1960: Pl. 11:A, B), Akhziv (*Treasures of the Holy Land*:175: No. 88) and others.

7. Musician Playing a Wind Instrument(?) (Fig. 7.7)
Tomb ZR XII (Reg. No. 70-8048).
Dimensions: H 15+ cm; D 5+ cm.
Brownish-buff clay, red paint on the front.

The bell-shaped body of this figurine was made on the potter's wheel. The head was moldmade, and clay was added and smoothed to form the back of the head, which has an airhole. The eyes are almond shaped, and the nose is large and crude. The lips are slightly indicated. The hairstyle is short, covering part of the forehead and falling behind oversized ears. Despite the poor condition of this figurine, some interesting details are visible. On the chin there is an impression of what was probably part of an elongated attachment, traces of which are also noticeable along the bust of the figurine. The similarity to our double-flute player suggests that the figurine may have been playing the flute, or some other single-reed wind instrument.

8. Female Figurine (Fig. 7.8)
Tomb ZR XXVI (Reg. No. 70-8436).
Dimensions: H 10+ cm; D 8 cm.
Handmade, pinkish-buff ware.

The hollow body of this crude figurine was handmade. The head, now missing, was made separately and inserted

Fig. 7.8. Female figurine.

into the body at the top. A strip of clay was added to the base of the body to level it. Though the breasts are rendered in a fairly naturalistic manner, the figure's proportions are clearly distorted. The right arm ends in a flat, crude hand, held just below the right breast. The thick left arm, also crudely shaped, is much longer than the right and extends down the side of the body, practically reaching the base.

9. Head of Female Figurine (Fig. 7.9)
Tomb ZR V (Reg. No. 70-8319).
Dimensions: H 7 cm; W 4 cm.
Moldmade, pinkish-buff clay. Traces of red and black paint.

The face is rather expressionless, with almond-shaped and slightly protruding eyes delineated by red paint. The lips are also painted red, and there is a red band along the

Fig. 7.7. Musician playing a wind instrument(?).

Fig. 7.9. Head of female figurine.

base of the neck. The hair, with traces of black paint, falls behind the ears and covers part of the forehead, where it is accentuated by parallel grooves. The face was cast in a mold and clay was added and smoothed to form the back of the head. There is an airhole at the back of the head. The head ends in a peg inserted into the body of the figurine, which has not survived. This head is characteristic of the Phoenician figurines found at Akhziv, particularly with regard to the parallel grooves in the hair over the forehead.

10. Bathing Woman (Fig. 7.10)
Tomb ZR XXIX (Reg. No. 44.57).
Dimensions: L 10.5 cm; W 6.5 cm; H 7.5 cm.
Handmade, orange-buff ware with white and black grits.

Figurine of a woman seated in a shallow rectangular tub with a flat base. The bath has rounded corners, with a flat rim, wide at the short sides and narrow at the long ones. The seated woman, probably nude, is washing her left leg, with the left hand rubbing the toes while the right holds the leg. The head of the figurine is moldmade, hand-smoothed at the back. The hair falls along the sides of the head behind the ears and covers part of the forehead, where it is indicated by parallel grooves. The face is fairly crude, the expression placid.

There are several parallels to this scene. Three are from Cyprus; one comes from Tomb 190 in the necropolis of Amathus, dated to the Cypro-Archaic II period, mid 6th century BCE and representing a human figure seated in a bathtub and a second figure standing outside and assisting the first (Karageorghis 1987: Pl. I:4). Two others are of unknown origin (Ginouvés 1962: Pls. III:8, IV:10, 11). Further parallels, from the necropolis of Carthage, were attributed to the 6th century BCE (Vandenabeele 1986:355). Such terracottas may have been imitated in Rhodes (Higgins 1954: Pl. 39:236).

The petrographic analysis conducted by Y. Goren showed that the clay of this figurine originated either in southern Lebanon or in the Galilee. Due to the relatively large amount of bathers found in Cyprus, the origin of the type seems to be there, though our bather was probably locally made in Phoenicia.

11. Breadmaker (Fig. 7.11)
Tomb Z III (Reg. No. 44.51).
Dimensions: L 7.5 cm; W 5.5 cm; H 7 cm.
Handmade, pinkish-buff ware.

Figure of a woman(?), standing over a three-legged trough, kneading dough. The figure is bent over the trough, with its long neck and head turned slightly to the

Fig. 7.10. Bathing woman.

left. The outstretched hands are preparing a loaf of bread in the trough. Another lump of dough is placed near one of the short sides of the trough. The shallow trough has a wide flat rim. The three-legged trough and the figure are standing on a rectangular plinth. The body of the figure is plump, the legs are short, and the face is pinched, with pellets attached to represent the eyes and mouth. The figure wears a conical headdress.

The subjects of kneading dough, sieving flour and baking bread were popular in the coroplastic art of Cyprus in the Early–Middle Bronze Ages and later in the Cypro-Archaic period (Karageorghis 1987:16; Myres 1914:347–348). Two close parallels are known from Amathus, Cyprus (Karageorghis 1987: Pl. 1: T302/27; T232/64). A fragmentary example comes from Salamis (Monloup 1984:150 No. 574). This scene appears later in Rhodes (Higgins 1954: Pl. 39:233, 234).

Fig. 7.12. Figure of potter (or phallus holder?).

Fig. 7.11. Breadmaker.

12. Figure of Potter (or Phallus Holder?) (Fig. 7.12)
Tomb ZR XXXVI (Reg. No. 44.58).
Dimensions: H 12 cm; W 5 cm; L 8.9 cm.
Handmade, pinkish-brown clay with white grits.

The crudely formed figure, whose gender is not evident, stands on an oval base in an unnaturally inclined position, grasping a phallus. The torso is rather flat, while the legs are plump and rounded. The face, which is also flattish,

has large, almond-shaped eyes, a delicate nose, and a long, prominent, pointed chin. The hair style partly conceals the forehead, where it is indicated by parallel grooves, and descends along the sides of the face. The back of the entire figure was smoothed over and flattened. Like the legs, the arms were also crudely rounded. They extend forward, clasping a potter's wheel or a phallus, just below the glans.

No parallels to this type of figurine could be traced. Yet, as most of the figurines in the Akhziv repertoire depict everyday activities, it is likely that our figure represents a potter engaged in his craft. Such scenes appear on Middle Bronze Age pottery jars from Cyprus (Karageorghis 1991:33–37). However, phallus-like objects similar to ours are known from Cyprus (Ohnefalsch-Richter 1893: Pl. LXXVI:10–12). The custom of burying or planting phalli outside sanctuaries as part of a fertility ritual is known from Greece, where it was associated with the cult of Dionysus, as the god of fertility and vegetation. Depictions of such practices appear on Greek vases such as a red-figured cup of the 5th century BCE, bearing the scene of hetairai dancing round a model phallus (Johns 1993:43).

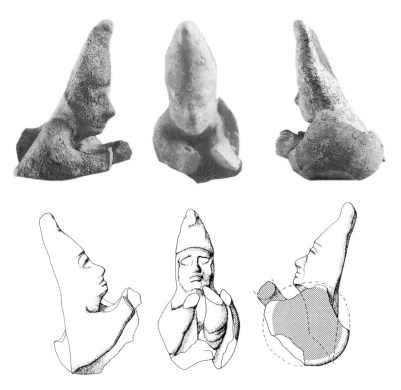

Fig. 7.13. Horseman.

13. Horseman (Fig. 7.13)
No information is available concerning the precise prove-
nance of this figure in the Akhziv cemetery.
Dimensions: H 9.1 cm; W 4 cm.
Partially moldmade, pinkish-buff clay.

All that remains of this figure is the head, arms and
shield. The rider's face and his high, peaked cap were
moldmade. Clay was then added by hand to the back of
the head and smoothed over, and the tip of the cap was
bent forward. The figure appears to have been seated on a
horse in a slightly inclined position, his handmade arms
extending forward to grasp its neck. On his left arm the
rider bears a round, wheelmade shield, which is covered
with red paint.

Several horse-and-rider figurines dated to the Persian
period, some with pointed caps, were uncovered at
Tel Ṣippor (Negbi 1966: Pl. XIII:101). The rider's headdress reflects Persian influence (Young and Young
1955:202).

14. Horse-and-Rider (Fig. 7.14)
Tomb Z IW (Reg. No. 70-7102).
Dimensions: L 8.2 cm; H 10.2 cm.
Handmade, brownish-buff ware with black grits.

The crudely formed horse has a long body and neck, and
an accentuated mane. It stands stiffly on its four legs,
which are short and stumpy in relation to the body. The
forelegs are straight and plump, while the shorter, tapered
hindlegs project from the body at a slight angle. The
prominent tail dangles between the hindlegs. Though the
rider is missing, the place where he was originally attached to the horse can be seen clearly on the animal's
back. Traces of black lines and red paint are visible on the
horse's chest and on the front of the forelegs.

Horse-and-rider figurines were popular gifts offered
to the dead. They have been found both in tombs and in
sanctuaries. A similar horse is known from Sarepta
(Pritchard 1975:4). Other examples come from Amathus
(Karageorghis 1987: Pl. XIX:92, 93).

15. Horse-and-Rider Horse Head (Fig. 7.15)

The head was found/purchased during the excavation(?) (Reg. No. 48-824).

Dimensions: L 9.5 cm; W 8 cm.

Handmade, buff ware. Traces of red paint on the neck.

The horse has a long and flattened neck with an accentuated mane. The protruding muzzle, which is partly hollow, terminates in a swollen nose with accentuated nostrils and a groove for the mouth—all of which lend the horse a naturalistic expression. Two pellets represent the eyes. The head is crowned by a separately made flat 'turban', from which two cone-shaped ears emerge. The head and neck of the horse are all that remain of a 'horse-and-rider' figurine, a popular type of figurine that was either offered to the gods in sanctuaries or placed as a funerary offering in tombs, probably belonging to warriors.

Three identical horse-and-rider figurines were discovered in the 'horsemen's tomb' at Akhziv, excavated by E. Mazar and dated to the 7th century BCE (E. Mazar 1990:104–109). Two more identical horse heads were excavated by M. Dothan at 'Akko (unpublished), and another identical example comes from Tel Dor (Stern 1989:27). A similar horse's head, also dated to the 7th century BCE, is known from Tell Keisan (Briend and Humbert 1980: Pl. 138:104.28–32). Reminiscent in shape is a horse-and-rider figurine found at Amathus

Fig. 7.15. Horse-and-rider horse head.

(Karageorghis 1987: Pl. XX:97). A large number of horse-and-rider figurines were recovered at Kurion, dated to the 7th–6th centuries BCE (Young and Young 1955:54 ff.; Winter 1991: Pl. LVIIIb).

ANIMAL FIGURINES

16. Head of a Horse Figurine (Fig. 7.16)

Tomb Z III (Reg. No. 48-15).

Dimensions: L 7 cm; W 4.8 cm.

Handmade, pinkish-buff ware. Only the neck and head have survived.

The horse has a long neck and a mane falling over the brow, emphasized by an additional strip of clay applied along the back of the neck. The horse's head is long and detailed. The open mouth was apparently cut to accommodate a bit, which may have been made of a different material, perhaps bronze or string. The nose and nostrils are carefully modeled and fairly pronounced. The ears are naturalistically rendered. The eyes are made from separately applied clay pellets. The detailed harness is also separately attached. The head was separately modeled and inserted into the horse's body.

A similar horse head is known from Tel Keisan (Briend and Humbert 1980: Pl. 104:34), dated to the late 7th or 6th–5th centuries BCE. Somewhat reminiscent in shape are horse heads from Lachish (Tufnell 1953:

Fig. 7.14. Horse-and-rider.

Fig. 7.16. Head of a horse figurine.

17. Cat Figurine (Fig. 7.17)
Tomb ZR XIV (Reg. No. 44.55).
Dimensions: H 13 cm; W 6.6 cm; D 7.6 cm.
The figure was found intact; moldmade, orange-buff clay. Traces of red and black paint on the front, sides and back.

The cat is represented as seated upright on its haunches, its flexed forelegs pressed closely together. The shanks are partially outlined in black. The head is held erect and faces forward. The face is softly modeled, and the nose was treated gently. The almond-shaped eyes are outlined with black paint. The whiskers are partly incised and partly indicated with black lines. The exceptionally large ears extend upward.

The figure was made in two parts. The front and sides were cast in a mold, while the back was added by hand and smoothed over, leaving the interior hollow and the base open. The ears were formed by hand, pinched between the thumbs and forefingers and pulled upward. A lump of clay was pulled from one side of the back, around the front, to the other side, in order to frame and level the uneven base.

Pl. 32:7, 8, 11). Other parallels include horse figurines from Kourion in Cyprus (Young and Young 1955:139:2942, 2943; 140:2950), probably dating to the late 4th century BCE.

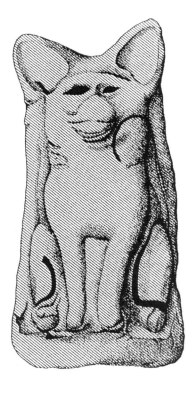
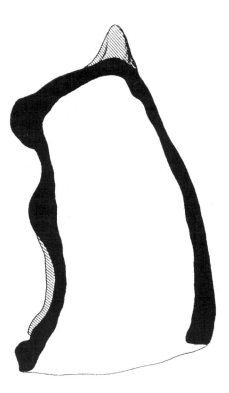

Fig. 7.17. Cat figurine.

The cat appears to be a Phoenician adaptation of the Egyptian sacred cat. A similar cat was found at Beth Gan (Liebowitz and Dehnisch 1998:175, Fig. 1). Additional cast animals in a seated position are known from other sites. The moldmade figure of a bear was found in another cemetery excavated at Akhziv by Prausnitz (unpublished). Figures of seated baboons were unearthed at Tel Keisan, Stratum IV, dated to the late 7th century BCE (Briend and Humbert 1980: Pl. 104:39–44).

BOATS

18. Model Boat (Fig. 7.18)
Purchased during the excavation (Reg. No. 44.48).
Dimensions: L 16.3 cm; W 5.6 cm; H 5.5 cm.
Handmade, light buff ware, red-painted on the interior, traces of red on the exterior and a wide red band along the curvature of the boat.

The model represents a double-ended boat with a carinated and crescent-shaped hull. There are no interior fittings. The stempost and the sternpost rise vertically, ending in a debased animal head. This could have been a horse's head, according to the Greek tradition which calls the Phoenician vessels *hippos* (horse) because of the horse heads on the prows of their boats (Stieglitz 1975). A depiction of such boats transporting timber from Lebanon appears on reliefs in Sargon's palace at Khorsabad of the 7th century BCE (Moscati 1988:40). Another depiction of a boat with the stern in the shape of a duck's head appears on a scapula found at Dor, dated to the Persian period (Stern 1994c:9). Our model probably represents a Phoenician boat, such as those used for transporting goods and passengers along the Mediterranean coast (Karageorghis 1996: Pl. XLIII).

19. Fragment of a Model Boat (Fig. 7.19)
Tomb ZR III (Reg. No. 70-8491).
Dimensions: L 13+ cm; W 7.8 cm; H 4 cm.
Handmade, light buff ware, traces of red paint.

The boat is broken, with scattered traces of red paint on the exterior. The model represents a double-ended boat, one-third of its length missing, with a carinated and wide hull. There are no interior fittings. The vertical stempost is very debased.

Yuval Goren's petrographic analysis shows that the ware consists of dense quantities of clay and is rich in minerals fairly uncommon in most soils of this country. As this clay is common in the delicate Cypriot pottery, the boat model may have originated in Cyprus.

Figs. 7.18, 7.19. Model boats.

Parallels to our boats are known from Tel Keisan (Briend and Humbert 1980: Pl. 106:60, 61). Several clay boats were excavated by M. Dothan at 'Akko (unpublished). A fragment of a similar pottery boat was discovered at Dor (Stern 1994a:37). Further comparisons come from Shavé Ẕiyyon (unpublished). A boat model on display at the Maritime Museum, Haifa, is dated to the 12th–11th centuries BCE (Wachsmann 1981:209). Boat models are frequently found in Cyprus from the Bronze Age onward (Karageorghis 1993: Pl. XXX 11:3, 4). An extensive group is known from Amathus (Karageorghis 1987:29, n. 83). The two models from Akhziv can be compared to Cypriot models, dated to Late Cypriot I or Late Cypriot II (Westerberg 1983: Fig. 10; Stieglitz 1975: Pl. VI:3). The presence of such boats in the Akhziv tombs may reflect the owner's maritime background.

MASKS

The Akhziv cemetery has yielded five masks: two represent female faces, one a male face, one a grotesque face, and a fifth mask depicts a bull's head.

The main facial features are indicated on the masks. Sometimes the eyes and/or the mouth are cut out, and most masks have suspension holes. All five masks are under life-size, and could thus not have been worn in the modern sense. However, they most certainly imitate actual masks of perishable material. They may have been hung by their suspension holes on the walls of a room or a tomb.

20. Female Mask (Fig. 7.20)
Tomb ZR XXIX (Reg. No. 44.255).
Dimensions: 15.2 cm; W 10.09 cm; D 7 cm.
Moldmade, orange-buff clay. Almost complete except for the right edge.

Three suspension holes, made before firing: two behind the ear lobes and one at the top. The face is sensitively shaped and marked by the soft and graceful modeling of the individual features. The cheeks are softly contoured; the lips are delicately outlined; the nose is well proportioned and carefully modeled with defined nostrils, forming a continuous line with the eyebrows. The almond-shaped eyes were cut out before firing. The well-defined eyebrows emerge from the upper part of the nose extending toward the temples. The left ear is placed behind the

Fig. 7.20. Female mask.

eyes. The forehead is straight and low. The hair is dressed in the style of an Egyptian wig, with the hair flowing behind the ears along the sides of the neck.

The mask belongs to the Phoenician–Egyptian style in Stern's categorization (Stern 1976:114–115). It has a parallel in a female mask from another excavation at Akhziv (*Treasures of the Holy Land*:172), as well as in a protome from Douimès in the vicinity of Carthage (Cintas 1946: Pl. VIII:66).

The mask was found in a tomb which contained a pottery assemblage extending over a long time span. Most of the pottery is of the 9th–8th centuries BCE, though it contains also earlier (10th century) and later vessels (7th century BCE).

21. Female Protome (Fig. 7.21)
Purchased during the excavation.
Dimensions: L 13.5 cm; W 7.0 cm.
Moldmade, buff clay with traces of red paint.

The face is broken and most of the left side is missing. Only one of the suspension holes has survived, behind and above the right ear. The protome includes the upper

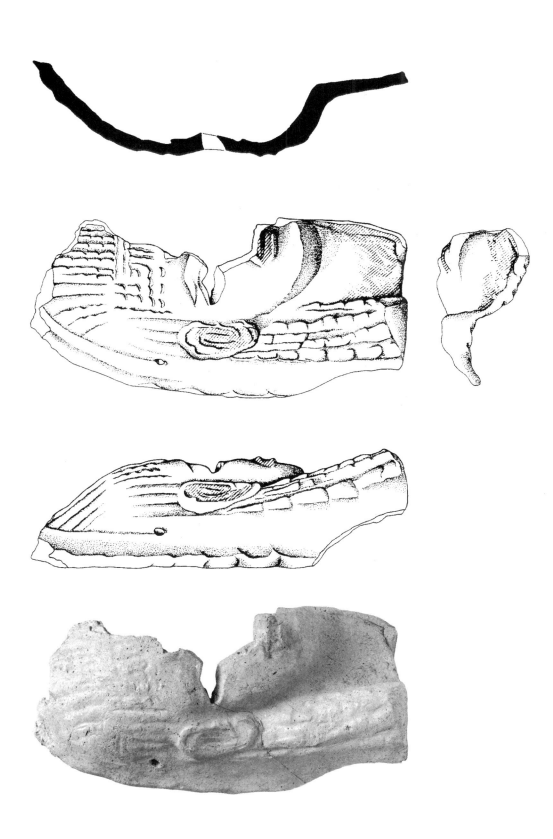

Fig. 7.21. Female protome.

part of the neck, the face and the hair. The lips are delicately outlined and painted red. The nose is missing. The slanted eyes were made before firing. The eyebrows are thick, but hardly noticeable. The right ear is well-defined with traces of red paint. The forehead is straight and low. The hair is shown as an Egyptian-style headdress, flowing behind the ears and along the sides of the neck, represented by an arrangement of vertical grooves. Like the other female protomai, this one also belongs to the Phoenician–Egyptian style. A protome with similar features comes from Tharros, dated to the 6th century BCE (Moscati 1988:363).

Protomai, mainly of women, were widespread in burials in the western Mediterranean. They appear in two main styles: one under strong Phoenician–Egyptian inspiration, the other showing Phoenician–Greek influence (Stern 1976:114–116). Stern suggests that the Phoenician–Egyptian group dates from the 7th–6th centuries, while the Phoenician–Greek group, which does not appear at Akhziv, is later, dating from the 6th–4th centuries BCE (Stern 1976:114).

Fig. 7.22. Male mask

22. Male Mask (Fig. 7.22)
Purchased during the excavation (Reg. No. 45.1).
Dimensions: L 12.5 cm; W 10 cm; D 4 cm.
Moldmade, pinkish-buff clay. The face is covered with a red wash, with some features painted in black. It was found in perfect condition.

Three suspension holes, two below the ears and one at the top, were made before firing. The carefully modeled features include many naturalistic details. The elongated oval eyes are cut out, the cheekbones are high, the ears are well sculpted and the prominent nose forms a continuous line from the well-defined black painted eyebrows. The full lower lip of the closed mouth is visible, while the upper lip is concealed by a black mustache. A black beard, together with sideburns and hairline, frames the face. The black-painted hair and beard contrast vividly with the red-slipped face. Parallel grooves define the hair, which partially covers the forehead and continues upward.

The lower half of a male mask was excavated by M. Dothan at 'Akko (unpublished). Masks of bearded males are known from Tyre (Bikai 1978b: Pl. XXIV:7), Sarepta (Pritchard 1988: Fig. 16), Kition (Karageorghis and Demas 1985: Pl. CLXXVI:4148, 3809) and Enkomi (Karageorghis 1993:33, No. 2, Pl. XX:1); a miniature

male mask was found in an Iron Age child's grave at Khalde (Parrot, Chéhab and Moscati 1975:100, Fig. 103).

23. Grotesque Mask (Fig. 7.23)
Tomb Z III (Reg. No. 44.52).
Dimensions: L 13.5 cm; W 13.8 cm; D 5 cm.
Moldmade, pinkish-buff ware, traces of red paint.

The mask is almost complete, with the right cheek, bottom of the right eye and part of the nose missing. There are cracks all over. Three suspension holes, two located above the ears and one at the top, were made before firing. The wrinkled face lends the mask a frightening expression. The slanted narrow eyes were cut out before firing, as was the crescent-shaped mouth, different in shape from the other Akhziv masks. The nose is squashed, forming a continuous line with the eyebrows. The cheekbones are exceptionally high. The relatively large ears are carelessly shaped. Red paint covers the left ear.

This type of old, beardless face, characterized by its deep lines, is known as the 'grimacing mask' and has been found mainly at Punic sites (Cintas 1946: Pl. XI:78–80). Fragments of grotesque masks were recently discovered at Dor (Stern 1994b:175). It has been suggested that some of the male grotesque masks are iconographically derived from the Mesopotamian masks of Pazuzu and

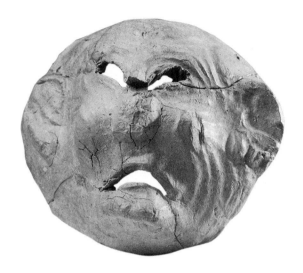

Fig. 7.23. Grotesque mask.

Humbaba (Culican 1975–1976:67). According to Stern, they represent demonic figures and their essential function was apotropaic (Stern 1976:117).

The mask was discovered in context with ceramics dated mainly to the 8th–7th centuries BCE, as well as a few items of the 6th–5th centuries BCE.

24. Bull Mask (Fig. 7.24)
Purchased during the excavation (Reg. No. 44.47).
Dimensions: H 9.5 cm; Diam. 8.5 cm; D 7 cm.

The head is intact. Pinkish-buff clay with red paint on ears and mouth. Traces of red paint on other parts of the face. A white-painted band confined on top by a black line defines the collar.

The mask was formed as a cylindrical cup on the potter's wheel, and its upper part was shaped by hand. Of the three suspension holes made before firing, two are located on either side and the third at the top center of the neck.

The bull head has a wide neck, a naturalistic muzzle with a grooved mouth and cut-out nostrils. A swelling between the horns depicts the hump, and two applied pellets mark the eyes. The two upright horns (ends missing) and the ears protruding below them were shaped separately and added later.

In contrast to the human masks, a limited number of animal masks have been found. An identical bull mask was excavated in another cemetery at Akhziv by E. Mazar (1994:33). A calf mask is in the collections of

the Israel Museum (Hestrin and Dayagi-Mendels 1980:84–87). This category of animal masks includes a number of lion masks from Tell Qasile (A. Mazar 1980:85–86). At Kition and Enkomi, bull skulls were used as ritual masks in Late Cypriot III temples, where the bull probably served as the symbol of the fertility deity. A bull mask from Cyprus also has suspension holes (Myres 1914:342, No. 2073). Male figures wearing bull masks, probably priests participating in a ritual ceremony, are known from Cyprus (Karageorghis 1987: Pl. II:5, 6). The Cypro-Archaic clay figurines representing priests wearing bull masks may allude to one function of the masks (Karageorghis 1971:262). Three bull masks, defined by their excavators as *oscilla*, were discovered at Kourion in Cyprus (Young and Young 1955:949–951). The small size of the Akhziv mask seems to indicate a similar function to that of the *oscillum*, i.e. to be hung on the wall.

Fig. 7.24. Bull mask.

Summary
Pottery masks and protomai executed in naturalistic or grotesque style are well known in the Phoenician sphere, particularly in the western Mediterranean. A substantial number of masks, mainly of pottery but some of stone, have been uncovered along the Levantine coastline. Many were found in tombs, while others came from sanctuaries. They have been discovered in the Phoenician homeland, at Khalde (Saidah 1966:51–90) and at Sarepta in connection with the Phoenician temple (Pritchard

1975: Fig. 62:1–3), as well as at Tyre (Bikai 1978b: Pl. XXIV:7) and Sidon (Macridy 1903).

In Palestine, pottery masks were found at Ḥazor, one of them associated with a Canaanite shrine of the Late Bronze Age, dedicated to the moon god (Yadin et al. 1958:117, Pl. CLXIII; 1960:108, Pl. CLXXXIII); fragments are known from Gezer (Macalister 1912:233, Fig. 383) and Bet She'an (Rowe 1940:23). A pottery mask was uncovered in an 11th century BCE temple at Tell Qasile (A. Mazar 1980:84–85) and another mask comes from a 10th century BCE level at Tel Sera' (unpublished).

Several masks are known from Cyprus, where at least some have been found in sanctuaries. An early 11th century BCE mask was discovered on Floor I of a building in Kition which may have been a sanctuary (Karageorghis 1976:102). A similar clay mask was located in the sanctuary of the Ingot god at Enkomi dating from the same period (Caubet and Courtois 1975:44, n. 102). A life-size mask uncovered at Amathus was probably intended to be worn over a human face (Karageorghis 1990:3–15).

In the wake of the Phoenician expansion westward, such masks appeared at Punic sites, where they became particularly common (Cintas 1946:32–64). Most of the masks found in the western regions were uncovered in tombs together with other funerary equipment. In Sicily a number of masks were discovered in the Tophet at Motya, dated to the 6th century BCE (Ciasca et al. 1964: Pls. XLIV–LI).

Many suggestions have been made concerning the exact function of the Phoenician masks and protomai (Culican 1975–1976; Stern 1976; Hestrin and Dayagi-Mendels 1980). In the case of life-size masks, the cut-out eyes and mouth suggest that they were worn by living persons, perhaps by priests or worshippers during religious rituals. For instance, they were found in the sanctuary of Artemis Orthia in Sparta (Boardman 1963; Carter 1987). The smaller masks could have been placed on statues like those found in the sanctuary at Ḥazor (see above). Yadin suggests that the masks should be identified as a representation of Tanit in the form of פני בעל, 'Face of Ba'al' (Yadin 1970:229). When placed in tombs, it is believed they served an apotropaic purpose. Their widespread use in burials in the Punic world led Culican (1975–1976:71) to posit that they were part of a burial custom which involved the use of the mask of a specific demon or deity. Moscati (1968:164) hypothesizes that the female protomai were probably divine images, so that the protective and votive function would be fundamental.

It seems probable that when placed in tombs, the masks were meant to ward off evil spirits. When found in shrines, they could have either formed part of the cult equipment or may have served as votive offerings.

ARCHITECTURAL MODELS

25. Model Shrine (Fig. 7.25)
Purchased during the excavation (Reg. No. 44.46).
Cubiculum: W 8.8 cm; H 12 cm.
Entablature: W 14.5 cm; H 5 cm.
Base of shrine: W 6.8 cm; L 9 cm.
Handmade, reddish-orange clay, well fired.

This carefully executed model shrine has a rectangular cubiculum, whose floor extends forward to form a threshold. A large rectangular entablature rises above the opening of the cubiculum, with a disk-shaped knob on the lower center (Maier and Dayagi-Mendels, forthcoming). A broad strap of clay, spanning the full width of the cubiculum opening, emerges from the front edge of the threshold. At the midpoint of the cubiculum, it bends back toward the rear wall. Rising from the strap, at a point just before it meets the back wall, is a square, flat projection bearing a double row of four flattened knobs or pellets. The shrine was originally covered with a white wash and decorated with red paint. The lower part of the entablature is embellished with a red band. Traces of red paint are also visible on the strap, the square projection and the flattened knobs.

Models of houses from Mesopotamia and the Levant, some bearing symbols attributed to specific deities, date back to the third millennium BCE (Epstein 1989). Such models are believed to represent the houses of deities. They were probably presented to the gods in their temples, kept at home for private cult use, or placed in tombs.

Two main types of model shrines are known. One type, which dates to the Late Bronze and Iron Ages, is made from the pottery jars of that period. In these models, an opening, sometimes embellished with architectural elements, is cut into one of the walls, giving the appearance of a façade. These openings could be easily closed with a clay door. According to some scholars, such models may have served for storing treasures (Amiran et al. 1978:53), or as 'cages' for keeping the sacred snakes in the Ḥazor temple (Yadin 1975:90).

The other type of model shrine is house-shaped, and dates to the Iron Age. A growing number of models of

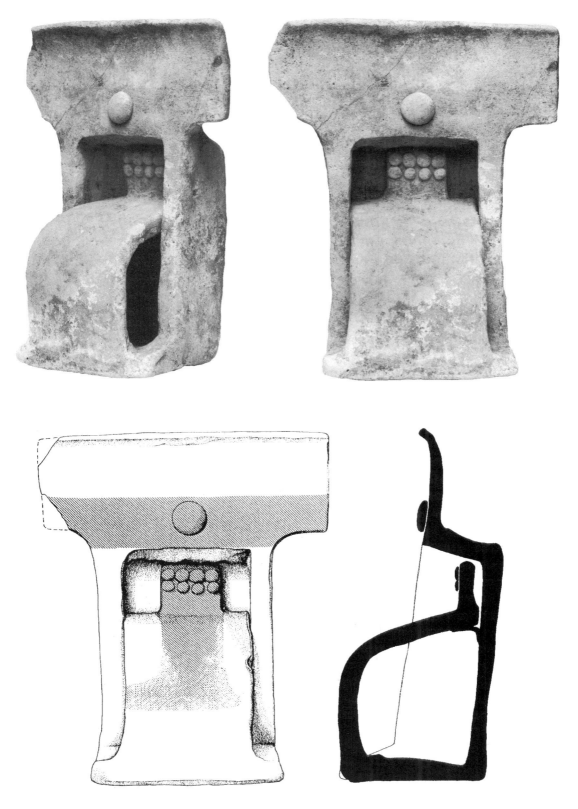

Fig. 7.25. Model shrine.

this type continue to come to light. These model shrines are believed to represent temple architecture and are usually characterized by an elaborate entablature, indicating the façade of the shrine, and a cubiculum, standing for the shrine's interior. The Akhziv model shrine belongs to this category, though it is unique in terms of some of its features, as has already been discussed (Culican 1976b; Weinberg 1978:42–43). Its façade is minimally decorated, and unlike many other models of this type, it has no columns and capitals and a fairly simple entablature. The circular knob on the entablature may represent a lunar disk, though this symbol usually appears together with a crescent, and was described as such by Culican (1976b:47) and Karageorghis (1996: Pls. XXXIV, XXXV). However, no traces of a crescent can be seen on this model. The red-painted band that decorates the entablature may represent a wooden beam, or some other architectural feature.

Clay model shrines similar to ours sometimes contain a figure, presumably that of a deity, in the cubiculum (Bretschneider 1991). In other model shrines, figures are entwined in the entablature (Culican 1976b: Pl. 5:B). Many of the models, however, were discovered empty. In those cases, the cubiculum may have held a figure made of a perishable material. Alternatively, the absence of a permanent figurine may have been intended to allow the worshipper to remove the figure and replace it with that of another deity. The deity whose figure or symbols are most frequently found in the cubiculum is Astarte. Culican has suggested that the Phoenician proclivity to aniconic representation accounts for the absence of figures in some of the models (Culican 1976b:49). This view, however, is difficult to accept, given the representation of deities in some of the model shrines and their frequent depiction in naiskoi and on Punic funerary stelae (Lilliu 1940:296–418; A. Mazar 1985b:5).

While at first glance, the Akhziv model shrine appears to lack a figure, the broad curved strap filling most of the interior cannot be ignored. The frequent presence of a female figure suggests that a female deity was also present in our shrine. The strap is reminiscent of figurines depicting seated goddesses, whose torsos merge with their thrones, such as the 'Ashdoda' type (T. Dothan 1982:235–236; regarding seated deities, see also Van Buren 1939/1941:277 ff.; Mollard-Besques 1954: Pl. IX:B75; Bisi 1973:73, No. 7, Pl. XXXVII.1; 1974:217–218, Pls. LXXIII–LXXIV). It may thus be interpreted as the schematization of a seated deity, perhaps in line with an aniconic conception (Karageorghis 1996:63, Fig. 46). Similarly, the square projection emerging from the strap may be regarded as an abstraction of the goddess' neck and head, in which case the eight pellets represent her crown. Another possibility is that the goddess' head is missing, and that the projection depicts only her long neck, graced by a necklace of eight beads (cf. a terracotta shrine from Amathus with a female figure wearing a crown of pellets, Culican 1976b: Pl. 2:c) and another model shrine from Amathus with a schematic image wearing a 'rose crown' (Culican 1976b: Pl. 3:A). It is of interest to compare this figure with that of a seated deity from Haraib (Culican 1976b: Pl. 6:B), whose body also forms part of the throne but whose head is rendered quite clearly.

The eight pellets on the projection are reminiscent of the *sibitti*—the seven-star motif known from Mesopotamian art (Seidl 1989:101–103). Another model shrine from Cyprus, now in the Cesnola collection, is decorated with six pellets (Culican 1976b: Pl. 2a), representing, perhaps, another deviation from the original number of seven. It is conceivable, therefore, that our eight pellets did indeed derive from the original seven-star motif that, over the centuries, apparently lost its initial meaning and became a purely decorative element.

A strikingly similar model shrine was found in a necropolis at Tyre, dated to the 8th century BCE (Institut du monde arabe 1998:141).

CHAPTER 8

SUMMARY

To date, very few of the 11th–6th century BCE cemeteries of the eastern Mediterranean coastal cities have been investigated. The publication of the finds from the Akhziv cemeteries, therefore, not only brings to light the rich assemblages excavated in the 1940s by Ben-Dor, but also contributes to our knowledge of the Phoenicians in their homeland.

The two cemeteries excavated by Ben-Dor reflect a fairly long period of use. The earliest datable material suggests that the cemeteries were first utilized in the late 11th–10th centuries BCE. The bulk of the pottery, however, dates to the 9th–7th centuries BCE, with a notable decrease of examples from the 7th century BCE. A few finds of the Persian period indicate that some of the tombs either remained in use until the 6th–5th centuries BCE or were re-used at that time.

One of the major characteristics of the Akhziv cemeteries is the uniformity of the tombs. While different tomb types were observed in the cemeteries, one type prevailed in each. This is particularly interesting in view of the proximity of the cemeteries, their chronological closeness and the similarity of their contents. There are few other Phoenician cemeteries with such a large number of tombs of a similar plan for which the research findings have been published. However, it should be noted that although the tombs of a given cemetery usually have the same orientation, we cannot be certain that this was the case at Akhziv, given a lack of information.

With the exception of a single trough tomb and one masonry tomb, the Akhziv tombs under discussion were rock-hewn shaft tombs, almost all of which had a single burial chamber. One tomb, however, had two chambers. The entrances were generally sealed with large stone slabs, some of which have been recovered. The approach by a shaft is somewhat surprising, as many other Phoenician tombs were approached by a *dromos*, such as those uncovered at Byblos and Sidon. The shafts were vertical, and sometimes had stairways along the walls to facilitate the descent. The burial chambers were located at a right angle to the lower part of the shaft, and sometimes there were steps leading from the passage to the standing pit that was frequently found in the chamber floor. Some of the chambers had niches hewn into the walls. These niches were at times separated from the main burial chamber by a low partition. The ceilings were generally rock cut, though some of the tombs had open ceilings that were roofed with stone slabs.

From the late second millennium BCE to the early first millennium BCE the most common burial practice at Akhziv and in Phoenicia in general was inhumation. The rite of cremation, so well-known in the Phoenician–Punic sphere in the 8th–6th centuries BCE, is also recorded at various sites along the eastern Mediterranean coast (Hestrin and Dayagi-Mendels 1983:56), where it was usually carried out in open fields. Evidence of this practice was observed by Elat Mazar in her excavations at Akhziv. The custom of placing urns with human ashes inside a tomb is known from several Phoenician sites (Gras, Rouillard and Texidor 1991:134). It should be noted that cremation together with inhumation, although rare, was sometimes carried out in the same tomb at the Akhziv cemeteries, as, for instance, in Tomb ZR XLVI. In this same tomb two urns were uncovered, one containing a skull and bone fragments. Although inhumation was the common burial practice at Akhziv, Prausnitz reports evidence of cremation in tombs dated to the 9th–7th centuries BCE in the southern (ez-Zib [Buqbaq]) cemetery of Akhziv (Prausnitz 1993:35).

Unfortunately, no skeletal remains from Akhziv have reached us, and we therefore have no estimate of how many individuals were interred in each tomb (though we can probably assume it was more than one); nor can we draw any conclusions regarding the ages and gender of the deceased. There is no clear-cut evidence attesting to the holding of banquets or offering of funerary sacrifices at the cemeteries under discussion. However, holes in the ceilings of several tombs are considered to be openings for libations. In addition, within the pottery assemblage originating in the trenches, there are fragments of what seem to be chalices; this suggests that, after the burial ceremony, banquets or some sacrificial activity may have been held.

At Akhziv, the body of the deceased was placed on the chamber floor and surrounded by burial offerings. Since many of the tombs, however, were looted, much information has been lost. Nonetheless, it seems that most of the offerings were pottery; these finds have greatly enriched our knowledge of the Phoenician ceramic repertoire. The pottery assemblage from Akhziv is rather homogeneous, consisting primarily of jugs, juglets and bowls, a considerable number of which are of a rather poor quality and were apparently made especially for funerary purposes. Domestic vessels such as cooking pots and oil lamps are rare. A distinctive group among the pottery vessels are the red-slipped jugs with 'Akhziv' bases, as well as crude imitations of these types. Imported Cypriot vessels, such as the White-Painted and Black-on-Red types, also occupy a significant place, attesting to ties between the two regions.

Another type of burial gift that was popular at Akhziv is the terracotta figurine. Some of these figurines also demonstrate a strong Cypriot influence. Included among these are human figurines, horses with riders, masks and a model shrine. Many of these depict scenes from everyday life—bread-making, bathing, etc. A remarkably large number of the terracottas represent musicians.

A relatively limited repertoire of small finds was recovered from Akhziv, even from tombs containing rich and varied pottery assemblages. Objects made of gold, silver and precious stones were rare, whereas bronze and faience were more common. Among the adornments were rings, bracelets, earrings, fibulae, pendants, and amulets. The amulets were of apotropaic significance intended to ward off evil; the many scarabs found in the tombs symbolized regeneration. Unfortunately, most of these finds are chronologically non-diagnostic, consisting of motifs that were popular over a long span of time. Some of the jewelry, such as the basket-shaped earrings and the amulet case, have their closest parallels in the western Mediterranean. It is interesting that very little material from Israel and Judah was recovered in the cemeteries. This raises many questions regarding the relations between the community interred at Akhziv and these kingdoms.

The settlement that corresponds to the Akhziv cemeteries is as yet unidentified, a situation well-known from other Phoenician cemeteries (Gras, Rouillard and Texidor 1991:127). This could be attributed to the fact that the deceased were individuals who met their deaths far from their homes, as may have been the case with sailors, craftsmen or traveling merchants. Though there are many unanswered questions regarding the origin, age and gender of the individuals buried in the Akhziv cemeteries, the impression is that these were people of a similar social background, probably belonging to the middle class. This assumption is based on the common nature of the tombs and the burial offerings. While the origin of the individuals buried in the cemeteries of Akhziv remains unknown, the contents of the tombs clearly reflect Phoenician culture and strong ties to Cyprus and areas further west.

REFERENCES

Aharoni M. 1979. The Askos: Is it the Biblical Nebel? *Tel Aviv* 6:95–97.

Aharoni Y. 1970. *The Beersheba Excavations* I. Tel Aviv.

Albright W.F. 1932. *The Excavations of Tell Beit Mirsim* I. *The Pottery of the First Three Campaigns* (AASOR XII). New Haven.

Albright W.F. 1933. *The Excavations of Tell Beit Mirsim* IA. *The Bronze Age Pottery of the Fourth Campaign* (AASOR XIII). New Haven. Pp. 55–128.

Albright W.F. 1938. *The Excavations of Tell Beit Mirsim* II. *The Bronze Age* (AASOR XVII). New Haven.

Albright W.F. 1943. *The Excavations of Tell Beit Mirsim* III. *The Iron Age* (AASOR XXI–XXII). New Haven.

Amiran R. 1969. *Ancient Pottery of the Holy Land*. Jerusalem.

Amiran R. et al. 1978. *Early Arad* I. Jerusalem.

Anderson W.P. 1988. *Sarepta* I. *The Late Bronze and Early Iron Age Strata of Area II.Y*. Beirut.

Andrae W. 1943. *Die Kleinfunde von Sendschirli* (Mitteilungen aus den Orientalischen Sammlungen 15). Berlin.

Avigad N. 1960. Excavations at Makmish, 1958. *IEJ* 10:90–96.

Avigad N. 1989. The Inscribed Pomegranate from the "House of the Lord". *IMJ* 8:7–16.

Barkay G. 1986. *Ketef Hinom: A Treasure Facing Jerusalem's Walls* (Israel Museum Cat. 274). Jerusalem.

Barnett R.D. 1957. *The Nimrud Ivories*. London.

Barnett R.D. and Mendelson C. eds. 1987. *Tharros. A Catalogue of Material in the British Museum from Phoenician and Other Tombs at Tharros, Sardinia*. London.

Bayer B. 1982. Ancient Musical Instruments. *BAR* 8:18–57.

Beck H.C. 1928. *Classification and Nomenclature of Beads and Pendants*. Oxford.

Beit-Arieh I. 1995. *Horvat Qitmit—An Edomite Shrine in the Biblical Negev*. Tel Aviv.

Bikai P.M. 1978a. The Late Phoenician Pottery Complex and Chronology. *BASOR* 229:47–56.

Bikai P.M. 1978b. *The Pottery of Tyre*. Warminster.

Bikai P.M. 1981. The Phoenician Imports. In V. Karageorghis ed. *Excavations at Kition* IV. *The Non-Cypriote Pottery*. Nicosia. Pp. 23–35.

Bikai P.M. 1987a. The Phoenician Pottery. In V. Karageorghis and O. Picard eds. *La nécropole d'Amathonte, Tombes 113–367* II. *Céramiques non-chypriotes*. Nicosia. Pp. 1–19.

Bikai P.M. 1987b. *The Phoenician Pottery of Cyprus*. Nicosia.

Biran A. 1985. Tel 'Ira. *Qadmoniot* 18:25–28 (Hebrew).

Birmingham J. 1963. The Chronology of Some Early and Middle Iron Age Cypriote Sites. *AJA* 67:15–42.

Bisi A.M. 1973. Le terrecotte figurate di tipo greco-punico de Ibiza. *RSF* 1:69–89.

Bisi A.M. 1974. Le terrecotte figurate di tipo greco-punico de Ibiza. *RSF* 2:201–244.

Boardman J. 1963. Arthemis Orthia and Chronology. *ABSA* 58:1–7.

Bosanquet R.C. 1905–1906. The Cult of Arthemis Orthia as Illustrated by the Finds. *ABSA* 12:338–339.

Braidwood L. 1940. Report on Two Sondages on the Coast of Syria, South of Tartous. *Syria* 21:183–226.

Braun J. 1999. *Die Musikkultur Altisraels/Palästinas: Studien zu archäologischen, schriftlichen und vergleichenden Quellen* (Orbis Biblicus et Orientalis 164). Freiburg.

Bretschneider J. 1991. Götter in Schreinen. *Ugarit Forschungen* 23:13–32.

Briend J. and Humbert J. eds. 1980. *Tell Keisan (1971–1976). Une cité phénicienne en Galilée*. Fribourg.

Carter J.B. 1987. The Masks of Ortheia. *AJA* 91:355–383.

Cassimatis H. 1986. Terres cuites chypriotes à Dublin. *RDAC*:173–182.

Catalan M.P. 1963. Ein altpunisches Graberfeld bei Almunecar. *Madrider Mitteilungen* 4:9–38.

Caubet A. and Courtois J.C. 1975. Masques chypriotes en terre cuite du XIIe s. av. J.-C. *RDAC*:43–49.

Chambon A. 1984. *Tell el Far'ah* I. *L'âge du Fer*. Paris.

Chapman S.V. 1972. A Catalogue of Iron Age Pottery from the Cemeteries of Khirbet Silm, Joya, Qraye and Qasmieh of South Lebanon. *Berytus* 21:55–194.

Chéhab M. 1953–1954. *Les terres cuites de Kharayeb. Planches* (BMB XI). Beirut.

Christou D. 1986. Greek and Near Eastern Links with Cyprus in the Iron Age from the Tomb Evidence at Rizokarpaso and Amathus. In V. Karageorghis ed. *Acts of the International Archaeological Symposium—Cyprus between the Orient and the Occident*. Nicosia.

Ciasca A. et al. 1964. *Mozia* I. Rome.

Cintas P. 1946. *Amulettes puniques*. Tunis.

Cintas P. 1950. *Céramique punique*. Paris.

Clerc G. et al. 1976. *Fouilles de Kition* II. *Objets égyptiens et égyptisants*. Nicosia.

Coldstream J.N. 1982. Greeks and Phoenicians in the Aegean. In H.G. Niemeyer ed. *Phönizier im Westen*. Mainz am Rhein.

Crowfoot J.W., Crowfoot G.M. and Kenyon K.M. 1957. *Samaria-Sebaste* III. *The Objects*. London.

Culican W. 1970. Phoenician Oil Bottles and Tripod Bowls. *Berytus* 24:5–18.

Culican W. 1973. The Graves at Tell er-Reqeish. *AJBA* 2:66–105.

Culican W. 1975–1976. Some Phoenician Masks and Other Terracottas. *Berytus* 24:47–87.

Culican W. 1976a. Phoenician Demons. *JNES* 35:21–24.

Culican W. 1976b. A Terracotta Shrine from Achzib. *ZDPV* 92:47–53.

Culican W. 1976c. A Votive Model from the Sea. *PEQ* 108:119–123.

Culican W. 1982. The Repertoire of Phoenician Pottery. In H.G. Niemeyer ed. *Phönizier im Westen*. Mainz am Rhein. Pp. 45–82.

Dickins G. 1929. *Terracotta Masks*. In R.M. Dawkins ed. *The Sanctuary of Artemis Orthia at Sparta*. London. Pp. 163–186.

Dothan M. 1961. Excavations at Azor. *IEJ* 11:171–175.

Dothan M. 1964. Ashdod. Preliminary Report on the Excavations in Seasons 1962/1963. *IEJ* 14:79–95.

Dothan M. 1970. The Musicians of Ashdod. *Archaeology* 23:310–311.

Dothan M. 1971. *Ashdod* II–III (*'Atiqot* [*ES*] 9–10). Jerusalem.

Dothan M. and Freedman D.N. 1967. *Ashdod* I (*'Atiqot* [*ES*] 7). Jerusalem.

Dothan M. and Porath Y. 1982. *Ashdod* IV (*'Atiqot* [*ES*] 15). Jerusalem.

Dothan T. 1961. Excavations at Azor, 1960. *IEJ* 11:171–175.

Dothan T. 1963. Spinning Bowls. *IEJ* 13:97–112.

Dothan T. 1982. *The Philistines and Their Material Culture*. Jerusalem.

Duchesne-Guillemin M. 1981. Music in Ancient Mesopotamia and Egypt. *World Archaeology* 12:287–297.

Dunand M. 1950. *Fouilles de Byblos* II. Paris.

Elgavish J. 1968. *Archaeological Excavations at Shikmona* I. Haifa.

Elgavish J. 1993. Shiqmona. *NEAEHL* 4:1373–1378.

Epstein C. 1989. Temple Model Shrines and Their Symbolism. *EI* 20:23–30 (Hebrew, English summary:193*–194*)

Fantalkin A. 2001. Meẓad Ḥashavyahu: Its Material Culture and Historical Background (*Tel Aviv* 28). Tel Aviv.

Flouerentzos P. 1991. Wind Musical Instruments from Cyprus. In P. Astrom ed. *Acta Cypria, Acts of an International Congress on Cypriote Archaeology Held in Göteborg, 22–24 August*. Göteborg. Pp. 41–47.

Fugmann E. 1958. *Hama. Fouilles et recherches 1931–1938*. Copenhagen.

Gal Z. 1989. *Ḥurvat Rosh Zayit, Biblical Cabul* (The Reuben and Edith Hecht Museum Cat. 5). Haifa.

Gal Z. 1992. Ḥurbat Rosh Zayit and the Early Phoenician Pottery. *Levant* 24:173–186.

Gal Z. and Alexandre Y. 2000. *Ḥorbat Rosh Zayit. An Iron Age Storage Fort and Village* (IAA Reports 8). Jerusalem.

Gehrig U. and Niemeyer H.J. 1990. *Die Phönizier im Zeitalter Homers*. Mainz.

Gilboa A. 1989. New Finds at Tel Dor and the Beginning of Cypro-Geometric Pottery Import to Palestine. *IEJ* 39:204–218.

Ginouvés R. 1962. *Balaneutiké. Recherches sur le bain dans l'antiquité grecque*. Paris.

Gitin S. 1990. *Gezer* III. Jerusalem.

Gjerstad E. 1948. *The Swedish Cyprus Expedition*. IV, 2. *The Cypro-Geometric, Cypro-Archaic and Cypro-Classical Periods*. Stockholm.

Gjerstad E. et al. 1935. *The Swedish Cyprus Expedition* II. *Plates*. Stockholm.

Goldstein S.M. 1979. *Pre-Roman and Early Roman Glass in the Corning Museum of Glass*. New York.

Gorali M. 1977. *Music in Ancient Israel*. Haifa.

Gras M., Rouillard P. and Texidor J. 1991. The Phoenicians and Death. *Berytus* 39:127–176.

Guy P.L.O. 1924. Mt. Carmel: An Early Iron Age Cemetery near Haifa, Excavated September 1922. *BBSAJ* 5:47–55.

Guy P.L.O. and Engberg R.M. 1938. *Megiddo Tombs*. Chicago.

Hamilton R.W. 1935. Excavations at Tell Abu Hawam. *QDAP* 4:1–69.

Harden D. 1962. *The Phoenicians*. London.

Herrmann C. 1994. *Ägyptische Amulette aus Palästina/Israel* (Orbis Biblicus et Orientalis 138). Freiburg, Switzerland.

Herzog Z., Rapp G. Jr. and Negbi O. 1989. *Excavations at Tel Michal, Israel*. Tel Aviv.

Hestrin R. and Dayagi-Mendels M. 1980. Two Phoenician Pottery Masks. *The Israel Museum News* 16:83–88.

Hestrin R. and Dayagi-Mendels M. 1983. Another Pottery Group from Abu Ruqeish. *IMJ* 2:49–57.

Higgins R.A. 1954. *Catalogue of the Terracottas in the Department of Greek and Roman Antiquities, the British Museum* I. *Text and Plates. Greek: 730–330 B.C.* London.

Institut du monde arabe. 1998. *Liban, l'autre rive: Exposition présentée à l'Institut du monde arabe du 27 octobre au 2 mai 1999*. Paris.

James F.W. 1966. *The Iron Age at Beth Shan*. Philadelphia.

Johns C. 1993. *Sex or Symbol—Erotic Images of Greece and Rome*. 4th ed. London.

Johns C.N. 1933. Excavations at Atlit (1930–31): The South-Eastern Cemetery. *QDAP* 2:41–104.

Johns C.N. 1938. Excavations at the Pilgrims' Castle, Atlit (1933): Cremated Burials of Phoenician Origin. *QDAP* 6:121–152.

Kaoukabani B. 1973. Rapport préliminaire sur les fouilles de Kharayeb 1969–70. *BMB* 26:41–59.

Karageorghis V. 1970. *Salamis Vol. 4. Excavation in the Necropolis of Salamis* II. Nicosia.

Karageorghis V. 1971. Notes on Some Cypriot Priests Wearing Bull-Masks. *HTR* 64:261–270.

Karageorghis V. 1973, 1974. *Salamis Vol. 5. Excavations in the Necropolis of Salamis* III. Nicosia.

Karageorghis V. 1976. *Kition-Mycenean and Phoenician Discoveries in Cyprus*. London.

Karageorghis V. 1978. *Salamis Vol. 7. Excavations in the Necropolis of Salamis* IV. Nicosia.

Karageoghis V. 1983. *Palaepaphos-Skales. An Iron Age Cemetery in Cyprus*. Konstanz.

Karageorghis V. 1987. The Terracottas. In V. Karageorghis and O. Picard eds. *La nécropole d'Amathonte Tombes 113–367* II. *Céramiques non-chypriotes*. Nicosia.

Karageorghis V. 1990. Notes on Some Teracotta Masks from Amathus now in the British Museum. *RSF* 18:3–15.

Karageorghis V. 1991. A Middle Bronze Age Scenic Composition: Copper-Leaching or Pot-Making. In F. Vandenabeele and R. Laffineur eds. *Cypriote Terracottas*. Brussels–Liège. Pp. 33–38.

Karageorghis V. 1993. *The Coroplastic Art of Ancient Cyprus* II. *Late Cypriote II–Cypro-Geometric III*. Nicosia.

Karageorghis V. 1996. *The Coroplastic Art of Ancient Cyprus* VI. *The Cypro-Archaic Period Monsters, Animals and Miscellanea*. Nicosia.

Karageorghis V. and Demas M. 1985. *The Excavations at Kition* V. *The Pre-Phoenician Levels*. Nicosia.

Karageorghis V. et al. 1981. *The Excavations at Kition* IV. *The Non-Cypriote Pottery*. Nicosia.

Keel O. 1978. *The Symbolism of the Biblical World*. London.

Keel O. 1997. *Corpus der Stempelsiegel—Amulette aus Palästina/Israel von den Anfängen bis zur Perserzeit* I. *Von Tell Abu Farağ bis 'Atlit* (Orbis Biblicus et Orientalis 13). Freiburg/Switzerland–Göttingen.

Kelm G.L. and Mazar A. 1985. Tel Batash (Timnah) Excavations, Second Preliminary Report (1981–1983) *BASOR Supplement* 23:93–120.

Khalifeh I.A. 1988. *Sarepta* II. *The Late Bronze and Iron Age Periods of Area II, X*. Beirut.

Koehl R.B. 1985. *Sarepta* III. *The Imported Bronze and Iron Age Wares from Area II, X*. Beirut.

Lamon R.S. and Shipton G.M. 1939. *Megiddo* I. *Seasons of 1925–34. Strata I–V*. Chicago.

Liebowitz H. and Dehnisch A.M. 1998. A Mould-Made Seated Terra-Cotta Cat from Beth Gan. *IEJ* 48:174–182.

Lilliu G. 1940. Le stele puniche di Sulcis (Cagliari). *Monumenti Antichi* 40:294–418.

Lindemann G. et al. 1972. Toscanos, Jardin und Alarcon. Vorbericht über die Grabungskampagne 1971. *Madrider Mitteilungen* 13:125–156.

Loffreda S. 1968. Typological Sequence of Iron Age Rock-Cut Tombs in Palestine. *Liber Annuus* 18:244–287.

Loud G. 1948. *Megiddo* II. *Seasons of 1935–39*. Chicago.

Luckenbill D.D. 1924. *Ancient Assyrian Annals*. Chicago.

Macalister R.A.S. 1912. *The Excavations of Gezer 1902–1905 and 1907–1909* II. London.

Macridy T. 1903. Le Temple d'Echmoun à Sidon. *RB* 12:69–77.

Maier A. and Dayagi-Mendels M. Forthcoming. A Decorated Model Shrine from the Shlomo Moussaieff Collection. In R. Deutsch ed. *Festschrift in Honor of Shlomo Moussaieff*.

Markoe G.E. 1985. *Phoenician Bronze and Silver Bowls from Cyprus and the Mediterranean*. Berkeley.

Maxwell-Hyslop K.R. 1971. *Western Asiatic Jewellery c. 3000–612 B.C.E.* London.

Mazar A. 1980. *Excavations at Tell Qasile* I (Qedem 12). Jerusalem.

Mazar A. 1985a. *Excavations at Tell Qasile* II (Qedem 20). Jerusalem.

Mazar A. 1985b. Pottery and Plaques Depicting Goddesses Standing in Temple Facades. *Michmanim* 2:5–18.

Mazar B. 1950–1951. The Excavations at Tell Qasile. Preliminary Report. *IEJ* 1:125–140.

Mazar B., Dothan T. and Dunayevsky I. 1966. *En Gedi. The First and Second Seasons of Excavations 1961–1962* ('Atiqot [ES] 5). Jerusalem.

Mazar E. 1990. A Horsemen's Tomb at Akhziv. *Qadmoniot* 23:104–109 (Hebrew).

Mazar E. 1994. Phoenician Ashlar-Built Iron Age Tombs at Achzib. *Qadmoniot* 27:29–33 (Hebrew).

Mazar E. and Mazar B. 1989. *Excavations in the South of the Temple Mount. The Ophel of Biblical Jerusalem* (Qedem 29). Jerusalem.

Meyers C. 1987. A Terracotta at the Harvard Semitic Museum and Disc-Holding Female Figures Reconsidered. *IEJ* 37:116–122.

Meyers C. 1991. Of Drums and Damsels: Women's Performance in Ancient Israel. *BA* 54:16–27.

Miroschedji P. de. 2001. Les "maquettes architecturales" palestiniennes. In B. Muller ed. *"Maquettes architecturales" de l'antiquité. Actes du Colloque de Strasbourg 3–5 décembre 1998* (Travaux du Centre de Recherche sur le Proche-Orient et la Grèce Antiques). Paris. Pp. 43–85.

Mollard-Besques S. 1954. *Catalogue raisonné des figures et reliefs en terre-cuite grecs étrusques et romains* I. Paris.

Monloup Th. 1984. *Salamine de Chypre* XII. *Les figurines de terre cuite de tradition archaïque*. Paris.

Moscati S. 1968. *The World of the Phoenicians*. London.

Moscati S. 1988. *The Phoenicians*. Venice.

Müller-Winkler C. 1987. *Die Ägyptischen Objekt-Amulette*. Fribourg.

Myres J.L. 1914. *Handbook of the Cesnola Collection of Antiquities from Cyprus*. New York.

Naveh J. 1962. The Excavations at Meṣad Ḥashavyahu; Preliminary Report. *IEJ* 12:89–113.

Negbi O. 1966. *A Deposit of Terracottas and Statuettes from Tel Ṣippor* ('Atiqot [ES] 6). Jerusalem.

Niemeyer H.G. et al. 1964. Altpunische Funde von der Mündung des Rio Algarrobo. *Madrider Mitteilungen* 5:73–90.

Ohata K. ed. 1967. *Tel Zeror* II. *Preliminary Report of the Excavations, Second Season 1965*. Tokyo.

Ohnefalsch-Richter M. 1893. *Kypros—Die Bibel und Homer*. Berlin.

Ornan T. 1986. *A Man and His Land: Highlights from the Moshe Dayan Collection* (Israel Museum Cat. 270). Jerusalem.

Parrot A., Chéhab M.H. and Moscati S. 1975. *Les Phéniciens*. Paris.

Perrot G. and Chipiez C. 1885. *History of Art in Phoenicia and its Dependencies* I. London.

Petrie W.M.F. 1914. *Amulets*. London.

Petrie W.M.F. 1927. *Objects of Daily Use*. London.

Petrie W.M.F. 1928. *Gerar*. London.

Petrie W.M.F. 1930. *Beth Pelet* I. *Tell Fara*. London.

Petrie W.M.F. 1932. *Ancient Gaza* II. *Tell el-Ajjul*. London.

Petrie W.M.F. 1934. *Ancient Gaza* IV. *Tell el-Ajjul.* London.

Posener G. 1962. *A Dictionary of Egyptian Civilization.* London.

Prausnitz M.W. 1972. Red-Polished and Black-on-Red Wares at Akhziv Israel and Cyprus in the Early–Middle Iron Age. *Praktika tou Protou Diethnous Kyprologikou Synderiou.* Nicosia. Pp. 151–156.

Prausnitz M.W. 1982. Die Nekropolen von Akhziv und die Entwicklung der Keramik vom 10. bis zum 7. Jh. v. Chr. in Akhziv, Samaria und Ashdod. In H.G. Niemeyer ed. *Phönizier im Westen.* Mainz am Rhein. Pp. 31–44.

Prausnitz M.W. 1993. Achzib. *NEAEHL* 1:32–35.

Pritchard J.B. 1975. *Sarepta. A Preliminary Report on the Iron Age.* Philadelphia.

Pritchard J.B. 1980. *The Cemetery at Tell es-Sa'idiyeh, Jordan.* Philadelphia.

Pritchard J.B. 1985. *Tell es-Sa'idiyeh Excavations on the Tell, 1964–1966.* Philadelphia.

Pritchard J.B. 1988. *Sarepta* IV. *The Objects from Area II, X.* Beirut.

Quillard B. 1979. *Bijoux carthaginois* I. *Les colliers.* Louvain-La-Neuve.

Quillard B. 1987. *Bijoux carthaginois* II. *Porte-amulettes, sceaux-pendentifs, pendants, boucles, anneaux et bagues.* Louvain-La-Neuve.

Rast W.E. 1978. *Taanach* I. *Studies in the Iron Age Pottery.* Cambridge, Mass.

Reich R. and Brandl B. 1985. Gezer under Assyrian Rule. *PEQ* 117:41–54.

Reifenberg A. 1950. *Ancient Hebrew Arts.* New York.

Renan E. 1864. *Mission de Phénicie.* Paris.

Riis P.J. 1948. *Hama. Fouilles et Recherches 1931–1938.* Copenhagen.

Rowe A. 1940. *The Four Canaanite Temples of Beth Shan.* Philadelphia.

Saidah R. 1966. Fouilles de Khaldé. Rapport préliminaire sur la première et deuxième campagnes (1961–1962). *BMB* 19:51–90.

Schumacher G. 1908. *Tell el-Mutesellim* I. Leipzig.

Seidl U. 1989. *Die Babylonischen Kudurru Reliefs.* Göttingen.

Shefton B.B. 1982. Greeks and Greek Imports in the South of the Iberian Peninsula. The Archaeological Evidence. In H.G. Niemeyer ed. *Phönizier im Westen.* Mainz am Rhein. Pp. 337–370.

Spaer M. 2001. *Ancient Glass in the Israel Museum: Beads and Other Small Objects* (Israel Museum Cat. No. 447). Jerusalem.

Stager L.W. and Wolff S.R. 1984. Child Sacrifice at Carthage: Religious Rite or Population Control? *BAR* 10:31–51.

Stern E. 1976. Phoenician Masks and Pendants. *PEQ* 108:109–118.

Stern E. 1978. *Excavations at Tel Mevorakh* (1973–1976) (Qedem 9). Jerusalem.

Stern E. 1982. *Material Culture of the Land of the Bible in the Persian Period.* Warminster.

Stern E. 1989. What Happened to the Cult Figurines? *BAR* 15:22–29.

Stern E. 1994a. A Cypro-Phoenician Dedicatory Offering from Tel Dor Depicting a Maritime Scene. *Qadmoniot* 27:34–38 (Hebrew).

Stern E. 1994b. *Dor—Ruler of the Seas.* Jerusalem.

Stern E. 1994c. A Phoenician-Cypriote Votive Scapula from Tel Dor: A Maritime Scene. *IEJ* 44:1–12.

Stieglitz R.R. 1975. An Ancient Terra-Cotta Ship from Cyprus. *Sefunim* 4:44–46.

Stronach D. 1959. The Development of the Fibula in the Near East. *Iraq* 21:181–206.

Taylor J. du P. 1959. The Cypriot and Syrian Pottery from Al Mina, Syria. *Iraq* 21:62–92.

Treasures of the Holy Land. Ancient Art from the Israel Museum. The Metropolitan Museum of Art. New York 1986.

Tufnell O. 1953. *Lachish* III. *The Iron Age.* London.

Ussishkin D. 1974. Tombs from the Israelite Period at Tel 'Eton. *Tel Aviv* 1:109–127.

Van Beek G.W. 1951. Cypriote Chronology and the Dating of Iron Age Sites in Israel. *BASOR* 124:26–29.

Van Buren D. 1939/1941. The Seven Dots in Mesopotamian Art and Their Meaning. *AfO* 13:277–289.

Vandenabeele F. 1986. Phoenician Influence on the Cypro-Archaic Terracotta Production and Cypriot Influence Abroad. In V. Karageorghis ed. *Acts of the International Archaeological Symposium 'Cyprus between the Orient and the Occident'.* Nicosia. Pp. 351–360.

Vercoutter J. 1945. *Les objets égyptiens et égyptisans.* Paris.

Wachsmann S. 1981. The Ships of the Sea Peoples. *International Journal of Nautical Archaeology* 10:187–220.

Wampler J.C. 1947. *Tell en-Nasbeh* II. *The Pottery.* Berkeley and New Haven.

Weinberg S.S. 1978. A Moabite Shrine Group. *MUSE* 12:30–48.

Westerberg K. 1983. *Cypriot Ships from the Bronze Age to c. 500 BC.* Gothenburg.

Winter N.A. 1991. Terracotta Figurines from Kourion: The Workshops. In F. Vandenabeele and R. Laffineur eds. *Cypriote Terracottas.* Brussels–Liège. Pp. 221–224.

Yadin Y. 1970. Symbols of Deities at Zinjirli, Carthage and Hazor. In J.A. Sanders ed. *Essays in Honor of Nelson Glueck: Near Eastern Archaeology in the Twentieth Century.* Garden City.

Yadin Y. 1972. *Hazor, the Head of All Those Kingdoms.* London.

Yadin Y. 1975. *Hazor. The Rediscovery of a Great Citadel of the Bible.* Tel Aviv.

Yadin Y. et al. 1958, 1960, 1961. *Hazor* I, II, III–IV. Jerusalem.

Young J.H. and Young B.H. 1955. *Terracotta Figurines from Kourion in Cyprus.* Philadelphia.

Zimhoni O. 1985. The Iron Age Pottery of Tel 'Eton. *Tel Aviv* 12:63–90.

PHOENICIAN TOMB STELAE FROM AKHZIV

FRANK MOORE CROSS, JR.
Harvard University

Six funerary stelae from the necropolis of ez-Zib, ancient Akhziv, are now known from various sources: the excavations of I. Ben-Dor, the recent excavations of M.W. Prausnitz, and a local antiquities dealer. Three were published by G.R. Driver (1953:62–65, Pl. VIII:6–8), and are republished below (Nos. 1–3), since the initial publication requires extensive correction. No. 4, the epitaph of " 'Ama' the smith", is published here thanks to the kindness of the excavator, I. Ben-Dor. No. 5 was excavated above Tomb 645 by M.W. Prausnitz in 1960; No. 6, attributed by its seller to Akhziv, completes the group. Illustrations are not to scale.

No. 1 (Fig. App. 1.1; Reg. No. 42.251)

לעמסכ

ר

(the stele) of 'Amaskar

Found in shaft of Tomb ZR VI.
Dimensions: 0.78 × 0.36 × 0.35 m.
Sandstone.

The personal name *'mskr* is known in Punic as well as in similar names compounded with the divine name *mškr*: *grmskr*, *htrmskr* and *'bdmskr* (Donner and Röllig 1964:142). Driver read *l'mhwd*, which is paleographically and orthographically impossible.

Probably the name 'Amaskar should be understood as a haplology of *'amas-skar*.[1]

The script of the stele of 'Amaskar is relatively early. The vertical of the *samek* does not break through the

Fig. App.1.1.

horizontals, but the latter show no sign of cursive ticks, a feature which develops in cursive, 8th century scripts.[2] *Mem*, with the medial vertical well broken through the horizontal, appears in the 8th century, but has a long life. *Kaf* is difficult to place owing to the doubtful character of the far-left strokes on the horizontal. It fits best with 8th–7th century forms. The 'square-headed' *res* appears as early as the Karatepe Inscription (late 8th century BCE). In view of these traits, the script is best dated to the 7th century, perhaps to the second half of the century.[3]

No. 2 (Fig. App. 1.2; Reg. No. 42.252)

לעבדשמש

שבן אשי

the stele of 'Abdšamš son of 'šy

Outside Tomb Z I.
Dimensions: 0.73 × 0.43 × 0.26 m.
Sandstone.

The stele, written in a semi-cursive script, was correctly read by Driver. Both names, 'Abdšamš and 'šy, are well known in Phoenician.[4]

The paucity of cursive scripts in the era of this inscription hinders dating. Its script stands close to that of the Amrit Stela,[5] and the early cursives from Saqqarah and Elephantine, that is, between the early 6th and early 5th centuries BCE (cf. Peckham 1968:111, Pl. X:3, 4). Peckham dates the stele in the early 6th century BCE; this date may be low, but cannot be far off.

Noteworthy is the šin, intermediate between the older zigzag ('double-check') form, and the full cursive (three strokes, converging to a point). The yod also is significant for dating; it is still upright, not having rotated as it has normally in 6th century scripts. Note that the medial horizontal does not touch the vertical stroke as is often the case in late 7th–early 6th century scripts. The 'alef is an early example of a cursive, made with three horizontal strokes. It appears first in the late 7th century.

The cross at the bottom of the stele may be compared with the 'anḫ sign (crux ansata) on Stele No. 4, as well as

the cross in a rectangle (not a ṭet!) on No. 5 and the cross on No. 6. At the top of the cross in No. 2 there is a gouged out area, roughly circular, which could be regarded as the vestigial circle of the 'anḫ.

No. 3 (Fig. App. 1.3; Reg. No. 42.253)

לזכרמ

לך

(stele) of Zakarmilk

Outside Tomb Z I.
Dimensions: 0.78 × 0.38 × 0.22 m.
Sandstone.

Driver prefers to read "to Zecher (the son of) Melech," but there is no reason to divide the elements of the name. The divine epithet milk preceded by a verbal element is frequent in Canaanite, e.g. 'zrmlk, ytnmlk, 'msmlk, etc.

The typological elements of the script are remarkably close to those of Stele No. 1. Compare mem, lamed, reš, and even kaf. Kaf has the horizontal only slightly tipped downward to the left, if at all. The downward tick on the end is a relatively rare element, but is found often at Karatepe in the late 8th century, in the Gold Pendant from Carthage (c. 700 BCE), and sporadically until quite late times. The zayn, unfortunately, is slightly damaged, almost certainly by the false start of a samek.[6] If the zayn reading (rather than samek) is correct, its stance and form are archaic. A date in the late 7th century is likely.

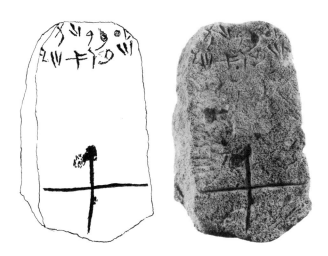

Fig. App.1.2.

Fig. App.1.3.

No. 4 (Fig. App. 1.4; Reg. No. 44.323)[7]

לעמא

הנסך

(stele) of 'Ama' the smith

Found in Tomb ZR XVI.
Dimensions: 0.76 × 0.38 × 0.22 m.
Sandstone.

The name '*m* and the similar hypocoristicon '*my* are known in Phoenician. Probably it is not to be taken as a shortened form of an '*amm* name; such formations had fallen out of use in Canaanite in this period. Rather it may be analyzed as the hypocoristicon of a name with the element '*ms,* which had come into great popularity. *Hannosek* (or *nusek*), 'the smith', is found both in Ugaritic and in Phoenician in this sense.

Below the inscription is an '*anḥ* sign, the Egyptian symbol of life, stylized and used commonly on seals and jewelry as well as on funerary monuments.

The script of the stele is relatively archaic. The *lamed* has a rounded base and no tendency to add a tick downward. The '*alef* has a characteristic form, most closely paralleled on the Ur Box (7th century BCE). Most important palaeographically are the *samek* and the *kaf*. *Samek* is inscribed with the vertical cutting through the horizontals, a style not found after the 8th century BCE. The *kaf,* with its left stroke slanted upward and thickened, is found in the Tabnit and Esmun'azor sarcophagi, and earlier on

the Ur Box. These typological elements of the script point to the 7th century, perhaps to the first half of that century.

No. 5 (Fig. App. 1.5)[8]

לתב

(stele) of Tab[nit?]

Tomb 645, Prausnitz excavation, 1960.

The stone-cutter has inscribed three letters only on the stela. He seems to have abbreviated a name of the type *taqtil*, possibly *Tabnit*.

The letters are relatively archaic. *Lamed* tends to the vertical, and has no tick on the right of the basal hook.[9] *Taw* is broad, and the left crossbar is not shortened perceptibly. The *bet* is large with the leg angling from the base of the head. Such a form is early (e.g. in the Ba'l Lebanon Inscription, *CIS* I, 5) and reappears late in the cursive. A date in the 8th or early 7th century seems likely if not certain (to judge from palaeographical data and the pottery associated with the tomb).

Above the inscription at the top of the stone is a rectangle raised in relief, inside of which a cross is engraved. It should be stressed that this is not a Phoenician *ṭet* which is regularly a cross within a circle (not an oval) in this period. Apparently the symbol is to be related to the other crosses on Phoenician stelae, and ultimately to the *crux ansata.*

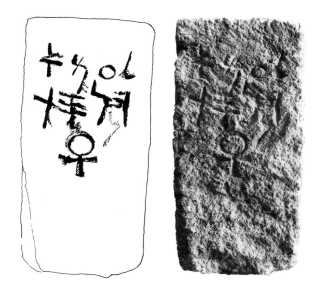

Fig. App.1.4.

Fig. App.1.5.

No. 6 (Fig. App. 1.6)[10]

בדי

(stele of) Boday(?)

The reading of the inscription is not certain. On the right is a cross, not to be taken for a letter.[11] Presumably it is a vestigial *crux ansata*, or the like. *Bet* is clear, as are *dalet* (or *reš*) and *yod*. Between the *dalet* and *yod* is a gouged-out place which appears to have been there when the stele was inscribed. Probably we are to read *Boday*, a hypocoristicon of a *bod* name. The parallel form *bd', Boda'* does appear. Greek βοδης, βοωδη[12] may reflect either *Bōday* or *Bōda'*.

The rotating *yod* is advanced beyond that of the Ur Box, and resembles strongly those of Ipsambul (*CIS* I, 112, dated 591 BCE) and of Esmun'azor. The other letters are not especially helpful. The forms of the letters permit attribution of the inscription tentatively to the 6th–5th centuries BCE.

Above the inscription is a face in relief. The stele appears broken at the top (to judge by the usual proportions of such stele). It is not out of the question that the face is carved secondarily, i.e. in modern times, to enhance the value of the monument, despite the fact that the break in the stone runs just above the eyes of the face. I know of no good parallel to the relief among Phoenician monuments.[13]

This crude little monument bristles with problems.[14] The inscription itself seems, however, to be authentic.

Fig. App.1.6.

NOTES

[1]As suggested to the writer by W.F. Albright, who compares the haplologic forms *yawkin, yawqin, yehu.* Z. Harris (1936:134) had already guessed the etymology of this name, if not its linguistic development.

[2]In this element, the Karatepe Inscription (late 8th century BCE) already exhibits the more developed cursive form; however, the Karatepe *samek* exhibits the older treatment of the vertical.

[3]The downward slant of the horizontal tends to be late; unhappily *lamed* and *'ayn* are of no help in dating.

[4]On biblical and extra-biblical parallels to the latter, see Cross (1966: n. 16). On the vocalization of 'Abdšamš, cf. Assyrian *Ab-di-*[d]*šam-ši.*

[5]A drawing of the Amrit script based on unpublished photographs may be found in Peckham (1968:109, Pl. IX:2).

[6]On the interchange in this root between *z* and *s*, which produces late Phoenician *skr* for *zkr*, see Harris (1939:79).

[7]Permission to publish this stele had been graciously given by Prof. Ben-Dor. It was correctly read by him.

[8]The burial contained red-burnished Phoenician ware of the 8th–7th centuries BCE (Dr. Prausnitz, pers. comm.).

[9]There is damage on the stone below the hook; this must not be taken as part of the letter.

[10]Attributed to Akhziv by seller. Neg. No. 31.595. The registration number is not available to me. My thanks to Prof. Ben-Dor for the photograph.

[11]The horizontal of the cross is much too long left and right for *taw*. The slight indentation over the crossbar on the left is not part of the sign.

[12]Polybius, *Histories* I, 21, 6 (βοωδη) and Dio 11 (βοδης), cited by Harris (1936:85, n. 4).

[13]One may find a remote parallel in the 8th century(?) South Arabian stele published by A. Jamme (1954:25 f.).

[14]We may add to the problems discussed above the unexpected omission of *lamed* before the name.

REFERENCES

CIS: Corpus Inscriptionum Semiticarum. Paris 1881–1962.

Cross F.M. 1966. An Aramaic Inscription from Daskyleion. *BASOR* 184:7–10.

Donner H. and Röllig W. 1964. *Kanaanäische und aramäische Inschriften* II. Wiesbaden.

Driver G.R. 1953. Seals and Tombstones. *ADAJ* 2:62–65.

Harris Z. 1936. *A Grammar of the Phoenician Language.* New Haven.

Harris Z. 1939. *Development of the Canaanite Dialects.* New Haven.

Jamme A. 1954. An Archaic Dextrograde Sabaean Inscription from Mareb. *BASOR* 134:25–26.

Peckham B. 1968. *The Development of the Late Phoenician Scripts* (Harvard Semitic Studies 20). Cambridge, Mass.

APPENDIX 2

SCARABS AND AMULETIC SEALS FROM AKHZIV*

OTHMAR KEEL
University of Freiburg, Switzerland

The Akhziv finds come from two cemeteries: Ez-Zib (Buqbaq), the southern cemetery (Z), late Iron Age I–Iron IIC (11th–6th centuries BCE); and er-Ras, the eastern cemetery (ZR), Iron I–early Persian period (1150–500 BCE).

The material excavated by Ben-Dor and Makhouly can be summarized as follows (Keel 1997:20–48):

Table 1. A Summary of the Excavated Seals from Akhziv, 1941–1942

Keel 1997	Item	Tomb: Item No./Attribution	IAA Reg. No./Fig.	Date (BCE)
1	Scarab	Z XI:43 (9th–8th c.)	48-82/3.10:43	XXII Dyn. (945–713)
2	Scarab	Z XVIII:23 (8th–7th c.)	48-87/3.14:23	2nd half XXII Dyn.–XXV Dyn. (c. 850–656)
3	Scarab	Z XVIII:24 (8th–7th c.)	48-117/1/3.14:24	XXII Dyn. (945–716) Phoenician-Israelite?
11	Conoid	ZR II:34 (9th–7th c.)	48-229/4.1:34	Iron IIB–C (c. 800–650)
12	Scarab	ZR III:19 (7th–6th c.)	48-201/4.2:19	7th–6th c.
13	Scarab	ZR VIII:7 (8th–6th c.)	48-224/4.6:7	XXVI Dyn. (664–525)
14	Scarab	ZR VIII:8 (8th–6th c.)	48-225	XXII Dyn. (945–716)
15	Round seal	ZR IX:118 (9th–7th c.)	48-234/4.7:118	Iron IB–IIA (1050–900) or slightly later**
16	Scarab	ZR IX:119 (9th–7th c.)	48-236/4.7:119	Iron IIA1–first half Iron IIB (1000–800)
17	Rectangular plaque	ZR IX:120 (9th–7th c.)	48-265/4.7:120	XXII Dyn. (945–713)**
18	Scarab	ZR IX:121 (9th–7th c.)	48-266/4.7:121	XXV–XXVI Dyn. (728–525)
19	Scarab	ZR IX:122 (9th–7th c.)	48-266A	XXV–XXVI Dyn. (728–525)
20	Scarab	ZR IX:123 (9th–7th c.)	48-295/4.7:123	XXV–XXVI Dyn. (728–525)
21	Scarab[1]	ZR IX:124 (9th–7th c.)	48-307/4.7:124	XXVI Dyn. (664–525)**

*The material presented here was excavated by I. Ben-Dor and N. Makhouly at Akhziv, 1941–1942, on behalf of the Department of Antiquities, Mandatory Government of Palestine. I am grateful to Michal Dayagi-Mendels and the late Ruth Hestrin of the Israel Museum for allowing me to publish the scarabs and other stamp seals. Due to the length of time that has elapsed between the submission of the original manuscript and the final publication of this volume, the material has already appeared in full in my corpus of scarabs and seals (Keel 1997), which also contains thirteen unprovenanced and illicitly excavated seals in the State Collections, as well as material from later excavations. Therefore, only a general discussion and conclusions relating to the 1941–1944 excavated material will be presented here, as well as the note of the scarabs having been taken in the tomb inventories above.

**I have been able to narrow the chronological span of this type since the publication of Keel 1997.

Table 1. (contd.)

Keel 1997	Item	Tomb: Item No./Attribution	IAA Reg. No./Fig.	Date (BCE)
22	Scarab	ZR IX:125 (9th–7th c.)	48-308/4.7:125	Context suggests a date in the 8th–7th c., perhaps even 9th–8th c.; the item is rather typical of the XXI Dyn (664–525)**
23	Scarab	ZR IX:126 (9th–7th c.)	48-321/4.7:126	8th–7th c.
24	Scarab	ZR IX:127 (9th–7th c.)	48-322/4.7:127	Probably a XIX Dyn. (1292–1190) imitation of a XVth Dyn. piece (1630–1522)**
25	Conoid	ZR IX:128 (9th–7th c.)	48-347	Any time during the Iron Age**
26	Scarab	ZR IX:129 (9th–7th c.)	48-351/4.7:129	Reminiscent in style of the XV Dyn.–early XVIII Dyn. (1630–1400), but XXII Dyn. (945–713)**
27	Scarab	ZR X:27 (7th–6th c.)	48-381/4.8:27	XXVI Dyn. (664–525)
28	Scarab	ZR X:28 (7th–6th c.)	48-385/4.8:28	XXVI Dyn. (664–525)
29	Scarab	ZR X:29 (7th–6th c.)	48-386/4.8:29	XXVI Dyn. (664–525)**
30	Scarab	ZR X:30 (7th–6th c.)	48-387/4.8:30	XXVI Dyn. (664–525)**
31	Rectangular plaque[2]	ZR XIII:58 (7th–6th c.)	48-402/4.11:58	XXV Dyn. (728–656)
32	Scaraboid	ZR XIII:32 (7th–6th c.)	48-422	Iron IIA–B (1000–700)
33	Scarab	ZR XII:20 (8th–6/5th c.)	48-397/4.10:20	XXVI Dyn. (664–525), including some typical XVIII Dyn. (1540–1292) elements**
34	Scarab	ZR XVII:28 (11/10th–7/6th c.)	48-483/4.14:28	Reminiscent in style of XIII–XV Dyn. (1760–1530); 7th–6th c. on basis of carving of *nfr*; but more likely XIX–XXth Dyn. (1292–1075) or slightly later
35	Scarab	ZR XIX:10	48-501/4.15:10	XXII Dyn. (944–713)**
36	Scarab	ZR XXIV:4 (7th c.)	48-512/4.18:4	7th c.
37	Scarab	ZR XXVIII:20 (7th–6th c.)	48-520/4.20:20	XXII–XXV Dyn. (945–656) or even XXVI Dyn. (656–525)**
38	Scarab	ZR XXVIII:21 (7/6–5th c.)	48-521/4.20:21	XXVI Dyn. (664–525)**
39	Scarab	ZR XXVIII:22 (7/6–5th c.)	48-521A/4.20:22	XXV Dyn. (728–656)
40	Scarab	ZR XXIX:78 (9th–8th c.)	48-579/4.21:78	8th c.
41	Scarab	ZR XXIX:79 (9th–8th c.)	48-581/4.21:79	8th c.
42	Scarab	ZR XXX:3 (10th–7th c.)	48-595/4.22:3	XXII–XXV Dyn. (945–656)
43	Scarab	ZR XXX:4 (10th–7th c.)	48-596/4.22:4	XXII–XXV Dyn. (945–656)
44	Scarab	ZR XXX:5 (10th–7th c.)	48-597/4.22:5	
45	Scarab	ZR XXX:6 (10th–7th c.)	48-598/4.22:6	8th c.
46	Scarab	ZR XXXI:7 (8th–7th c.)	48-600/4.23:7	XXVI Dyn. (664–525)
47	Scarab	ZR XXXI:8 (8th–7th c.)	48-601/4.23:8	XXV–XXVI Dyn. (728–525)
48	Scarab	ZR XXXI:9 (8th–7th c.)	48-605/4.23:9	2nd half XV Dyn. (1600–1522)
49	Scarab	ZR XXXIII:2	48-610/4.24:2	XXVI Dyn. (664–525)
50	Scarab	ZR XXXIV:1	48-612/4.25:1	XXVI Dyn. (664–525)
51	Scarab	ZR XXXIV:2	48-613/4.25:2	XXVI Dyn. (664–525)
52	Scarab	ZR XXXIV:3	48-614/4.25:3	XXVI Dyn., Psamtik I (664–610)
53	Scarab	ZR XXXIV:4	48-615/4.25:4	XXVI Dyn. (664–525)
54	Scarab	ZR XXXVI:138 (10/9th–8/7th c.)	48-624/4.27:138	Probably 10th/9th c.
55	Rectangular plaque	ZR XXXVI:139 (10/9th–8/7th c.)	48-625/4.27:139	XXII–XXV Dyn. (945–656)**

Table 1. (contd.)

Keel 1997	Item	Tomb: Item No./Attribution	IAA Reg. No./Fig.	Date (BCE)
56	Scaraboid	ZR XXXVI:140 (10/9th–8/7th c.)	48-627/4.27:140	XXV–XXVI Dyn. (728–525)
57	Scarab	ZR XXXVI:141 (10/9th–8/7th c.)	48-628/4.27:141	XXII–XXV Dyn. (944–656)
58	Scarab	ZR XXXVI:142 (10/9th–8/7th c.)	48-630/4.27:142	End of Iron I–Iron IIA (1050–900)
59	Scarab	ZR XXXVI:143 (10/9th–8/7th c.)	48-631/4.27:143	XXI–XXII Dyn. (1075–716)
60	Scaraboid	ZR XXXVI:144 (10/9th–8/7th c.)	48-632/4.27:144	Iron IIB–C (*c.* 800–587)
61	Scarab	ZR XXXVI:145 (10/9th–8/7th c.)	48-633/4.27:145	XXII Dyn. (945–713)
62	Unfinished scarab	ZR XXXVI:146 (10/9th–8/7th c.)	48-634/4.27:146	
63	Scarab	ZR XXXVI:147 (10/9th–8/7th c.)	48-635/4.27:147	XXII Dyn. (944–713)**
64	Scarab	ZR XXXVI:148 (10/9th–8/7th c.)	48-636/4.27:148	XXII Dyn. (944–716) or slightly later
65	Scarab	ZR XXXVI:149 (10/9th–8/7th c.)	48-637/4.27:149	Probably XIX–XX Dyn. (1292–1075), but uncertain
66	Scarab	ZR XXXVI:150 (10/9th–8/7th c.)	48-638/4.27:150	Iron IIB (900–700)**
67	Scarab	ZR XXXIX:21 (10th–9th c.)	48-714/4.28:21	XX–XXI Dyn. (1186–945)
68	Scarab	ZR XXXIX:22 (10th–9th c.)	48-715/4.28:22	XXII Dyn. (944–713)
69	Scarab	ZR XXXIX:23 (10th–9th c.)	48-719/4.28:23	XXII Dyn. (944–713)
70[3]	Scarab	ZR LVI:5	44-330	XXVI Dyn. (664–525) or earlier

What stands out in this collection is that scarabs of greenstone facies and veined steatite, which are considered typically Phoenician and of which there is ample evidence in the Persian-period cemeteries of 'Atlit, are completely absent in the Phoenician cemeteries of Akhziv published here. This confirms that these groups cannot be documented for the pre-Persian period (cf. Keel-Leu 1991:87–89, 91 No. 107, 92–99 Nos. 109–115). The scarabs of light-blue composite material (Akhziv Nos. 3, 14, 41, 64; cf. also Nos. 28 and 40) could be of Phoenician–Israelite production of the late 8th–6th centuries. The Memphite themes (Nos. 21, 27, 30, 52, 53) featured on many scarabs of the XXVIth Dynasty (664–525 BCE) suggest that even during that period, many scarabs were imported from Egypt and subsequently traded by the Phoenicians all over the Mediterranean. A more detailed evaluation of the finds published here appears in Keel 1997.

NOTES

[1]Scarab No. 21 in Keel 1997 and here is not the scarab illustrated in Fig. 4.7:124 above (M. D-M.).

[2]The tomb number has been corrected to match the attribution of the scarab in the State of Israel collection (M. D-M.).

[3]No tomb of this number is recorded in the Ben-Dor notebooks (M. D-M.).

REFERENCES

Keel O. 1997. *Corpus der Stempelsiegel—Amulette aus Palästina/Israel von den Anfängen bis zur Perserzeit* I. *Von Tell Abu Farağ bis 'Atlit* (Orbis Biblicus et Orientalis 13). Freiburg/Switzerland–Göttingen.

Keel-Leu H. 1991. *Vorderasiatische Stempelsiegel. Die Sammlung des Biblischen Intituts der Universität Freiburg Schweiz* (Orbis Biblicus et Orientalis 110). Freiburg/Switzerland–Göttingen.

IAA REPORTS

No. 1

G. Avni and Z. Greenhut, *The Akeldama Tombs: Three Burial Caves in the Kidron Valley, Jerusalem*, 1996. 129 pp.

No. 2

E. Braun, *Yiftaḥ'el: Salvage and Rescue Excavations at a Prehistoric Village in Lower Galilee*, 1997. 249 pp. + plans.

No. 3

G. Edelstein, I. Milevski and S. Aurant, *Villages, Terraces and Stone Mounds: Excavations at Manaḥat, Jerusalem, 1987–1989*, 1998. 149 pp.

No. 4

C. Epstein, *The Chalcolithic Culture of the Golan*, 1998. 352 pp. + plans. Hardcover.

No. 5

T. Schick, *The Cave of the Warrior: A Fourth Millennium Burial in the Judean Desert*, 1998. 137 pp.

No. 6

ר' כהן, **ההתיישבות הקדומה בהר הנגב: התקופה הכלקוליתית, תקופת הברונזה הקדומה ותקופת הברונזה התיכונה א', תש"ס.** 396 עמ'.

R. Cohen, *Ancient Settlement of the Central Negev: The Chalcolithic Period, the Early Bronze Age and the Middle Bronze Age I* (Hebrew, English Summary), 1999. 396 pp.

No. 7

R. Hachlili and A. Killebrew, *Jericho: The Jewish Cemetery of the Second Temple Period*, 1999. 202 pp.

No. 8

Z. Gal and Y. Alexandre, *Ḥorbat Rosh Zayit: An Iron Age Storage Fort and Village*, 2000. 247 pp.

No. 9

U. Dahari, *Monastic Settlements in South Sinai in the Byzantine Period: The Archaeological Remains*, 2000. 250 pp. + map.

No. 10

ז' ייבין, **בית הכנסת בכורזים: חפירות בשנים 1962–1964, 1980–1987**, תשס"א. 216 עמ'.

Z. Yeivin, *The Synagogue at Korazim: The 1962–1964, 1980–1987 Excavations*, 2000. 216 pp.

No. 11

M. Hartal, *The al-Ṣubayba (Nimrod) Fortress: Towers 11 and 9*, 2001. 129 pp.

No. 12

R. Gonen, *Excavations at Efrata: A Burial Ground from the Intermediate and Middle Bronze Ages*, 2001. 154 pp.

No. 13

E. Eisenberg, A. Gopher and R. Greenberg, *Tel Te'o: A Neolithic, Chalcolithic, and Early Bronze Age Site in the Ḥula Valley*, 2001. 232 pp.

No. 14

R. Frankel, N. Getzov, M. Aviam and A. Degani, *Settlement Dynamics and Regional Diversity in Ancient Upper Galilee: Archeological Survey of Upper Galilee*, 2001. 198 pp. (including color distribution maps) + foldout map.

No. 15

M. Dayagi-Mendels, *The Akhziv Cemeteries: The Ben-Dor Excavations, 1941–1944*, 2002. 182 pp.

No. 16

Y. Goren and P. Fabian, *Kissufim Road: A Chalcolithic Mortuary Site*, 2002. 108 pp.

Forthcoming:

A. Kloner, *Maresha* I.